With the best wishes
of the author

May 1956

A JOURNEY TO GREATNESS

The Encyclopedia of the Opera

The Home Book of Musical Knowledge

Milton Cross' Encyclopedia of the Great Composers and Their
    Music (with Milton Cross)

The Complete Book of 20th Century Music

Music for the Millions

Men of Popular Music

Dictators of the Baton

Music Comes to America

From Bach to Stravinsky

Mr. Ewen has also written a young people's biography of
George Gershwin, The Story of George Gershwin (Holt, 1944).
Other books by Mr. Ewen for the Holt Musical Biography Series
for Young People are: The Story of Jerome Kern; Tales from the
Vienna Woods: The Story of the Johann Strausses; Haydn: A
Good Life; The Story of Irving Berlin; The Story of Arturo Tosca-
nini.

DAVID EWEN

A Journey

THE LIFE AND

GEORGE

Illustrated with photographs

to Greatness

M U S I C   O F

GERSHWIN

Henry Holt and Company   *New York*

To the memory of my Mother

ACKNOWLEDGMENTS

Without the cooperation of George Gershwin's relatives, friends, and associates in the worlds of the theater and music, this book could not have been written. With few, and negligible, exceptions, they have all been unsparing of time and energy in providing me with all the materials at their disposal to help me prepare this first complete and definitive biography of a man they loved and will never forget. They gave me access to letters, documents, diaries, guest books, programs—as well as their memories and often most personal confidences—which have been invaluable to me.

I owe a special debt to Ira Gershwin, with whom I spent two extended periods at his home in Beverly Hills. His formidable memory, and his equally formidable archives gathered over a period of more than three decades, served me well, and are responsible for making this book as complete, authoritative, and accurate as I could make it. His wife, Leonore, was equally cooperative. Her comments on the manuscript, which she read in the first draft, were often as penetrating as they were useful.

It would be impossible to list here the more than sixty people who were interviewed, but I would surely be remiss if I did not single out at least a handful for special gratitude: George Pallay, Kay Swift, Henry Botkin, Jules Glaenzer, Alexander Steinert, Irving Caesar, Phil Charig, Vinton Freedley, Frances Godowsky, Edward Kilenyi, Samuel Chotzinoff, Harry Ruby, Emily Paley, Max Dreyfus, Dr. Albert Sirmay, and Mrs. Hambitzer Reel.

I am indebted to the office of Robert Breen for the extensive materials it provided me about the foreign tours of *Porgy and Bess;* to the Congressional Library in Washington, D.C., for the opportunity of inspecting Gershwin's manuscripts and sketchbooks; to the Drama and Music Divisions of the New York Public Library for their clipping files; to Mischa Portnoff, who spent many an hour at the piano playing for me Gershwin music, particularly all of the early songs, many of them unknown to me; finally, to the many, many people in all parts of the country who were so patient and responsive to my avalanche of inquiries submitted by letter, telephone, and telegram.

For permission to use lyrics, or excerpts from lyrics, by Ira Gershwin, I am indebted to two sources: to the Gershwin Publishing Company, New York, for "Love Is Here to Stay" and "Love Walked In," both copyrighted in 1938; to the New World Music Corporation, New York, for "Sweet and Low Down," copyrighted in 1925, "The Babbitt and the Bromide," copyrighted in 1927, "Soon," copyrighted in 1929; "Bidin' My Time" and "Could You Use Me," both copyrighted in 1930; "Some Girls Can Bake a Pie," copyrighted in 1932; "Mine" and "Union Square," both copyrighted in 1933.

I am grateful to Little, Brown & Company, for permission to use quotations from Vernon Duke's *Passport to Paris* and Sir Osbert Sitwell's *Laughter in the Next Room,* and Doubleday & Company for an extract from Ethel Merman's *Who Could Ask for Anything More.*

D. E.

Little Neck, N.Y.

contents

A JOURNEY TO GREATNESS

introduction

GERSHWIN TODAY

In the history of music there are many composers who were neglected during their lifetime and discovered after their death. There were others who were first honored, then forgotten. There are still others who were honored, then ignored, and ultimately rediscovered.

The case of George Gershwin is still more curious. In 1937, when he died suddenly at the age of thirty-eight, he was, without question, one of the most successful composers the United States has ever produced. He made a fortune from his music, he was respected by many serious musicians and music critics in Europe and America, and he was sung, whistled, and played by millions. Yet not even his staunchest supporters then could have guessed how his artistic stature and his popularity were to grow in the years that followed.

Today, his music is heard more often and in more places than it was two decades ago. A survey conducted by *Musical America* among the foremost symphony orchestras of this country discloses the startling fact that in the period between 1945 and 1954, he consistently received more performances than did such world-famous personalities as Stravinsky, Bartók, Milhaud, Vaughan Williams, Shostakovich, Hindemith, Britten, or Honegger. In six of those years he was performed more often than any other American composer; one year, he was tied for first place; and in two other years he held second place.

He is the only American composer, and one of the few moderns anywhere, whose works continually occupy a complete program. Besides the all-Gershwin concerts that have become something of a yearly ritual on both coasts to commemorate his death, all-Gershwin programs are frequently presented by major American symphony orchestras, and just as frequently these programs become the invitations for sold-out auditoriums. Before Gershwin's time, only all-Beethoven, or all-Tchaikovsky, or all-Wagner programs had such box-office appeal. In 1953, the Gershwin Concert Orchestra was organized to tour the United States in all-Gershwin programs. This was the first time in the history of musical performance that a one-man orchestral program was taken on tour by a single organization. The project was so successful that, in 1954, the orchestra embarked on a second cross-country tour, visiting seventy-four cities in a four-month period.

In Europe, too, Gershwin's music has taken a firm hold

on the living repertory. None of his larger works is now a novelty in any major European city. Before the intensification of the cold war, the *Rhapsody in Blue* was acclaimed in Moscow in an American music concert given by the Moscow State Symphony on July 3, 1945. Before the iron curtain was lowered on Czechoslovakia, this same *Rhapsody* was performed, and cheered, in Prague, played by Eugene List and the Czech Philharmonic Orchestra conducted by Leonard Bernstein; the occasion was an international festival held there in May 1946 to celebrate the fiftieth anniversary of the Czech Philharmonic. In Florence, Italy, at the Teatro Communale in 1953, so many disappointed music-lovers were turned away from an all-Gershwin concert that a Beethoven program scheduled for a few days later had to be canceled and the Gershwin concert repeated.

According to Edwin Hughes, director of the National Music Council in New York, Gershwin's music had by far more performances in Europe in 1954 than that of any other American. That year, the Council made its first survey of American music performed abroad and was able to compile a partial list of the cities that had heard Gershwin's orchestral works, either individually or in all-Gershwin programs. The impressive list is as follows: Arras (France), Avesta (Sweden), Biarritz, Birmingham, Bologna, Cannes, Catania, Edinburgh, Florence, Gävleborg (Sweden), Gothenburg (Sweden), Halle, Kareskoga (Sweden), Lille, London (four major orchestras), Luleå (Sweden), Malmö (Sweden), Milan, Monte Carlo, Mulhouse, Nancy, Nantes, Naples, Palermo, Paris (three major orchestras), Rennes, Rome, Strasbourg, Toulon, Toulouse, Trieste, Turin, Valenciennes, Venice, and Vichy.

What is particularly interesting about the frequency

of all-Gershwin programs both here and abroad is that Gershwin left only a handful of orchestral works: two rhapsodies, one piano concerto, one tone poem, one overture, and one set of variations for piano and orchestra. This limited repertory has been played and replayed to meet an apparently insatiable demand. Far from becoming bored with this continual repetition of the same works, audiences everywhere appear to grow more and more responsive to them with each rehearing, more and more enthusiastic. Repetition has not robbed this music of its impact.

So great is Gershwin's appeal in Europe that he is the first American composer about whom books have been published in Austria, Germany, France, Italy, and Holland. Five of these were biographies written by foreign authors. And in Holland and Germany not one, but two, such books were issued.

Gershwin's popular songs have also done well since the composer's death, this despite the notoriously high mortality rate of popular music. To this day Gershwin has remained one of the five or six highest-paid members of ASCAP: the American Society of Composers, Authors, and Publishers. ASCAP protects the copyright interests of its members and licenses their works for performances in public places, over radio, television, and on records. It is, consequently, an accurate barometer of the frequency with which the music of any popular composer is performed in this country.

The full significance of Gershwin's present-day standing in ASCAP strikes us when we remember that other composers or lyricists in his select group are such men as Irving Berlin and Cole Porter, both of whom receive dual ratings as composers *and* lyricists, and Richard Rodgers and Oscar Hammerstein II. Each of these men has remained richly productive for the past two decades, a period during which Gershwin was silenced by death. Despite his death, their continuing activity, and the acknowledged evanescence of popular songs, Gershwin continues to be one of the most frequently heard composers through popular media—a composer represented by songs written a quarter of a century ago. And some Gershwin songs—such as "The Man I Love," "I've Got a Crush on You," and "Love Is Here To Stay"—are more popular today than when they were first released.

Probably nothing points up more vividly the expansion of Gershwin's posthumous importance than the history of his opera, *Porgy and Bess.* When first produced, it was a failure. Only after the composer's death did it, phoenix-like, rise from the ashes of its initial defeat to soar in triumph. It was hailed in America as our greatest folk opera, and often by the very critics who had originally condemned it. Then it went on to conquer Europe in a way no other American opera has done. That story—the conquest of Europe, the Near East, South America, Mexico, and the Soviet Union by *Porgy and Bess*—is a saga without parallel in American music, and is told in a later chapter.

One of the most impressive and singularly significant facts about Gershwin is the way he progressed toward a single goal from his boyhood on. He sought from the very first to achieve artistic validity as a composer through popular music. It is surely significant that he should have sensed, and become convinced of, the destiny of American popular music at a time when it was in its unkempt infancy; when it was regarded by all serious musicians with the distaste of an

impatient adult for an irresponsible child. In discussing ragtime or Irving Berlin's songs with his first important teacher,
Charles Hambitzer, Gershwin said: "This is American music. This is the way an American should write. This is the kind
of music I want to write." He was only sixteen years old then,
but already he was convinced that a serious composer could
produce important art by bringing to popular music the
harmonic, rhythmic, and contrapuntal resources of serious
music. And he felt that the use of large musical forms for
popular idioms could provide a creative artist with a broad
avenue for self-expression.

Later in life, when he already was successful, he
wrote: "Jazz is music; it uses the same notes as Bach used.
. . . Jazz is the result of the energy stored in America. . . .
Jazz has contributed an enduring value to America in the
sense that it has expressed ourselves. It is an original American achievement that will endure, not as jazz perhaps, but
which will leave its mark on future music in one way or
another."

And again: "I regard jazz as an American folk music,
a very powerful one which is probably in the blood of the
American people more than any other style of folk music. I
believe that it can be made the basis of serious symphonic
works of lasting value."

His North Star, then, was the mission to write popular
songs with the techniques and approaches of serious music,
and serious music with the techniques and approaches of
popular music. As an apprentice in Tin Pan Alley, writing
his first popular songs, he also wrote *Rialto Ripples* (with
Will Donaldson), a first effort to transfer a jazz style to piano
writing. And as the mature creator of a three-act opera, almost twenty years later, he was still writing popular songs.

If he kept on writing popular music after becoming celebrated with more serious efforts, it was not only for the money it brought him; on several occasions he proved his willingness to brush aside a fortune in contracts when his conscience demanded that he turn to ambitious projects. He wrote popular music because it brought him profound artistic satisfaction. He brought to it all the skill, high principle, and artistry of which he was capable. As he worked on his best songs, he subjected them to continual revision, refinement, and editing in his pursuit of the *mot juste*. The popular song was one facet of his art, and an important one; the larger works were another. He needed both media to give complete expression to his artistic personality.

And his popular songs revealed genuine mastery of means. There was much more to them than a caressing melody, or a kinesthetic rhythm, or a poignant emotion. His songs abound in subtle details: skillful enharmonic changes, dexterous setting of one rhythm against another, piquant use of after-beats and staggered accents, and intriguing changes of meter. He had his own personal mannerisms. The way he would suddenly inject a minor third in the melody, or use anticipatory harmonies in the bass, or pass from one key to another without the proper harmonic transitions, or allow the chordal structure of an accompaniment to follow its own design rather than serve as a prop for the melody, or give musical significance and harmonic inventiveness to his verses—all this gives his songs an unmistakable Gershwin identity. His song technique was usually so unorthodox and complex that considerable familiarity was required before parts of it could be properly appreciated.

It may come as a surprise to many to discover that, from the point of view of sales figures, Gershwin's only genuine song hit was the early, "Swanee." Other songs, though frequently performed, fell far short of marks achieved by such men as Irving Berlin and Jerome Kern whose sheet and record sales consistently hit a million copies. Indeed, many of Gershwin's songs required the passing of several years before they achieved wide acceptance. This was due not only to his advanced writing but also to the fact that his harmonic structure was often so germane to the melodic idea that—unlike popular songs by Berlin, Kern, or, for that matter, virtually anybody else—they lose their appeal if sung without an accompaniment, and thus could not become the kind of tunes that a nation catches at first hearing and then at once begins to sing and whistle all the time.

On the other hand, Gershwin's best songs are heard more often today, and are better known, than they were when he was alive. They have become classics, and not exclusively in popular music. The enthusiasm of one serious music critic, Henry Pleasants, for Gershwin's songs has even led him to make the following excessive statement in *The Agony of Modern Music*: "Certainly there is nothing in the *Rhapsody in Blue* or *An American in Paris* to compare in simple, spontaneous creative genius with 'The Man I Love' or 'Embraceable You.' " Others may not go so far as Pleasants in placing Gershwin's songs so far above and beyond his serious works; but there should be no hesitancy in finding for those songs a rightful place in the repertory of serious American music.

Gershwin had the sure instincts from which genius derives so much of its strength. He had had an inadequate training in music, yet a powerful creative intuition more than compensated for his shortcomings as a technician. No textbook or teacher would have led him where his own intuition did many times. The opening measure of the *Rhapsody in Blue* is a case in point. When Gershwin conceived the ascending clarinet glissando, he knew precisely the effect for which he was reaching: a hyperthyroid, hysterical wail, almost the voice for a hyperthyroid, hysterical era. He explained to Paul Whiteman's clarinetist, Ross Gorman, precisely how he wanted that passage to sound. At first Gorman insisted that no clarinetist could produce the effect Gershwin had in mind. The composer, however, was so intransigent that Gorman had to keep on experimenting with various reeds and techniques until, at last, he brought to life Gershwin's music exactly as Gershwin had heard it with his inner ear.

That opening is surely one of the unforgettable moments in contemporary music; a single bar establishes the atmosphere and mood of the entire work. In his serious works, Gershwin was particularly fortunate with his opening passages. He had the showman's instinct for seizing the listener's attention immediately. And he had the creator's instinct for bringing to his openings something fresh and original, and sometimes something altogether unexpected. The Concerto in F begins with an exciting Charleston rhythm. *An American in Paris* opens with an insouciant, Parisian walking theme which, before many measures pass, is punctuated with the startling sounds of actual taxi horns. The opening theme of the *Second Rhapsody* is an incisive, machine-like rivet motive. *Porgy and Bess* has for its opening aria one of the most beautiful melodies in the opera, "Summertime."

If Gershwin knew how to begin, he also had an infallible instinct for providing his works with the big, sweeping idea at every major climactic moment. Gershwin rarely fails us after an exciting build-up. He may at times fumble and

grope while reaching toward the high ground of a composition, but once he gets there he invariably is able to produce a
breath-taking vista. There are, as examples, the unforgettable
slow sections of the *Rhapsody in Blue* and the *Second Rhapsody;* the sensual melody that is the core of the second movement of the Concerto; the whirling percussive ending of the
Cuban Overture; and the wake scene, the Kittiwah Island
scene, and the finale of *Porgy and Bess.*

Gershwin's spotty musical education would have
spelled doom for any composer who was not a genius. Gershwin was saved by his instincts and intuition; and also by a
phenomenal capacity to absorb, almost by a kind of subtle
osmosis, musical knowledge wherever and whenever he came
in contact with it, and then to adapt that knowledge for his
own creative purposes. Some of his basic musical knowledge
came from study with various teachers who are discussed in
later chapters. But most of what he knew came autodidacti-
cally: from imitation; self-analysis; experimentation; painstaking listening at concerts, which he attended from the time
he was twelve; from studying musical scores which he learned
to dissect with a kind of scientific exactitude; from poring
over texts like Percy Goetschius' *Material Used in Musical
Composition,* Cecil Forsyth's *Orchestration,* and Benjamin
Cutter's *Harmonic Analysis.* He picked up here and there
numerous methods, approaches, and stylistic tricks which
soon become permanently fixed in his own equipment. He
continually hounded his musician-friends with questions
about their own work, or sought criticisms of his own. "Anything he wanted to learn," says Kay Swift, "he hit with a
terrific sock. He just tore into it." He had such a keen and
perceptive mind and memory, and such an insatiable appetite for information, that in time he was able, through this

haphazard way, to accumulate an impressive storehouse of musical knowledge.

He could not always give the proper textbook definition to a specific method. But, generally, he knew what he was doing, why he was doing it, and where he was going. He consciously used polyrhythms, changing meters, unresolved discords, ambiguous tonalities, bold modulations—always toward a precise artistic effect. No teacher had shown him how; he had seen them used in works by others and had tried them out for himself. "Why," he once remarked with the amazement of a Monsieur Jourdain discovering he was talking in prose, "I wrote a whole thirty-two bar chorus in canon, and if someone told me it was a canon, I'd laugh in his face."

It was this unquenchable thirst for musical information, this restless search for answers to his creative problems, that made it possible for him to grow the way he did, creatively and technically. The advance in know-how and musical articulateness during the ten-year period separating his one-act opera, *135th Street,* and his grand opera, *Porgy and Bess,* has few parallels in modern music. It is an advance from fumbling apprenticeship to full mastery. An examination of his serious works reveals a step-by-step development in technical skill, an increasing self-assurance and *savoir-faire,* a growing command of the materials of his trade. From a structural consideration, the *Second Rhapsody* is notable progress over the *Rhapsody in Blue* in organic unity, compactness of form, adroitness of thematic growth; if the *Rhapsody in Blue* remains the more popular work it is because the basic material is more inspired. The *Cuban Overture* represents a remarkable step forward in the use of contrapuntal means, just as the *Variations on I Got Rhythm* reveals a new virtuosity in thematic variation. And from every possible consideration—orchestration, idiomatic writing, complexity of means, variety of materials, artistic sureness, and profound insight—*Porgy and Bess* dwarfs everything that preceded it.

In time he became a much better informed musician than he was credited with being. He knew and loved the chamber music of Mozart and Brahms, and Mozart's operas. He admired almost everything by Bach, Beethoven, and Debussy. Among the moderns, his favorites were Schoenberg, Ravel, Hindemith, Stravinsky, and Alban Berg. In the last year or so of his life he made an intensive study of Schoenberg's string quartets through scores and private recordings, and acquired an intimate knowledge and penetrating understanding of this abstruse music. At a time when many a sophisticated and well-informed musician knew almost nothing about Alban Berg's music, Gershwin was a passionate advocate of his, and made a special trip to Philadelphia to attend the première of *Wozzeck*.

Gershwin had the courage and stamina of genius to cut new paths for music, and to make these paths broad highways upon which many others would follow his lead. His significance as a pioneer can hardly be overestimated; in *Makers of the Modern World,* Louis Untermeyer considers Gershwin to be one of the four most important composers to shape musical trends in the past century (the other three being Wagner, Debussy, and Stravinsky). When Gershwin started in popular music, a trained musician was a *rara avis* in Tin Pan Alley. Men such as Jerome Kern or Victor Herbert, both well equipped by training, were phenomena not usually encountered in the song industry. But not even Kern or Herbert brought to their popular writing the wealth of inventiveness, the imagination, the daring, and the complexity of means we find in Gershwin. In an area where entertainment-appeal was the primary, if not the exclusive, goal, Gershwin bravely introduced artistic considerations. More than any other single person he made it possible for later composers like Kurt Weill, Richard Rodgers, Vernon Duke, and Leonard Bernstein to write the kind of popular music they did and to find a large audience receptive to it.

It was also Gershwin who convinced serious musicians throughout the world of the value of using American popular idioms in classical music. He was not the first to do so. Before the *Rhapsody in Blue,* Stravinsky had written *Ragtime,* for piano, and Milhaud *La Création du monde,* a ballet in jazz style; and before them there had been the tentative efforts of Debussy and Satie to employ American popular styles. But this music had little or no impact on the musical thought of our time. It was regarded by the intelligentsia as a spicy exotic dish to pique the jaded musical appetite. It was Gershwin who brought full acceptance to our popular styles, techniques, and materials in the world of serious music. After the *Rhapsody in Blue* came the deluge: Křenek's *Jonny spielt auf,* Hindemith's *Neues vom Tage,* Kurt Weill's *Mahagonny* and *Die Dreigroschenoper,* Ravel's "Blues" Sonata and the *Concerto for the Left Hand,* Constant Lambert's *Rio Grande,* Aaron Copland's Concerto for Piano and Orchestra, and John Alden Carpenter's ballet, *Skyscrapers.*

One more point: Gershwin helped create and establish an American musical art which no longer aped the speech of Europe, and which could have been produced nowhere but in this country. In this tendency, our music has taken a giant leap forward since the 1920s. Many of our gifted composers are producing music deeply rooted in American backgrounds, psychology, experiences, and culture; and it is for this reason, above all others, that American music is now regarded with respect in foreign capitals. Today we are beginning to recognize—perhaps for the first time—what a role George Gershwin played in bringing about this development.

1

T H E   G E R S H V I N S

George Gershwin's life was no rags-to-riches story. Many writers, drawing a false inference from the fact that Gershwin lived most of his childhood and youth in New York's East Side, have described the poverty in which he was raised. There was never such poverty. One of the things in Gershwin's screen biography that most upset the composer's mother was this distorted picture of George's boyhood. "There was always money for piano lessons," she remarked sadly. "My husband always made enough money to take care of the family."

The Gershwin family resided for so many years in the

East Side because that was where the father's varied business establishments were usually located, and he was a man
who had made it a practice to live where he worked. But most
of the apartments in which the family lived were roomy, airy,
comfortable, and at times comparatively expensive.

Since Mrs. Gershwin frequently helped her husband
in business, the family usually employed a maid. George's
sister, Frances, cannot remember the time when the family
was without one. When the father did comparatively well,
the mother would invest her savings in diamonds. (The pan-
ics of 1893 and 1907 had left among many New Yorkers a
profound distrust in banks.) When bad times came, Ira was
sent to the Provident Loan Society, or some other reputable
loan agency, to pawn one of the diamonds, and on one or two
occasions, it had to be sold outright. But even during the
leaner years, the family never really knew want. The mother
was a level-headed administrator of the family finances,
and when fortunes sank there was still enough around to pay
not only for basic necessities but even for some luxuries.
Frances recalls that during one of the hardest periods in the
family history she was sent to a summer camp for two successive seasons. None of the children can remember when the
mother did not dress well; nor can they recall when they
themselves did not have spending money jingling in their
pockets, or the price to pay for a show or an expedition to
Coney Island. They clearly recollect the occasions when their
parents hired a private limousine to go to the races.

Both of Gershwin's parents came from St. Petersburg.
The mother, Rose Bruskin, belonged to a prosperous family,
her father was a successful furrier. The father, Morris Gershovitz, was also well esteemed in the old country since his
father had invented a model gun which was sold to the Tsar.

Rose was in her early 'teens, and strikingly beautiful, when Morris met and fell in love with her. The Bruskins migrated to America sometime in or about 1891 and, like so many other immigrants, took root in New York's East Side. Morris Gershovitz followed their trail soon after, attracted to the new world not so much by the opportunities it offered a young, ambitious man as by Rose's intense eyes and her sensitive face.

Once in America, Morris shortened his name to Gershvin, and found a well-paying job as a designer of fancy uppers for women's shoes. He did not delay in pursuing and winning Rose. They were married July 21, 1895 in a rathskeller on Houston Street in the East Side; she was nineteen, he twenty-four. Family hearsay has it that the marriage festivities lasted three days. But Morris long insisted that it was fact and not hearsay that one of those who stepped into the rathskeller to drink the health of the young couple was young Theodore Roosevelt, then president of the Board of Police Commissioners in New York City.

The Gershvins settled in a small apartment on the corner of Hester and Eldridge streets, right above Simpson's pawn and loan shop. There, Ira Gershwin was born, December 6, 1896. The parents always called him Isidore, and that is the name he retained until early manhood. But his real name was Israel, a fact not known to him until 1928 when he applied for a passport.

About a year after Ira's birth, the family moved to the Williamsburg section of Brooklyn, where the father found a new job as a leather worker. They acquired roomy quarters at 252 Snedicker Avenue, a two-story brick house which rented for $15.00 a month. It was there that George Gershwin was born, September 26, 1898. The name which appeared on the birth certificate was Jacob Gershwine. The "Gersh-wine" is apparently a misspelling for Gershvin, but "Jacob" was both correct and official. As was the case with Ira, the parents preferred using another name for him, and the name they chose from the very beginning was George. Ira cannot remember any time when he called his brother anything but George. When George stepped out into the world of music he changed the spelling of his second name to "Gershwin," and the other members of the immediate family followed suit.

With the birth of two more children the family was complete. Arthur came on March 14, 1900. Later in life he enjoyed some success as a salesman of motion-picture films, and after that as a stockbroker. But his heart—like George's—was in music. He has written over one hundred and fifty songs, some of which are not without some charm. "I am," he will tell you, "a leading composer of unpublished songs." George liked one of them well enough to play it on his radio program. Arthur also wrote the score for a musical comedy, *The Lady Says Yes*, which came to Broadway in 1945 and departed after only eighty-seven performances. After an un-happy marriage, Arthur was separated from his wife, Judy; they have one son, Mark George.

Frances (or as her brothers call her, "Frankie") was born on the same birthday as Ira, on December 6, but in 1906. She appeared on the Broadway musical-comedy stage in such intimate revues as *Merry-Go-Round* and the second *Americana*. She was also popular at parties as a singer of her brother George's songs; though she had a small, somewhat husky voice, George always praised the way she sang his music, particularly the way she could keep the rhythm mov-ing. In 1930, she married Leopold Godowsky, Jr., son of the world-famous pianist of the same name, and himself an excellent violinist. The son was a celebrity in his own right, being the inventor, with Leopold Mannes, of the Kodachrome process of color photography. The Godowskys live on an estate in Westport, Connecticut, where they have raised four children: one of them, Georgia, is named after her famous uncle. Leopold's laboratory, built by the Eastman-Kodak Co., where he continues his experiments, is within a hundred yards or so of his home.

Since Morris Gershvin was so insistent on living close to his place of employment, the Gershvins were a nomadic tribe. The family remained on Snedicker Avenue only eight months before returning to the East Side of Manhattan. After that they occupied several different East Side apartments (at Forsyth Street near Delancey, Second Avenue on 7th Street, Grand Street, Second Avenue and 4th Street) between periods that brought them either to Coney Island, or to 129th Street in Harlem. Even Ira's retentive memory is incapable of following accurately all the movements of the family between 1900 and 1917. He has, however, computed that up to 1917 the family occupied twenty-eight different apartments: twenty-five in New York, and three in Brooklyn.

The mother was the strong hand of the family. She was a proud and self-centered woman whose driving ambition for herself and her family made her continually restless. Filled with energies that found few outlets and frequently aspiring toward financial and social goals well beyond her reach, she was frequently an unhappy woman. She dominated the household with the imperious authority of an empress.

It has sometimes been said that George "adored" his mother. He actually did say once that "she is the kind of woman about whom composers write mammy songs—only *I* mean them." But this was not strictly the case. Having inherited much of her strength of will and purpose, pride, and even selfishness, he was often at odds with her. In his maturity, he became the dutiful son, solicitous, respectful, considerate, and generous. But his letters reveal that if he adored anybody at all—outside of his brother, Ira—it was not his mother but his father. His psychoanalyst, Dr. Gregory Zilboorg, has said that in his opinion, had the situation been otherwise, had Gershwin adored his mother and only respected his father, he would have become a hopeless psychoneurotic. Gershwin's adjustment to his work and to his life, says Dr. Zilboorg, was made possible only because his relations to his mother and father were exactly what they were.

The father was a gentle, mild-mannered man, who had an easygoing nature, and was as soft as velvet. Partly influenced by his wife, and partly by his own wishes to be a good provider, he soon came to the conclusion that a salaried job held no promise for him. He opened a small stationery store in Brooklyn. Before long, he abandoned it for a restaurant on the East Side, in partnership with his brother-in-law, Harry Wolpin. After that he passed from one business venture to another, always in partnership with his brother-in-law. At different periods he owned several restaurants: one on Forsyth Street, another on downtown Broadway, a third on upper Broadway near 145th Street, a fourth near the Hotel McAlpin on 34th Street and Broadway. There was one period when he ran four restaurants simultaneously. Also at different times he owned and operated several Turkish and Russian baths, including the St. Nicholas Baths on Lenox Avenue and 111th Street, and the Lafayette Baths downtown. He was also at one time or another the proprietor of several bakeries, and of two rooming houses at or near 42nd Street; the owner of a cigar store which included a pool parlor on what is now the Grand Central Station; and a bookmaking establishment at the Belmont Race Track. One summer, in 1904, he operated a summer hotel in Spring Valley, New York, which accommodated two hundred guests.

Despite these many and varied adventures in the world of business, he was not really an ambitious man, and the accumulation of money meant little to him. When he was well off, he would have allowed all the money to dribble through his fingers had not his wife taken charge of the funds. Usually he provided comfortably for his family. But there were times when business reverses made things difficult. His three weeks as a bookmaker, for example, were a major financial disaster. And so many nonpaying relatives came to stay at his Spring Valley hotel that he was lucky to break even.

His highly personal and at times quixotic attitude toward life in general, and his Pickwickian comments, made him something of a legend. There was a time when intimate friends of George and Ira talked of gathering anecdotes about him into a book. In any event, they enjoyed circulating them by word of mouth.

Papa Gershwin's individual attitudes toward George and his music were the source for more than one choice story. When George was writing the *Rhapsody in Blue,* his father counseled him: "Make it good, George, it's liable to be important." When *An American in Paris* was written, the father proudly told a critic: "It is very important music—it takes twenty minutes to play." A few years later he learned George was wondering what to call his *Second Rhapsody,* and in all seriousness he advised: "Call it *Rhapsody in Blue No. 2*, George. Then you can write *Rhapsody in Blue No. 3*, *No. 4*, and *No. 5*—you know, just like Beethoven."

He once told George how much he liked one of the songs in the then current *Scandals*, but he could not remember the title. George played for him the hit song of that production, "Somebody Loves Me." The father shook his head; this wasn't it. George then played the rest of the score. No, the song wasn't there, either. "Well," George said at last, "it must be something from another show, because I played everything there is." As he spoke his fingers passed over the piano keys aimlessly and struck a few bars from "Somebody Loves Me." "*That's it, that's it*," the father cried excitedly. Then with undisguised anger he added: "Why didn't you play it for me in the first place?"

His approaches to subjects other than George's music were equally his own. George once showed his father the photograph of a famous Renoir painting of two women. When the father heard that the original was worth about $50,000 he whistled with amazement. "Why," he inquired, looking more intently at the photograph and pointing to each of the two figures there, "who is *she*—and who is *she*?"

Informed that the Einstein theory of relativity, which had taken twenty-five years to be evolved, required only three pages, his explanation was brief: "It must have been very close print." He knew that a certain magazine article on George was significant because—though he could not remember the name of the magazine or the author—he remembered that it cost thirty-five cents. In the early days of radio, he tried to convince George to buy a set because a friend of the family had just acquired one. He reported to George the wonder of the new invention. "Why, they even get Cuba. Not only Cuba

—but even England!" "Not England," remarked George skeptically. The father snapped back: "Cuba—guaranteed!"

He once asked George to buy him a gift of a dog. "Sure," George replied. "Go out and select a dog you like, and here's a check to cover the price." Papa's gratitude was cautious: "Thanks for the present so far, George."

Papa Gershwin died of leukemia at the Lenox Hill Hospital in New York City on May 14, 1932, in his sixty-first year. Mrs. Gershwin survived not only her husband, but also her son George. She died of a heart attack at her apartment at 25 Central Park West, New York, on December 16, 1948, in her seventy-second year—almost twelve years after George. Even George's maternal grandmother outlived him —by five years.

2

CHILDHOOD

George and Ira grew up on the East Side. The two boys were opposites. Ira was the son of his father: even-tempered, somewhat withdrawn, malleable to discipline, gentle by nature. Even as a boy his favorite pastime was reading. He would devour nickel novels by the dozen, borrowing them for two cents apiece from a nickel-novel circulating library located in the back of a laundry on Broome Street. His first clue to the pleasure to be found in good books came in 1906 when he read Conan Doyle's *A Study in Scarlet;* from then on hard-covered volumes displaced the more lurid paperbacks. He also enjoyed doing sketching, and was an ardent theatergoer. The theaters he went to were neighborhood ones: the Unique Theater, a nickelodeon on Grand Street, the first movie-house to open on the East Side; the Grand Street Theater where sensational melodramas of Owen Davis and others were performed in the flesh; and variety houses at Union Square. He still recalls vividly his first visit to a burlesque house, the Palace on Third Avenue near 129th Street; but what remains in his memory is not a provocative blackout, but the way one of the singers did "Wait Till the Sun Shines, Nellie."

Ira received from his mother a weekly allowance of twenty-five cents, but he did not have to rely exclusively on this stipend for his books and theaters. On most Saturday evenings, his mother and relatives of the family played poker. A special kitty was created to pay for the refreshments. It was Ira's responsibility to get the delicatessen and the drinks for the players, and he was permitted to keep the change, which usually amounted to about a dollar.

George was of a stripe different from Ira. He would not touch a book if he could help it, not even the nickel novels which were a passion with all the neighborhood kids. George's pleasures came from the pastimes of the city streets: games like "cat," street hockey, and punch ball, in all three of which he was highly proficient. His companions regarded him as the roller-skating champion of Forsyth Street. In the brawls of the streets he was capable of taking care of himself.

His temperament was like his mother's. He was headstrong, restless, assertive, dominating, dynamic. He was always getting into trouble. In school, he was often brought to task for failing to do his homework, misbehaving in class, and getting involved in various peccadilloes. In three or four instances Ira had to go to their school—P.S. 20, on Rivington and Forsyth streets—to straighten out George's difficulties. Things went somewhat more smoothly for George when he went on to P.S. 25, on First Avenue and Second Street. But there, as earlier, he was no scholar. His marks were just passable. When he was graduated from the school, in 1912, his mother sent him to the High School of Commerce for commercial training for a career in accounting.

Ira, of course, did much better in public school. He was graduated from P.S. 20 in 1910 with an average high enough to enable him to enter Townsend Harris Hall, a high school which demanded the highest scholastic ratings from its students. His mother wanted Ira to become a school-teacher.

By the mores of the city streets, anybody who studied music was a "sissy" or "Maggie." George accepted the values of his comrades. In his early childhood music meant little to him, for there was not much of it at home. Several generations of Bruskins and Gershovitzes had failed to produce a single musician, and the Gershwin parents were themselves not particularly musical. The father sang fairly well and sometimes went to the opera. When he wanted to make music it was not by any traditional method but by blowing through a comb which had tissue paper entwined through the teeth, or by vibrating a clothes pin in his mouth, or by giving a vocal imitation of a cornet. George sang the popular tunes of the day; one of these, "Put Your Arms Around Me, Honey," was a favorite. At school he learned such semiclassics as "Loch Lomond," "Annie Laurie," and "The Lost Chord."

In spite of his assumed superiority to all kids of the neighborhood who were forced to take music lessons, and despite his seeming indifference toward all music except

popular songs, George responded with an instinctive sym-
pathy to music whenever he came into contact with it. He was
about six years old when, strolling along 125th Street, he
stopped outside a penny arcade and heard Anton Rubinstein's
Melody in F on an automatic piano. "The peculiar jumps in
the music held me rooted," he later recalled. "To this very
day, I can't hear the tune without picturing myself outside
that arcade . . . standing there barefoot and in overalls,
drinking it all in avidly." One day, during the same period, while roller-skating in Harlem, he heard jazz music
outside the Baron Wilkins Club where Jim Europe and his
band performed regularly. The exciting rhythms and raucous
tunes made such an impression on him that he never forgot
them. From then on he often skated up to the club and sat
down on the sidewalk outside to listen to the music. He later
told a friend that his lifelong fascination for Negro rags,
blues, and spirituals undoubtedly began at this time; that
Jim Europe's music was partially responsible for his writing
works like *135th Street* and parts of *Porgy and Bess.*

There were other musical associations. When he was
about seven or eight he attended two free concerts at the
Educational Alliance on East Broadway. A year later he was
the victim of a puppy-love affair with a little girl of the
neighborhood; what attracted him to her was the way she
sang. There were excursions to the local penny arcades
where, at the drop of a penny, automatic machines would
disgorge recorded music through rubber ear tubings.

However, the most significant of George's musical adventures came in his tenth year. He was playing ball outside
P.S. 25 when, through the open window, he heard the
strains of Dvořák's *Humoresque* played on a violin. The
performer was one of his fellow students, an eight-year-old

prodigy by the name of Maxie Rosenzweig, who was appearing at a school entertainment. (Beginning with 1916, Maxie Rosenzweig—now called Max Rosen—enjoyed a meteoric success on the concert stages of the world.) Many years later Gershwin described his reactions to this music: "It was, to me, a flashing revelation of beauty. I made up my mind to get acquainted with this fellow, and I waited outside from three to four-thirty that afternoon, in the hopes of greeting him. It was pouring cats and dogs, and I got soaked to the skin. No luck. I returned to the school building. Rosen had long since gone; he must have left by the teachers' entrance. I found out where he lived, and dripping wet as I was, trekked to his house, unceremoniously presenting myself as an admirer. Maxie by this time had left. His family were so amused, however, that they arranged a meeting. From the first moment we became the closest of friends. We chummed about arm-in-arm; we lavished childish affection upon each other in true Jean Christophe fashion; we exchanged letters even when only a week and some hundred blocks lay between us."

Maxie was the one who opened the world of good music to George. He played for George, talked to him about the great composers, explained to him what made up the elements of a musical composition. Gershwin's curiosity now aroused, he began experimenting at the keyboard at a friend's house on 7th Street. He started by trying to reproduce the tunes he knew with the right hand while inventing some kind of harmonic background with the left. Then he tried making up melodies of his own. One of these he brought to the attention of Maxie who told him firmly and candidly: "You haven't got it in you to be a musician, George. Take my word for it. I know."

In 1910 a piano was brought into the Gershwin household on Second Avenue and 7th Street. Rose Gershwin's sister had recently acquired one and Rose was instantly fired
with the ambition of having one in her own home. Actually
she was thinking more of Ira than of George when she
planned some musical training for her family, for Ira had
been taking lessons with his aunt, Kate Wolpin, on and off
since 1908. As soon as the upright was put in place in the
living-room, George attacked it, amazing the family by playing some of the tunes he had already picked up on his
friend's piano. But the mother still intended the piano for Ira.
Kate Wolpin says that Ira was above average in musical
intelligence and receptivity. But his progress through Beyer's
exercise book was sluggish. Suspecting that the fault lay in
the fact that a doting aunt did not make for good instruction,
she decided to step aside for another teacher. It was at this
point—and not long after the appearance of a piano in the
Gershwin home—that Ira called it a day, having completed
only thirty-two pages in Beyer's. From then on, the piano was
George's.

George's first teacher was a Miss Green who, for fifty
cents a lesson, led him rigidly through Beyer's. From the
beginning George brought to the piano an intensity he had
shown for little else. He was now continually at the keyboard:
sometimes practicing, most often improvising and inventing.
Instinctively he sensed that Miss Green's formal and unimaginative instruction was not what he was looking for in his
determination to uncover for himself the hidden mysteries in
music. He changed teachers three times without finding an
answer to his needs. Two of them, like Miss Green, were
American. The third was a Hungarian named Mr. Goldfarb
who was so highly regarded in the neighborhood that he

could command $1.50 a lesson. Mr. Goldfarb had a flowing mustache and a lordly air. His approach to piano instruction was unique, avoiding scales, exercises, or even the simpler works of the masters, and concentrating exclusively on potpourris from the operas which he himself devised. It was this diet that he fed George.

With music rapidly relegating all other interests and diversions to insignificance, George now sought out friends able to satisfy his hunger for musical knowledge. One of those was a young pianist, Jack Miller, who played in the Beethoven Symphony, an amateur orchestra then giving concerts in New York. Impressed by George's enthusiasm, Miller brought him, one day in 1912, to the studio of Charles Hambitzer, a composer-pianist whom he regarded highly. George played for Hambitzer the *William Tell Overture* the way Goldfarb had taught him—with exaggerated dynamics, rubati, and uneven tempi. "Listen," Hambitzer told Gershwin, "let's hunt out the guy who taught you to play this way and shoot him—and not with an apple on his head, either."

Hambitzer later said that what attracted him immediately to Gershwin was the boy's deadly seriousness. Hambitzer offered to teach the boy, refusing to accept any payment for lessons. He became the most important single influence in Gershwin's musical development, probably the decisive influence.

Charles Hambitzer had come to New York in 1908 from Milwaukee where his father owned a music store. He had been born seventy miles from Milwaukee, in Beloit, on September 12, 1878. In Milwaukee he received a comprehensive musical training from Julius Albert Jahn, one of the finest piano teachers of the midwest, and Hugo Kaun, a visiting musician from Germany who taught him harmony, counterpoint, theory, and orchestration. Hambitzer absorbed musical knowledge effortlessly. As a child he could play the piano, violin, and cello, though none of his immediate family knew when or how he acquired this training. In short order he mastered musical theory, and became a virtuoso of the piano. As a young man he taught music at the Wisconsin Conservatory and later directed the Arthur Friend Stock Company orchestra at the Pabst Theater.

Kaun prevailed on Hambitzer to leave Milwaukee for New York. Hambitzer did so and opened a piano studio in the Morningside Park district where he became so popular that within a brief period he had seventy pupils. He also became a member of a thirty-two piece orchestra, conducted by Joseph Knecht, which gave concerts seven days a week, two to four hours a day, at the Waldorf-Astoria Hotel. These were by no means merely salon concerts devoted to popular and semiclassical favorites, but presented excellent symphonic music; the New York *Times* often listed these concerts among the major musical events of the city. Hambitzer was soloist in important piano concertos, and one of the violinists in the orchestra remembers his appearing also as a violin and cello soloist. However, a search among old Waldorf-Astoria Orchestra programs has failed to substantiate this.

Hambitzer was one of those rare musicians to whom musical expression of every kind comes as naturally as breathing. He could give a competent account of himself on about half a dozen orchestral instruments, besides the piano, violin, and cello. He could read fluently at the piano a complicated piano score, and his sight-reading was phenomenal.

He had a fantastic memory and a fabulous ear. A keen student of modern music, he was one of the first in America to perform publicly Schoenberg's piano pieces.

He was a composer of both classical works and popular music. In a serious vein he wrote several orchestral tone poems, and a suite for *Twelfth Night* which was used for a Sothern and Marlowe production. Some of his music was played by the Waldorf-Astoria Orchestra, while the suite was given by the Beethoven Symphony. In the year Gershwin came to study with him, Hambitzer completed an operetta score, *The Love Wager,* which starred Fritzi Scheff and toured the country for a year. Later he wrote a second operetta which was never performed, and also some popular songs.

Hambitzer made little effort to get any of his works published: partly because he was impractical, partly because he seemed devoid of any ambition for financial success or personal glory, and mostly out of a stifling sense of creative inadequacy. As soon as he finished a composition he would toss his manuscript aside, forget about it, and start something else. About the only works of his that were performed were those that had been commissioned. Everything else collected dust in closets and on shelves without any attempt on his part to get them recognition. After his death, most of his manuscripts disappeared mysteriously; it is more than probable that he had destroyed them.

He was a man dogged by tragedy as well as artistic frustration. A marriage in Milwaukee when he was twenty-two proved unhappy and divorce followed four years later. In 1905 he married a girl from Waukesha with whom he had fallen madly in love. After they came to New York she became a victim of tuberculosis and, returning one day in

1914 to his studio, he found her dead in bed of a lung hemorrhage. Their child, Mitzi, was adopted by the mother's family in Waukesha where she lives today, the wife of a surgeon, and the mother of three children. The death of his beloved wife sent Hambitzer to feverish work and long hours as an escape from memories. He pursued teaching, composition, and performance with an almost fanatic intensity. He now disregarded his health completely. Always delicate of constitution, this self-neglect did much to hasten his death. He died of tuberculosis in 1918, four years after his wife; he was thirty-seven.

Hambitzer was the right man at the right time in Gershwin's life. He gave the boy direction and purpose, background and training. He stimulated and inspired him. Gershwin's piano technique was strengthened through a rigorous application to exercises and scales; he was initiated into the great literature for the piano by Bach, Beethoven, Chopin, Liszt, and even such modern composers as Debussy and (remarkable when the year is considered, 1913) Ravel. Hambitzer was primarily concerned with teaching Gershwin the piano, but he did not fail to make the boy conscious of harmony, theory, and instrumentation. "I was crazy about that man," Gershwin later confessed. He scouted his neighborhood to recruit more pupils for him and found ten candidates. As a successful composer, Gershwin never failed to acknowledge his indebtedness to Hambitzer.

Hambitzer appears to have been conscious of Gershwin's latent ability from the beginning. He wrote to one sister: "I have a new pupil who will make his mark in music if anybody will. The boy is a genius, without a doubt; he's crazy about music and can't wait until it's time to take his lessons. No watching the clock for this boy." To another sister he later wrote about Gershwin: "The kid has talent, and I believe I can make something of him."

The teacher inflamed the boy with his own passion for music. Gershwin acquired a gray bookkeeper's ledger into which he neatly pasted pictures of great composers and performers which he found in current newspapers and magazines. He also carefully attached programs of the concerts he attended, for by now George was a devoted concertgoer. "I listened not only with my ears, but with my nerves, my mind, my heart. I listened so earnestly that I became saturated with music. Then I went home and listened in memory. I sat at the piano and repeated the motives." Between 1912 and 1913 he heard performances of the New York Philharmonic Orchestra, the New York Symphony Society, the Beethoven Orchestra, the Russian Symphony Orchestra, and virtuosos like Leo Ornstein (then the *enfant terrible* of modern music), Leopold Godowsky, and his friend Maxie Rosenzweig. He also attended various concerts at such local auditoriums as those at Wanamaker's and Cooper Union. Of course, he also attended performances at the Waldorf-Astoria whenever Hambitzer was soloist; a program for April 13, 1913 presented his teacher in the Rubinstein D Minor Concerto.

Gershwin was soon appearing publicly as a pianist. At the High School of Commerce, which he entered in 1912, he played at the school assembly. In the summer of 1913 he found a job as a pianist for $5.00 a week at a New York State resort in the Catskill Mountains.

He was also composing—mostly popular music. Sometime in 1913 he wrote his first song, "Since I Found You," which was never published; years later he remarked with considerable amusement how, midway in that song, his course was arrested by his inability to progress from G major to F. His second composition, while never published, was publicly performed. Early in 1914, the Finley Club, a literary society to which Ira belonged, held its annual entertainment at the Christadora House on Avenue B. Since Ira was on the arrangement committee, he put George on the musical program for the third and fifth numbers. In the fifth, George appeared as piano accompanist for several vocal selections, but in the third he gave a piano solo. Neither the composition nor its author are identified—the program merely reads "piano solo by George Gershvin"—but the piece was a tango for the piano, and the author was Gershwin himself hiding modestly behind anonymity.

This concern for popular rather than classical idioms in his first creative efforts is not without significance. It reveals that even at this early stage Gershwin's future direction was clear to him. Not even Hambitzer's determination to put him on a strict classical diet could keep George from those succulent dishes which were his favorite food. In the letter in which Hambitzer described George to his sister as a "genius" he also makes the following observation: "He wants to go in for this modern stuff, jazz and what not. But I'm not going to let him for a while. I'll see that he gets a firm foundation in the standard music first."

The formal lessons might be devoted exclusively to the masters, but George's private hours of creation belonged to Tin Pan Alley. Already, in 1913, he was a passionate admirer of Irving Berlin's, particularly of Berlin's "Alexander's Ragtime Band" which was then a rage. Again and again he tried convincing his teacher that there was musical significance to good popular music, that an American composer should use such native materials. Hambitzer was not convinced, and said so. But then, as later, Gershwin knew his mind; nobody, not even the teacher he admired, could shake him.

One idea now became fixed in his mind: to get a job in Tin Pan Alley. This meant he would have to leave school, and his mother was far from sympathetic. Though by now she had become convinced that George was not suited for a career as an accountant, she had vague ideas of setting him up in the fur business. One thing she said firmly: she would never tolerate her son becoming a popular pianist, a profession which, she said, promised only uncertainty, if not outright disaster. But George was uncompromising. After heated words had been exchanged, the mother had to yield her ground. The father, from the beginning, shrugged his shoulders with indifference at George's ambitions, since he always wanted his children to decide their own future for themselves.

Through Ben Bloom, a friend of the family, George was introduced to Mose Gumble, who held a managerial post in an up-and-coming song-publishing house called Remick's. Gumble liked the way George played the piano and offered him a job as a song plugger and staff pianist at a salary of $15.00 a week. In his own way Gershwin was already making modest history in popular music. He was the youngest song plugger in Tin Pan Alley (fifteen years old), and the first inexperienced employee hired by Remick's for that job.

3

TIN PAN ALLEY

The firm of Jerome K. Remick had originated in Detroit where, as the Whitney-Warner Publishing Company, it was swept to success on the crest of hits like "Creole Belles" and "Hiawatha." In 1902, the establishment moved to New York City, to join there several other reputable or up-and-coming publishers, including Broder and Schlam (recently from San Francisco), Joseph W. Stern, Charles K. Harris, Witmark, Leo Feist, Shapiro and Bernstein, and Harry von Tilzer. By 1914, the year in which Gershwin came to work for Remick, it was one of the most powerful publishing houses in Tin Pan Alley, by virtue of an impressive succession of song hits: "In the Shade of the Old Apple Tree," "China-town, My Chinatown," "Shine on, Harvest Moon," "By the Light of the Silvery Moon," "Put on Your Old Gray Bonnet," "Oh, You Beautiful Doll," and, in 1914, "Rebecca of Sunnybrook Farm."

Gershwin was engaged as a pianist; actually he was a song plugger. The song plugger was the catalytic agent be-tween the publisher who issued a song and the performers who made it popular with the public. Selling songs was a highly skilled and specialized science in Tin Pan Alley; the plugger was the most important single element in making a song a hit. It was the plugger's job to get his firm's songs rep-resented, sung, or played wherever there was an audience: in theaters, restaurants, dance halls, saloons, music shops. Upon his personal charm, his contacts, and his talent as salesman rested the success with which he sold his songs to vaudevillians, performers in musical comedy and burlesque, leaders of dance bands and restaurant orchestras, theater managers, singing waiters, and proprietors of stores selling sheet music.

The most direct way of getting a song performed was through stars of the theater, many of whom were given hand-some bribes to include specific songs in their acts and shows. But Tin Pan Alley had evolved other effective means of reaching the public's ear in an age before radio, television, talking pictures, extensive recordings, juke boxes, and disk jockies. In 1903 a Brooklyn electrician created the motion-picture slide. Pluggers would introduce these slides as part of the program of local motion-picture theaters, then plant a singer in the audience to perform the song while the screen flashed the lyrics and appropriate illustrations. Song plug-gers would also be planted in variety theaters. When an actor performed his song, the plugger would rise in his seat in the auditorium and sing the chorus several times until it was impressed on the consciousness and memory of the audience.

Gershwin's boss at Remick's was one of the ace song pluggers of all time, Mose Gumble. His career in popular music began at seventeen, when he started to play popular songs on the piano in a Cincinnati song shop. In the 1890s, Gumble came to New York, where he found a post as staff pianist for Shapiro, Bernstein and Company. He soon became the liaison between his firm and such theatrical stars as George M. Cohan, Weber and Fields, and Nora Bayes. In 1903 he scored his first major coup by lifting "Bedelia" to nationwide popularity and a million-copy sale. Subsequently he was engaged by Remick's where he was personally responsible for the success of "In the Shade of the Old Apple Tree" and "Oh, You Beautiful Doll," among other songs. Many years later, as representative of the Music Publishers Holding Corporation, Gumble's job was still to sell old-time song favorites, but this time to movie producers and radio performers.

As head of the song-plugging division of Remick's, Gumble had under his wing a string of pianists, of whom Gershwin was one. Each pianist occupied his own cubicle. From eight to ten hours a day, Gershwin was a prisoner to the keyboard, pounding out the current Remick song releases for visiting performers in search of new numbers. "Colored people used to come in and get me to play them 'God Send You Back to Me' in seven keys. Chorus ladies used to breathe down my back. Some of the customers treated me like dirt. Others were charming."

Among the most charming was Fred Astaire, then touring vaudeville with his sister Adele in a song and dance routine. "Wouldn't it be wonderful," Gershwin once asked Astaire, "if some day I could write a show and you and Adele would star in it?" Remembering that incident, Gershwin commented years later: "We just laughed then—but it came true."

Another visitor to the cubicle was a newspaperman working for *The Clipper,* a voice of the theater world. He was Max Abramson, who was so taken with the quality of Gershwin's piano playing that he consistently referred to him as "the genius" and did everything in his power to further the young man's career. Still another visitor was a young lyricist named Irving Caesar. Caesar haunted the halls of Remick's to try to sell his lyrics or to convince some of the firm's staff composers to set his words to music. But, before long, he found himself drawn to Remick's just to hear Gershwin play. "His rhythms had the impact of a sledge hammer. His harmonies were years ahead of the time. I had never before heard such playing of popular music."

There were times when Gumble sent Gershwin out of Remick's—to cafés, restaurants, or music stores to play Remick songs or accompany singers in them. One such mission took him to Atlantic City, New Jersey: to the sheet-music department of the local five-and-ten-cent store. At night, when the store was closed, Gershwin would have to make the rounds of nickelodeons, saloons, and smaller restaurants to place Remick songs and play them. (The swankier places were the domain of only first-string pluggers.)

It was in Atlantic City that Gershwin first met Harry Ruby, in later days a highly successful popular-song composer and one of Gershwin's lifelong friends. Like Gershwin, Ruby was at that time a humble song plugger, working for Harry von Tilzer; and like Gershwin, Ruby had come to Atlantic City to plug songs in a five-and-ten-cent store during the day, and in nickelodeons and saloons at night.

When work was over, long past midnight, all the song pluggers gathered at Child's Restaurant on the boardwalk to talk shop. "I still recall George's eagerness, his intense enthusiasm for his work, his passionate interest in every phase of the popular-music business," Harry Ruby relates. "Sometimes when he spoke of the artistic mission of popular music, we thought he was going highfalutin'. The height of artistic achievement to us was a 'pop' song that sold lots of copies, and we just didn't understand what he was talking about." But what impressed Ruby most, just as it had impressed Caesar, was Gershwin's piano playing. "It was far and beyond better than the piano playing of any of us. As I look back upon it I can say it was a completely different musical world from ours, and we did not completely understand it at the time, though we all reacted to it instinctively. I am also sure we were all jealous of him, too."

Day by day, hour by hour, Gershwin played the routine songs which Tin Pan Alley manufactured on an assembly belt. If he did not lose faith in the potentialities of American popular music it was because two Tin Pan Alley composers demonstrated even then that a popular song did not have to be derived from a matrix to be successful. The two composers were Irving Berlin and Jerome Kern.

Irving Berlin was already a giant figure in the Alley. As a boy he had been a busker in the Bowery, a song plugger for Harry von Tilzer at Tony Pastor's Music Hall in Union Square, and a singing waiter in Bowery saloons. His song-writing career was initiated in 1906 when, as a singing waiter for Pelham's Café, he wrote and published his first song lyric, "Marie from Sunny Italy," to music by the café pianist, Nick Michaelson. He kept on producing lyrics, and three years later had a two-hundred-thousand-copy song in "Sadie Salome Go Home." Then, as a salaried employee for the publishing house of Ted Snyder, he began writing music to his lyrics. In spite of the limitations then imposed upon composers by Tin Pan Alley, he was able, in 1911, to write a dynamic tune like "Alexander's Ragtime Band," which evoked a nationwide craze for ragtime music and for social dancing. Other rag tunes (notably "That Mysterious Rag," "Everybody's Doin' It," and "Everybody Step") made Berlin the "king of ragtime," as he was billed when he appeared at the Hippodrome Theatre in London in 1913. Meanwhile, in 1912, he had tapped for himself a new creative vein. The death of his young wife of typhoid fever, contracted during their honeymoon in Cuba, inspired "When I Lost You," the first of the Irving Berlin ballads. It added immeasurably to his popularity, for in short order it sold over a million copies. Then, in 1914, Berlin further extended his horizon by writing his first complete score for the Broadway stage, *Watch Your Step*, starring Vernon and Irene Castle.

The year of 1914 also saw the emergence of Jerome Kern as a major musical figure on Broadway. This was the year of his first stage triumph, *The Girl from Utah*. Its principal song "They Didn't Believe Me" accumulated the formidable sale of two million copies.

Kern was only fifteen years old when, in 1900, he walked into the publishing house of Harms and asked to see its head, Max Dreyfus. He had written a song he wanted Dreyfus to publish. Dreyfus did not accept it, but he saw enough value to it to offer Kern a salesman's job. Dreyfus' idea

was for Kern to learn something of the way Tin Pan Alley
operated from the inside; he also wanted to keep a vigilant
eye on the boy. Before long, Dreyfus published some of
Kern's songs and used his far-reaching influence to further
Kern's songs by getting him various commissions from
singers and producers. In 1905, Kern supplied a few songs
for *The Earl and the Girl;* six years later came his first complete stage score, for *La Belle Paree,* with which the Winter
Garden was opened.

Gershwin had known and played "Alexander's Ragtime Band" as a boy, and had used it as testimony to demonstrate to Hambitzer the positive values of popular music. In
Tin Pan Alley Gershwin came to know other Berlin ragtime
melodies as well as his first ballad, and his admiration for
the older man deepened. Many years later he wrote: "Irving
Berlin is the greatest American song composer . . . America's Franz Schubert." But he already felt that way in 1914.

As for Kern,. Gershwin first was attracted to his music
at the wedding of his aunt, Kate, at the Grand Central Hotel
in 1914. The band played a tune so exciting in its melodic
and harmonic construction that George rushed to the band-
stand to inquire after its title and composer. It was Kern's
"You're Here and I'm Here" from *The Girl from Utah.*
Then the band followed with "They Didn't Believe Me," and
Gershwin knew he had found a model and an inspiration.
"I followed Kern's work and studied each song he composed.
I paid him the tribute of frank imitation, and many things
I wrote at this period sounded as though Kern had written
them himself."

Gershwin was already writing popular songs. Some
appeared later in musical productions, but at the time he
wrote them, while still a hired hand at Remick's, they failed

to interest publishers. Among these efforts was "Drifting Along with the Tide," which turned up in the *Scandals of 1921* and "Some Rain Must Fall" and "Dancing Shoes" which found a haven in *A Dangerous Maid* in 1921. The first was pleasing for its neat structural balance, with the symmetrical rise and ebb of the melodic line; the second had interesting chromatic harmonies; the third was rhythmically alive. When Gershwin showed these songs to Mose Gumble, the latter dismissed them. "You're paid to play the piano not to write songs," he said. "We've plenty of song writers under contract."

Gershwin also brought these songs to Irving Berlin, who was now a publisher, a member of the house of Waterson, Berlin and Snyder. Berlin liked the songs, praised them, and foresaw a successful future for Gershwin, but made no move to take any of them for his firm. Louis Muir, who had written the ragtime classic "Waiting for the Robert E. Lee," was also generous in praise.

But in 1916 the name of George Gershwin finally appeared on a copy of sheet music. The song was "When You Want 'Em You Can't Get 'Em," with lyrics by Murray Roth, a young man Gershwin had met in Tin Pan Alley and who subsequently became a motion-picture executive. Sophie Tucker heard the song, liked the graceful arch of the melody with its occasional excursion into humor and colloquialism, and recommended it to Harry von Tilzer, who published it. Roth sold his lyrics outright for $15.00. George preferred gambling on royalties, and his total earnings were the $5.00 he had received as an advance. One of the now-rare printed copies is in Ira's possession.

The first published song was shortly followed by the first of Gershwin's songs to reach the musical-comedy stage.

Gershwin and Roth wrote "The Runaway Girl," a number they felt was suitable for a Winter Garden production. They played it for a Mr. Simmons of the Shubert office, who, in turn, sent them to Sigmund Romberg, then the official staff composer for Shubert. Romberg's career as one of the most successful composers of operetta in America was still in the future; but by 1916 (and within a period of only two years) he had completed scores for ten Shubert musicals, including two *Passing Shows,* and six Winter Garden productions. He was, then, already a person of some consequence in the theater.

Gershwin played for Romberg "The Runaway Girl," together with several other songs. Romberg accepted none of them, but he was sufficiently impressed with Gershwin's talent to suggest the possibility of their collaborating on some new Winter Garden production. Exhilarated by such a prospect, Gershwin kept bringing songs to Romberg, until one, "The Making of a Girl," was selected and used in *The Passing Show of 1916.* Harold Atteridge, who wrote the lyrics for most of Romberg's musicals, prepared the lyric. *The Passing Show* opened at the Winter Garden on June 22, 1916. Gershwin's song was in a score that included fourteen Romberg numbers, and passed unnoticed. His debut in the theater netted him about $7.00.

There was still another "first" for Gershwin in 1916. In collaboration with Will Donaldson, he wrote his first instrumental number in a popular style, a piano rag called *Rialto Ripples,* which Remick published in 1917. With its formal procedures, stilted syncopations, and a stilted melody marked by rippling triplets, *Rialto Ripples* marked no revolution in American popular music. It was not even much of a novelty. Piano rags had previously been written with outstanding success by many composers, including Scott Joplin, the composer of "The Maple Leaf Rag." One of the principal figures in the writing of such syncopated music for the piano at this time was Felix Arndt, composer of "Nola," which Vincent Lopez has used so effectively as his personal theme song. Arndt's influence on Gershwin has never been properly stressed. Gershwin often visited Arndt at his studio in the Aeolian Building on 42nd Street and was a great admirer of his piano music, which the composer played to him by the hour. It is this contact with Arndt that possibly stimulated Gershwin to write *Rialto Ripples*. In any event, Arndt's ragtime writing for the piano, which Gershwin learned and assimilated, was by no means a negligible influence in shaping Gershwin's own style of writing for the piano.

It was also through Arndt that Gershwin came to make piano rolls in January 1916, first for Perfection and later the same year for Universal. Gershwin originally received a fee of $25.00 for six rolls, and afterwards somewhat more than that. During 1916 he recorded about thirty popular numbers of the day, sometimes using his own name, and sometimes hiding under such pseudonyms as Bert Wynn, Fred Murtha, and James Baker.

Gershwin's attitude toward the songs of Berlin and Kern, and the piano music of Arndt, was characteristic. It reflected the enormous yearning to learn through imitation and assimilation. He knew that to become an important composer of popular music he had to acquire experiences other than those he could accumulate in Tin Pan Alley. Consequently, he went searching in other areas. The story is told that in his cubicle at Remick's, one day, he started practicing one of the Preludes and Fugues from Bach's *Well-Tempered Clavier*. A fellow song plugger asked: "Are you studying to be a concert pianist, George?" Gershwin answered: "No, I'm studying to be a great popular-song composer."

He kept going to concerts, always trying to uncover in the music of the masters harmonic, melodic, and rhythmic approaches that he could use advantageously. And he kept on with his music study. The piano lessons with Hambitzer continued until that teacher's death in 1918. And these were combined with the study of harmony, theory, and orchestration with Edward Kilenyi.

Kilenyi was a Hungarian-born musician who had studied with Pietro Mascagni in Rome and at the Cologne Conservatory. He came to the United States when he was twenty-two and attended Columbia University where he did graduate work on a Mosenthal Fellowship. While attending Columbia, Kilenyi supported himself by playing the violin in the Waldorf-Astoria Orchestra, of which Hambitzer was the pianist. Many years later, Kilenyi became famous as director of motion-picture theater orchestras in New York, and as a composer and musical director for various motion-picture studios in Hollywood, where he is now employed. His son, also named Edward Kilenyi, has achieved world-wide recognition as a concert pianist.

One day, in 1915, Hambitzer approached Kilenyi and urged him to accept Gershwin as a pupil in harmony and theory. "The boy is not only talented," Hambitzer said, "but is uncommonly serious in his love for music and in his search for knowledge. The modesty with which he comes to his piano lessons, the respect and gratitude with which he accepts instruction—all this has impressed and touched me. He wants to study harmony seriously, and I thought of you in this connection."

Kilenyi became the second of Gershwin's two most important teachers. There would be others, and they were helpful. But Gershwin himself always looked upon Hambitzer and Kilenyi as the ones who played the most vital role in shaping his musical development; and to the end of his life, Gershwin acknowledged his indebtedness to both men. Gershwin studied with Kilenyi, on and off, for about five years, but even after that he intermittently sought out his teacher for advice.

For the first eight months, Gershwin took two lessons a week. Kilenyi clearly recalls his first impression. He saw before him an earnest, soft-spoken young man, somewhat diffident, with a kind of melancholy expression on his face. Gershwin knew little about theory, and Kilenyi set out to teach him the fundamentals. After that came lessons in part-writing, transposition, modulation, and instrumentation. Three years later, Kilenyi engaged orchestral performers to come to the lessons and play for Gershwin each of the important instruments of the symphony orchestra. The following year Kilenyi led Gershwin through an analytical dissection of works like Beethoven's Eighth Symphony and the *Spring Sonata* to point up how a great composer worked, the devices he used and why, his harmonic techniques, and so forth. In this way, Gershwin acquired an intimate insight into many famous musical works from Haydn to Debussy and Richard Strauss.

Gershwin's exercise books still exist. They reveal how meticulous he was in being accurate and correct, how fastidious he was about neatness. They also betray the fact that once he learned basic rules Gershwin often tried to work out his personal ideas in direct opposition to established practice. In this he was encouraged by his teacher. While Kilenyi insisted that Gershwin must first learn the established styles, he was lenient when his pupil tried to violate them.

Kilenyi was also sympathetic to Gershwin's career in Tin Pan Alley. This was in direct opposition to many later musicians and teachers who felt he should devote himself only to serious creation. In fact, Kilenyi felt strongly (and said so in 1919) that Gershwin's popular music might easily be a short cut by which the young man might gain a sympathetic hearing for his more serious endeavors. "You will face the same difficulty all Americans do trying to have their works performed," Kilenyi told him—and this at a time when Americans were rarely performed. "It will bring you nearer your goal if you become a big success as a popular composer, for then conductors will come to you to ask for serious works."

After the first eight months, the lessons became less regular. Gershwin's varied commitments, in and out of New York, made a fixed schedule impossible between teacher and pupil. But once an assignment was completed, Gershwin always returned for more lessons. Sometimes he would bring Kilenyi numbers from a recently completed musical comedy for criticism and analysis. Sometimes he would come with the orchestrations others made of his scores in order to study them with his teacher and see if they could be improved. "He had an extraordinary faculty or genius," says Kilenyi, "to absorb everything, and to apply what he learned to his own music."

While George was working in Tin Pan Alley, his brother Ira was proceeding with his academic education in preparation for a teaching career. He attended Townsend Harris Hall, which was affiliated with the College of the City of New York. Of all the city high schools, this made the most exacting demands on students since it compressed the regular four year course in three. While at Townsend Harris, Ira edited, wrote, illustrated, and issued a one-page newspaper, *The Leaf*, which he diligently brought out once a week for twenty-six weeks for a single subscriber, his older second cousin. (George imitated his brother by starting a one-man periodical of his own, *The Merry Musician*. But he lost interest in it after one issue.) Ira soon found a wider audience for his talent by doing the illustrations for the school magazine.

Despite his passion for reading and his artistic temperament, Ira was no shining light at school. He had to stay an extra term at Townsend Harris to make up two subjects before going on to the College of the City of New York, which he finally entered in February 1914. Here he did hardly better. In his second year he was still taking first-year mathematics. "The only possible way, seemingly, of getting a diploma," he explained, "was to remain long enough in college to earn one by squatter's rights." He stayed at college only two years. In that time he wrote a regular column with Erwin Harburg (later "Yip" Harburg, the celebrated lyricist, and a close friend) for *The Campus*, and contributed sketches and verses to *The Mercury*, both college publications.

After transferring from day to night college, Ira worked during the day as a cashier in a Turkish bath partly owned by his father. But by now Ira had discarded all ideas

George Gershwin (1926). (*Portrait by Steichen*)

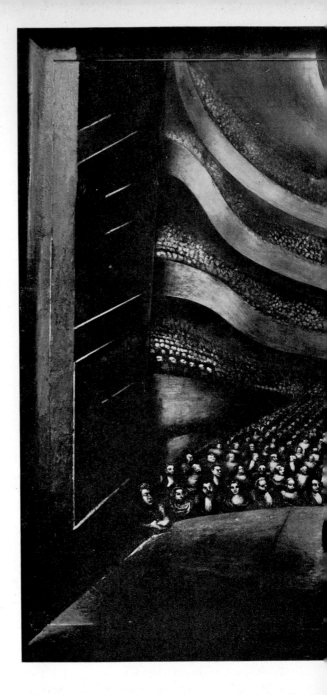

"Portrait of a Concert Hall," a painting by Siqueiros. The George Gershwin concert at the Metropolitan Opera House on November 1, 1932.

Left to right, front row: Siqueiros, Mabel Schirmer, Leopold Godowsky, Jr., Mrs. Godowsky (Frances Gershwin), Dr. Zilboorg, Leonore Gershwin, Ira Gershwin, and Leopold Godowsky, Sr. *Right to left, front row:* Bill Daly, Kay Swift, Lou and Emily Paley, Arthur Gershwin, Rose and Morris Gershwin. *Second row:* Oscar Levant and Henry Botkin (*left*); Max Dreyfus (*right*).

George Gershwin (1936).

George Gershwin (1933).
(*Portrait by Carl Van Vechten*)

A head of Gershwin by Isamu Noguchi.

George Gershwin, rehearsing the Los Angeles Philharmonic (1937). (*Photo by Otto Rothschild*)

George Gershwin in Seattle for concert appearance (1936).

George and Ira Gershwin (1930).

George and Ira Gershwin collaborating in Beverly Hills (1937).

Right, top:
Ira Gershwin (1938). (*Photo by ASCAP*)

Right, bottom:
Ira Gershwin today. (*Photo by Tommy Amer*)

Morris and Rose Gershwin (in the 1890's).

Morris Gershwin (1893).

Rose Gershwin (1936). A camera portrait by George Gershwin.

George Gershwin at the age of ten.   Ira Gershwin at the age of six.

George Gershwin's principal teachers: *above:* Edward Kilenyi (a drawing by Willy Pogany); *below:* Charles Hambitzer (*photo courtesy of Mrs. Hambitzer Reel*).

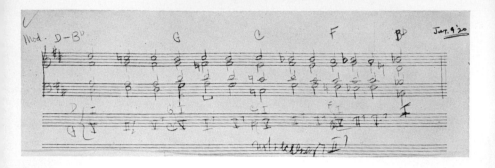

George Gershwin's student exercises: *above*, an exercise in modulation; *below*, this passage shows how systematically he studied orchestration.

Top, the comment, "devilish hard, you say," is Kilenyi's. George had expressed the opinion to his teacher that the use of chords other than those he was studying was a "devilishly hard" procedure. *Bottom*, this passage demonstrates how carefully he worked on his harmony exercises.

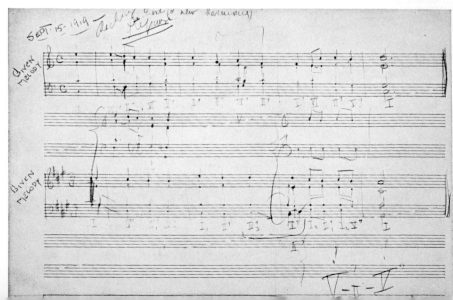

The Gershwin Circle at the Atlantic Hotel, Belmar, N. J., in 1926. Among those in the group are George, Ira, and Leonore Gershwin; S. N. Behrman; Milton and Celia Ager; Lou and Emily Paley; Mr. and Mrs. Bela Blau; Mischa Levitzki; Howard Dietz; Phil Charig.

of becoming a teacher, and for a time thought of studying medicine. As a preliminary, he went to Columbia University Extension. But when he failed chemistry in his first term he knew he would have to seek out his destiny away from the classroom.

In 1917 he worked as a cashier at The Lafayette Baths, which were owned jointly by his father and uncle. Above the baths there were three floors of hotel rooms. One of the hotel residents was Paul Potter, who had worked for the theatrical producer, Charles Frohman, and who had dramatized *Trilby* for the Broadway stage. One day, Ira Gershwin showed Potter one of his literary efforts, a brief sketch entitled "The Shrine." Potter liked it, and suggested that he send it to the magazine the *Smart Set,* then edited by H. L. Mencken and George Jean Nathan. It was accepted, and in the issue of February 1918 it appeared under the pseudonym of "Bruskin Gershwin." It reads as follows:

The Shrine

Fascinated, he would sit before it, glorifying at such times a sublime, shivery sensation . . . and incomprehensive wonder at the beauty of it all. Reverent before it, he felt invigorated with the spirit of eternal youth and happiness. Such soul-absorbing devotion to the embodiment of an ideal was unprecedented.

And one day it lay shattered to a thousand sharp, jagged fragments.

Panic-stricken, ashen-lined, he was scarcely able to mutter, "Gawd! Seven years bad luck."

For this Ira received the payment of $1.00. Bud De Sylva, already a successful lyricist at the time, told Gershwin

that he would have preferred getting a dollar check from
Mencken and Nathan than several thousands from Remick's.
"This was very charming of him," Ira remarks wryly, "but
the fact remains he left several millions."

THE APPRENTICE

After spending more than two years at Remick's, Gershwin had had enough of Tin Pan Alley. The cubicle was smothering him. Now that one of his songs had appeared in a Broadway revue he was thinking more and more in terms of writing for the stage. He felt that the theater provided a young composer with a wider scope for his talent than did Tin Pan Alley. Just as he had once sought out Tin Pan Alley as the logical school in which to learn the song-writing technique, so now he looked eagerly to the Broadway theater as the university in which to develop a personal style.

He told Mose Gumble he was through with Remick's early in 1917, then set out to find a new job. One of his friends, a Negro arranger, Will Vodery, found him a place as pianist at Fox's City Theater in 14th Street, for $25.00 a week. The City Theater was a vaudeville house with continuous performances. During the so-called "supper period," when the orchestra went out for the evening meal, a pianist took over the accompaniment for the acts. This was Gershwin's job, and his immediate predecessor at it had been Chico Marx. For the first few acts he did well, particularly since some of the numbers came from Remick's. But the headline act had original music which Gershwin was required to read at sight from manuscript. He missed a few cues and became flustered. Suddenly he discovered he was playing one song while the chorus was singing another. The comedian exploited this dilemma for laughs, making acidulous asides about the quality of the piano playing, guffawing, provoking laughs from the players on the stage and the people in the audience. Gershwin's humiliation was so intense that he could no longer play a note. The act continued without music. Gershwin fled from the piano and told the cashier he was quitting; he did not even bother to ask for his day's pay. "The whole experience left a scar on my memory," he said.

His next job brought him for the first time into everyday contact with Jerome Kern. Kern and Victor Herbert had collaborated on the score for a musical, *Miss 1917*, for which P. G. Wodehouse and Guy Bolton wrote the book, and which Ziegfeld and Dillingham decided to produce. Gershwin was hired as rehearsal pianist for $35.00 a week. His duties consisted of coaching the chorus and ensemble numbers, and rehearsing the principals. When he was not working, he entertained the cast and other members of the company, with improvised recitals. Everybody was deeply affected by his playing. Harry Askin, the company manager, became so convinced of Gershwin's talent after hearing him that he would soon be instrumental in bringing him to the attention of the most powerful publisher in Tin Pan Alley, Max Dreyfus. George White, one of the dancers in the cast, remembered Gershwin's musicianship when, three years later, he was looking for a new composer for his *Scandals*. Jerome Kern once said that it was during this period that he knew that "this was a young man who was going to go places." He urged Gershwin, however, to be sure to get plenty of experience working in the theater before trying to write music for it.

Miss 1917 overflowed with theatrical riches. Besides Ziegfeld, Dillingham, Kern, Herbert, Wodehouse, Bolton, and Wayburn—each already a person of some consequence on Broadway—the collaborators included: Joseph Urban as designer of sets and Adolph Bohm, choreographer. The star-filled cast included Vivienne Segal, Van and Schenck, Lilyan Tashman, Lew Fields, Irene Castle, Ann Pennington, George White, Marion Davies, and Peggy Hopkins. Yet *Miss 1917* was a failure, surviving only a little more than a month. The crowning paradox is that, despite the glittering array of names to crowd that production, *Miss 1917* is today remembered only for its rehearsal pianist.

Every Sunday evening leading members of the *Miss 1917* cast appeared in concerts at the Century Theater. Gershwin drew the assignment of accompanying. At one of these concerts, Vivienne Segal sang two Gershwin songs, "You—oo Just You" and "There's More to the Kiss than X-X-X." This concert was attended by a representative from Remick's who accepted "You—oo Just You" for publication. Thus a Gershwin song, with Vivienne Segal's picture on the cover, finally reached Remick's lists in 1918.

This publication linked for the first time the names of George Gershwin as composer and Irving Caesar as lyricist. Caesar, who was three years older than Gershwin, received his academic education in the city public schools and at the College of the City of New York. He came to know Henry Ford who, in 1915, made him the official stenographer of the Henry Ford Peace Ship which floated to Europe with the somewhat impractical intention of bringing World War I to an end. When the war did come to an end, through the more normal procedure of Germany's defeat on the battlefield, Ford prevailed on Caesar to work as a mechanic in his automobile plant so that the young man might acquire enough of the know-how of automobiles to be able to run a branch of his export division. Caesar's job was a menial one: he filled the grease in the rear axles on the conveyor belt. But already his hopes for the future lay in the song business. He spent his free time roaming around Tin Pan Alley and trying to market his lyrics.

Caesar first met Gershwin during his visits to Remick's, where he soon returned habitually not to sell lyrics but to hear Gershwin play the piano. They soon became collaborators. Their first published song, "You—oo Just You," was sung by Adele Rowland in *Hitchy-Koo of 1918*. Two other songs, both published in 1918, appeared in musicals a year later: "There's More to the Kiss than X-X-X" in both *Good Morning Judge* and *La, La Lucille*, and "I Was So Young, You Were So Beautiful" in *Good Morning Judge*.

One day Gershwin visited Caesar at the Ford plant, and as Caesar worked at the conveyor belt, they talked about song ideas. Ten rear axles passed Caesar by without his applying the necessary grease, and they all later burned out. The foreman decided to shift Caesar to a clerk's desk where he could do less damage. Not until he wrote his first major success with Gershwin did Caesar find the confidence to leave Ford's factory and concentrate on lyric writing.

Besides being collaborators, they became intimate friends. On Sunday evenings they would often go to a social club which met in a restaurant on 16th Street and Fifth Avenue. There Gershwin would play the piano and Caesar would sing and do improvisations for the enjoyment of their friends. Gershwin and Caesar often went to the theater together (mostly to Kern's musicals), or would sneak into concerts at Carnegie Hall through the back entrance on 56th Street, or play billiards in Broadway poolrooms.

Other close friends of Gershwin's during this period were Herman and Lou Paley, cousins of Max Abramson. Herman had studied with both of Gershwin's teachers, Hambitzer and Kilenyi, and by the time Gershwin came to know him well had already become a famous song composer through such hits as "Billy" and "I Can Hear the Ukeleles Calling Me." Herman Paley and Max Abramson, convinced of Gershwin's extraordinary talent, would often bring him to the Paley house. There George met Herman's brother, Lou, a schoolteacher who lived in the world of books and whose literary and cultural background George admired; also, Lou's girl friend, Emily Strunsky. After Lou and Emily got married, George was a frequent visitor to their home on Saturday evenings to participate with Buddy De Sylva, Howard Dietz, Morrie Ryskind, Joe Meyer, Irving Caesar, Groucho Marx, and others in the discussion of books and the theater that took place there regularly over steaming teacups, and in playing games of charades which usually followed the discussions. Once in a while, George would bring along Ira. Ira met and became attracted to Emily's dynamic and highly attractive sister, Leonore, who in the middle 1920s became his wife.

Gershwin remained singularly attached to both Lou and Emily Paley throughout his life; he sometimes said that Emily was the kind of woman he would have liked to marry. Another lifetime friendship for George began in the Paley household, with George Pallay, brother of Max Abramson, and Lou Paley's cousin. Pallay, who was two years younger than Gershwin, was a stockbroker who in 1918 had parlayed a $25.00-a-week job as clerk for a stock investment house into several hundreds of thousands of dollars of stock securities. He had a lust for living which the young and still inexperienced Gershwin admired and envied. They were drawn to each other and spent many an evening, late in 1918, making the rounds of night clubs, entertaining chorus girls, and spending money with a prodigal hand. In time their friendship deepened. Pallay eventually became one of the few friends to whom Gershwin entrusted his most personal confidences.

Already Gershwin had the zest for parties, night life, and beautiful women which remained with him permanently. But then, as later, his music came first. One of his friends recalls that once at a party Gershwin had a beautiful girl on his lap. When someone suddenly asked him to play the piano he completely forgot the girl and got up so fast to reach the piano that she fell on the floor. He was just as impatient and just as eager in advancing his career as a composer. His single passion was to get ahead, to become as good as Berlin or Kern. "He had such a drive," a colleague of his says, "and he tried to move so fast, that he left the rest of us far behind. We wouldn't, or couldn't, keep up with him."

He was playing his music to whoever would listen to

it. Thus it was that in 1918 he played for Sigmund Spaeth, then the music editor of the New York *Evening Mail*. Spaeth recalled the event a quarter of a century later in the *Herald Tribune:*

> The boy sat down at the piano, on one of those old-fashioned fringed stools, and played . . . with good technique and a nice musical feeling. But with almost daily virtuoso performances vivid in my ears, I did not repair to the street for dancing.

Then Gershwin played a few serious pieces he had written— some novelettes and a toccata that were weak distillations of Schumann and Liszt. Once again Spaeth felt that there was nothing to shout about. Finally, Gershwin performed some of his own popular tunes. Spaeth continues:

> The critic sat up and paid attention. . . . "If you want my advice, I'd suggest sticking to popular music for a while and saving your serious work until some time later."

Gershwin was continually on the alert for a position that could bring him further ahead as a composer. One day Irving Berlin came to him with an attractive offer. Gershwin had recently impressed him with the quiet competence with which he had put down on paper, from dictation, one of Berlin's ragtime melodies. (The manuscript today is one of Berlin's proud possessions.) Then Gershwin had played the tune. "I'll never forget his playing," Berlin says. "It sounded like a different song."

Berlin needed an arranger and musical secretary and

was ready to pay well for the right man. "The job is yours," Berlin told him, "if you want it. But I hope you don't take it. You are too talented to be an arranger and secretary. If you worked for me you might start writing the way I do, and your own style might become cramped. You are meant for big things."

Gershwin recognized the wisdom of Berlin's advice and had the courage to turn down the offer. He would wait for something more suitable to turn up. It did. While he was working as an accompanist for Louise Dresser—then touring the Keith vaudeville circuit—Harry Askin brought his name to the attention of Max Dreyfus.

Dreyfus was a power in the music industry. He was head of the publishing house of T. B. Harms where his keen musicianship and discernment were responsible for uncovering much latent talent and producing many a song hit. Dreyfus had worked his way up in Tin Pan Alley from the depths, having begun as an errand boy for the firm of Howley and Haviland. By gradual stages he progressed to the posts of shipping clerk, song plugger, arranger, and minor executive. His first major achievement as publisher was with Paul Dresser's ballad, "Just Tell Them That You Saw Me," which he accepted for Howley and Haviland in 1895; it sold a million copies and introduced into everyday conversation the title phrase. In the early 1900s he joined up with Tom and Alec Harms, first as arranger, then as song plugger, after that as composer, and finally as executive. Dreyfus was responsible for taking an obscure composer of piano pieces and overnight making him one of America's most successful operetta composers—for it was his decision that gave Rudolf Friml the assignment to write the music for *The Firefly* in 1911. He also helped discover Kern.

After Gershwin returned to New York from his tour with Louise Dresser he met Dreyfus for the first time. Dreyfus has said that when Gershwin came into the office he knew nothing about the composer other than what Askin had told him; Dreyfus, at the time, had not seen any of the songs Gershwin had published. But that first interview impressed him with the young man's earnestness, particularly when he tried to explain the kind of songs he wanted to write. "He was the kind of man I like to gamble on," Dreyfus said, "and I decided to gamble." He offered Gershwin a drawing account of $35.00 a week. There were to be no set duties or hours. All Gershwin had to do was to keep on writing songs and submitting them to Dreyfus. Under this novel arrangement, Gershwin began an association with the house of Harms that yielded lavish financial rewards to all concerned. For the next decade, beginning with "Some Wonderful Sort of Someone" in 1918, Harms was Gershwin's exclusive publisher.

Dreyfus today firmly denies that he "discovered" Gershwin or that he did anything more to advance Gershwin's career than to publish his songs. "A man with Gershwin's talent did not need anybody to push him ahead. His talent did all the pushing." But Dreyfus' modesty and consistent refusal to focus attention on himself is well known. There can be little question but that in that quiet, unassuming, and frequently inscrutable way of his, Dreyfus began pulling the strings for Gershwin from the moment he hired him.

One day in 1918 a producer by the name of Perkins came to Dreyfus with the idea for a revue starring Joe Cook, and including a bicycle act, a twenty-five piece colored band headed by Jim Europe, and sundry other attractions. Dreyfus

felt the production had some merit, gave the producer an
advance together with an offer to pay for all orchestrations.
When Perkins further explained he needed five more musical numbers, Dreyfus instantly suggested the name of George
Gershwin.

That revue, *Half-Past Eight,* proved to be a comedy of
errors and mishaps. It opened, and closed, in Syracuse, New
York. Since Perkins could not pay for the advertised bevy of
chorus girls, he had to resort to the use of his male performers—wearing Chinese pajamas, their faces covered by large
umbrellas; in the finale he tried to pass them off as the
chorus-girl line. On opening night the deception might have
worked but for the unfortunate development that three of
the umbrellas failed to function properly, mercilessly betray-
ing the sex of the chorus. *"Half-Past Eight,"* remarked the
local paper the following morning, "isn't worth even the
war tax."

By Wednesday matinee one of the principal acts, sens-
ing imminent disaster, precipitously left the cast, leaving
behind a yawning gap in the production. How to fill the
hole? The producer urged Gershwin to go out on the stage
and play the piano. Diffidently, hesitantly, Gershwin went
out and played some of his own songs. This was one of the
rare occasions when his piano playing failed to make an impression. Since none of his songs was known to anybody in
the audience, its reaction was both frigid and silent.

Half-Past Eight played its last performance that Friday evening. Then it expired unlamented. Gershwin never
received the money promised him for his share in the collaboration (about fifteen hundred dollars).

Another stage venture in which Gershwin was involved in 1918 did not turn out much happier. Nora Bayes,

the dynamic singing star of vaudeville, the Ziegfeld *Follies,*
and musical comedy, came upon Gershwin's "Some Wonderful Sort of Someone" and decided to include it in *Ladies
First,* in which she was then starring. Midway in the show
all action stopped dead as Bayes monopolized the limelight
and went through a program of her specialties. For this
part of the show she required the services of a piano accompanist, and when *Ladies First* went on a six-week tour she
hired Gershwin. During the tour other Gershwin numbers
were interpolated into parts of the show, among them "The
Real American Folk Song."

When *Ladies First* came to Pittsburgh, one of those
who saw it was Oscar Levant, then still only a boy. Levant,
of course, had never before heard the name of Gershwin. His
ear, consequently, was at first fixed on the dynamic singing
star. Soon he found the piano accompaniment seizing his ear
and attention. He wrote in *A Smattering of Ignorance:* "I
had never before heard such a brisk, unstudied, completely
free and inventive playing, all within a consistent frame-
work."

While on this tour Gershwin wrote Max Abramson
from Cleveland:

> Baldwin Sloane (composer of *Ladies First*) told me
> he received $400 royalty from Trenton and Pittsburgh.
> Zowie! Why didn't I write the show and let him interpo-
> late? He gets 3% of the gross. . . . I think Miss Bayes is
> having my name put on the program as a writer of interpo-
> lated songs. If she does, she'll be doing me a justice that I
> sorely need to get into the select circle of composers in New
> York. . . . Seriously, I am thinking of writing a show. In
> spite of what J. K. [Jerome Kern] told me. I am getting

confidence and encouragement from this show, and B. Sloane and his royalties. I'm going to make an attempt when I reach New York.

Gershwin and Nora Bayes did not get along well. Gershwin's creative approach to accompaniment upset her, particularly his sudden impromptu interpolations of a contrapuntal countertheme, his new treatments of a rhythmic phrase, or his sudden leap into a new key. Singer and accompanist parted when Gershwin stoutly refused to alter one of his songs at her suggestion. When informed by the proud lady that even Berlin and Kern changed their songs for her when she asked them, Gershwin answered: "I like the song the way it is."

THE FIRST SONG HIT —
THE FIRST MUSICAL
COMEDY

If 1918 had brought mostly frustration and defeat, 1919 was to be the first of Gershwin's banner years. Old songs found a haven in various Broadway productions, including *Look Who's Here, The Lady in Red,* and *Good Morning Judge.* New songs supplemented the old, sprouting out in *Morris Gest's Midnight Whirl, Sinbad,* and the stage show of the Capitol Theater.

Much more important to Gershwin than any individual song was the writing of his first complete score for a Broadway musical.

In 1919, Alex A. Aarons, a young man making his bow as a producer, commissioned Gershwin to write all the music for *La, La Lucille*. At this time, Aarons was twenty-nine, the proprietor of Finchley's, a New York clothing establishment since grown famous. His father, Alfred E. Aarons, was general manager of Klaw and Erlanger, and successful composer. Alex was born and raised in Philadelphia where he received some musical training and acquired a sensitive discrimination and acute discernment. He was ever partial to music with original approaches, new viewpoints, experimental techniques. The changing tonalities and chromatic harmonies in a song like Gershwin's "Some Wonderful Sort of Someone"; the new attitude toward the popular-song form in "Something About Love," in which the chorus ended in a protracted sequence; the surprise chromaticisms in the verse of "There's More to the Kiss than X-X-X"; the extended melodic line in "I Was So Young, You Were So Beautiful," where the melody of the chorus sweeps across twenty-four bars instead of the more usual sixteen—all this was the kind of iconoclasm that delighted young Aarons. When, therefore, Aarons decided to give up the clothing business for the theater, and made plans to produce *La, La Lucille* in 1919, he wanted the relatively inexperienced and unknown Gershwin for the music. His father had more practical ideas, he preferred Victor Herbert. But the younger Aarons was stubborn and Gershwin was hired.

The book by Fred Jackson, described as a "farce with music," concentrated on the bedroom. John Smith, a dentist, is left two millions by his aunt, but only on the condition that he divorce his wife, Lucille, whom he had picked up on the chorus line. An astute lawyer suggests to John that he divorce his wife, pick up the inheritance, and then remarry her. Most of the action takes place in a bridal suite of a Philadelphia hotel to which John Smith comes to be compromised by a corespondent who, carefully selected by Lucille, is the hotel scrubwoman. Since the hotel has no less than thirty-eight John Smiths on the register, and since the adjoining bridal suite is occupied by a newly married Mr. and Mrs. John Smith, complications ensue to the embarrassment and, at times, dismay of all concerned, including many innocent and soon outraged visitors.

With John E. Hazard as the dentist and Janet Velie as Lucille the musical tried out in Atlantic City and Boston. On May 26, 1919, it became the first musical to play the recently opened Henry Miller Theater. All things considered, *La, La Lucille* did well. It survived the summer heat and the Actors Equity strike to achieve a run of over one hundred performances.

The Gershwin score had a dozen numbers. Two of them were lifted out of the composer's trunk: "The Ten Commandments of Love," which he had written for *Half-Past Eight,* and "There's More to the Kiss Than X-X-X," in which he had collaborated with Irving Caesar. All the others —to lyrics by Arthur Jackson and B. G. De Sylva—were new, and six were published by Harms. The entire score is functional and articulate, but not even the best songs reveal much more than professional slickness. The principal song was "Nobody but You," which had an ingratiating Jerome Kern-ish charm; a secondary hit, "Tee-Oodle-Um-Bum-Bo," had a vital rhythmic impulse.

On October 24, 1919, a new motion-picture palace opened in New York City on Broadway and 51st Street, the Capitol Theater. For the opening week, Ned Wayburn prepared a sumptuous stage show prefacing the feature picture, and he used two new Gershwin songs including "Come to

the Moon" (lyrics by Lou Paley and Ned Wayburn) and
"Swanee."

The idea for "Swanee" was born during a lunch at
Dinty Moore's. Irving Caesar and Gershwin had met to discuss new ideas for songs. Caesar suggested that they write a
one-step in the style of "Hindustan," then in vogue. "Let's
use an American locale," Caesar suggested. And Gershwin
added: "Just like Stephen Foster did in 'Swanee River.'"
It did not take them long to agree on the subject of Swanee
River. They kept on discussing the idea and allowing it to
acquire a definite shape, as they rode atop a bus to Gershwin's apartment—then located at 520 West 144th Street
in the Washington Heights section of New York. By the time
they reached there, much of the song was clear in the minds
of both composer and lyricist. They went to the piano in the
living-room to work out the details.

At the moment, in the adjoining dining-room which
was separated by drawn portieres, a poker game was in progress. At first the poker players were annoyed at the disturb-
ance caused by George's playing and Caesar's singing as they
worked on their song. One of the card players called out:
"Can't you two work some other time?" But as the song began assuming a recognizable form and personality—and the
process had taken less than half an hour—and after Gershwin
had played it through several times, the card players became interested. The game was momentarily stopped. Papa
Gershwin improvised an obbligato for the melody by whis-
tling through tissue paper in the teeth of a comb.

"Swanee" was one of the songs Gershwin brought to
Ned Wayburn for the Capitol Theater show, and Wayburn
took it without hesitation. How well he thought of it can be
guessed by the impressive setting he provided. After the song

was introduced, sixty chorus girls, with electric lights glowing on their slippers, danced to its rhythms on an otherwise darkened stage. Since the orchestra then performing at the theater was the famous band of Arthur Pryor, "Swanee" was given in a band arrangement.

The audience reaction was, at best, only lukewarm. Gershwin and Caesar loitered outside the theater to see how the sheet music was moving in the lobby and were mortified to see how few buyers there were. The sale was just as poor in the shops. Max Dreyfus tried to console Gershwin by telling him that even if the song were not commercial, it was good, and a credit to both the composer and the publisher. Caesar was so discouraged that, one day, he offered to sell all his rights to the lyrics for $200.00, but was dissuaded by Gershwin from doing so.

The history of "Swanee" might have ended at this point but for the fact that one of the most magnetic stars of the Broadway stage became interested in it—Al Jolson. Jolson had recently met Gershwin in Atlantic City, New Jersey, when *La, La Lucille* tried out there; they were introduced by Charles Previn, the conductor of the Gershwin show. When Jolson ran an elaborate party in New York City sometime later he did not forget to invite Gershwin, who had made a good impression on him. Gershwin played some of his songs. When he came to "Swanee," Jolson seized it, saying he wanted it for one of his Winter Garden shows. Jolson made the difference. When he introduced it at a Sunday night concert at the Winter Garden he brought down the house. This reception encouraged him to interpolate it in *Sinbad*. The song now caught on, spreading through the country like contagion. In a year's time it sold over two million records and one million copies of sheet music. Each of the two collaborators earned approximately $10,000 in royalties during the first year, a sum that then represented to each something of a fortune.

The song also became popular in Europe, made famous in London by Laddy Cliff and in Paris by Harry Pilcer. It even reached Constantinople where, in 1920, a Russian musician named Vladimir Dukelsky—but subsequently famous as Vernon Duke—bought a copy of the sheet music and was "sent . . . into ecstasies. The bold sweep of the tune, its rhythmic freshness and, especially, its syncopated gait, hit me hard and I became an 'early-jazz' fiend." * And a dedicated Gershwin fan.

More than a quarter of a century after it was introduced, "Swanee" was still popular enough to deserve flattering treatment by the talking screen: first by Al Jolson in *The Jolson Story* and later by Judy Garland in *A Star Is Born.*

"Swanee" is very much like many another Southland song emanating from Tin Pan Alley—a lilting thirty-two bar sentimental melody with bounce. But there were important differences. There was pleasing contrast in mood from the F minor of the verse to the F major of the chorus, and the use of D-natural instead of D-flat in the ninth and twenty-five bars of the verse contributed novelty to the melodic line. Besides this, the unorthodox addition of a sixteen-bar "trio" after the chorus was an attempt to break through the constricting boundaries of the popular-song form.

Two other Gershwin items belong to the year 1919. One was a national anthem, "O Land of Mine," lyrics by Michael E. Rourke (better known as "Herbert Reynolds," the name he used writing lyrics for Jerome Kern), sub-

* *Passport to Paris,* by Vernon Duke. Boston: Little, Brown and Company, 1955.

mitted in a contest sponsored by the New York *American* for a first prize of $5,000. Gershwin's entry was published anonymously in the *American* on March 2, 1919. The judges—including John Philip Sousa, John McCormack, Irving Berlin, Joseph Stransky, and John Golden—gave Gershwin's anthem the lowest cash prize: $50.00.

In 1919, Gershwin also wrote a string quartet, entitled "Lullaby," which was never published or performed. The quartet provides evidence that Gershwin was already making notable progress in part writing, in tasteful harmonization, and in grateful writing for the four strings. The principal melody, which appears at once in the first violins, is a dolorous theme in the blues style which Gershwin later used for "Has Anybody Seen My Joe" in *135th Street*.

This quartet was the source for a familiar Gershwin anecdote. In 1923, he studied harmony for several months with Rubin Goldmark. It was not a rewarding experience since Goldmark's formal and traditional approach to harmony ran counter to Gershwin's own tendency toward deviation. One day, Gershwin showed his teacher the "Lullaby" which he had written four years earlier. Goldmark told him: "Good, very good. I see that you are already beginning to profit from your harmony lessons here."

Undoubtedly it was George's preoccupation with popular music that finally gave shape to Ira's nebulous literary aspirations and made him concentrate on the song lyric.

After making his initial sale to the *Smart Set*, Ira Gershwin kept on writing little humorous pieces and epigrams, two of which were marketable: a humorous questionnaire for song writers for which the New York *Sun* paid him $3.00, and a verse published in *Life* which brought him $12.00. The idea of writing song lyrics occurred to him sometime in 1918. If George was making headway in popular music, why not try his hand in the same field, but with words? Thus he began writing his first lyrics, for which he assumed the name of Arthur Francis (expropriated from the first names of his brother and sister) so that he might not be suspected of capitalizing on his brother's budding reputation. While doing this, he earned his living holding down different jobs: a cashier for the Col. Lagg Empire Show, a traveling circus; a reviewer of vaudeville for *The Clipper;* an assistant in a photographer's dark room; an employee in the receiving department of Altman's department store.

George set one of Ira's lyrics to music, "The Real American Folk Song," which Nora Bayes interpolated in *Ladies First.* This was the first song which George and Ira Gershwin wrote together, and it was Ira's first lyric to receive public performance. It was never published.

The Real American Folk Song

Near Barcelona the peasant croons
The old traditional Spanish tunes;
The Neapolitan Street Song sighs—
You think of Italian skies.
Each nation has a creative vein
Originating a native strain.
With folk songs plaintive and others gay,
In their own peculiar way.
American folk songs, I feel
Have a much stronger appeal.

CHORUS
The real American folk song is a rag—
   A mental jag—

A rhythmic tonic for the chronic blues.
The critics called it a joke song,
  But now—
They've changed their tune and they like it
  Somehow.
  For it's inoculated
  With a syncopated
    Sort of meter,
    Sweeter
  Than a classic strain;
  Boy! you can't remain
    Still and quiet—
    For it's a riot!
The real American folk song is like a Fountain of Youth;
  You taste, and it elates you
  And then invigorates you.
The real American folk song
A master stroke song
  Is a rag!

The collaboration of the Gershwins began with this brisk, at times skillful, and quite professional, verse, and with equally slick music which, in the chorus, makes a daring and characteristically Gershwinian excursion from D major to B-flat major (on the words, "but now they've changed their tune").

For the time being the brothers worked together only by fits and starts. Not until 1924, when Ira became successful in his own right, and without the benefit of George's music, did the partnership become permanent.

" "HE IS THE BEGINNING OF SOPHISTICATED JAZZ" "

For over a decade, George White had been appearing as a dancer in leading musical comedies and revues, including the *Passing Show of 1914* and the *Ziegfeld Follies of 1915*. In 1919 he decided to turn to producing, planning a revue that would out-Ziegfeld the *Follies* and out-folly Ziegfeld in lavish displays for the eye in sets, costuming, and beautiful girls.

On June 2, he presented the *Scandals of 1919*, whose cast included himself, Ann Pennington, Lou Holtz, Yvette Rugel, and Ona Munson. Except for the dancing of Ann Pennington, the "shimmie queen," the first *Scandals* did not have much distinction. The book and lyrics by Arthur Jackson and George White, and the music by Richard Whiting, were so routine that Arthur Hornblow complained in the *Theater Magazine:* "When there was so much money to be spent, Mr. White might have set aside a few dollars for a good scenario writer."

But Ziegfeld apparently saw in the *Scandals* a serious competitor. Soon after its opening he wired White a serious offer of $3,000 a week for him and Ann Pennington to appear in the *Follies*. White countered by offering $7,000 a week for Ziegfeld and his wife, Billie Burke, to appear in the *Scandals*.

In succeeding editions, White did manage to become a rival to Ziegfeld. The sinuous stairways down which beautiful girls descended in stately procession, the living curtains draped with nude females, the orgy of colors in sets and costuming, the breath-taking stage effects—all this in the *Scandals* were in the grand Ziegfeld manner.

Unlike Ziegfeld, who preferred buying stars and top-flight collaborators rather than developing them, George White gambled on lesser-known personalities when he had faith in their ability. For his second edition, in 1920, he asked George Gershwin to write all the music, even though up to this time Gershwin had produced only one song hit and had written only one complete Broadway score. White had never forgotten the way Gershwin played the piano when both of them worked in *Miss 1917*.

It was not a lucrative assignment for the composer. All White paid Gershwin was $50.00 a week. In later editions, Gershwin's salary went up to $75.00, then $125.00—supplemented, of course, by the royalties he received from publication. But the *Scandals* was an attractive showcase for any composer, and Gershwin accepted the offer eagerly.

Gershwin provided the music for five editions, up to and including the *Scandals of 1924*. In the first two editions his lyricist was Arthur Jackson; in the last three, E. Ray Goetz, Bud De Sylva, and Ballard McDonald. Many of the forty-four songs Gershwin contributed to the five *Scandals* are hardly indicative of his creative potential. Some are forgotten, and deservedly so. Others are sometimes revived; but these are too obviously machine-made to appeal to tastes made so discriminating by Gershwin's best music. Still others are interesting only in passing details, noteworthy in that they betray the occasional restlessness of the composer to search out new ways of saying old things. But two songs are truly Gershwinian in their freshness and originality: "I'll Build a Stairway to Paradise," a production number in the 1922 edition which Carl van Vechten at the time said represented "the most perfect piece of jazz yet written"; and "Somebody Loves Me," which was unforgettably interpreted by Winnie Lightner in 1924.

The first had its source in a lyric which Ira Gershwin had previously written and called "New Step Everyday." Ira showed this lyric to Bud De Sylva, who liked one line particularly—"I'll build a stairway to paradise." De Sylva suggested that a new lyric be written using that line as a title, and he helped Ira write it; George provided the music. Since both De Sylva and George Gershwin were then planning the songs and lyrics for the 1922 *Scandals*, the song went into the score. White gave it a lavish background: a gleaming white stairway dominated the stage, and dancers in black cavorted up and down the stairway as the song was sung. The song itself had an intriguing melody characterized by a five-step ascent and a five-step descent. What gave the melody particular interest was the unexpected intrusion of flatted thirds and sevenths, the subtle enharmonic changes, and the daring accentuation.

The appeal of "Somebody Loves Me" is primarily melodic, for in this song Gershwin tapped the rich, full-blooded lyricism that henceforth would identify his best-loved songs. Gershwin's way of suddenly interpolating a flatted third in the melody once again personalized his writing. The nebulous harmony was also a part of the song's charm.

"Somebody Loves Me" was one of Gershwin's greatest hits since "Swanee." It became a rage in Paris where it was introduced at the Moulin Rouge by Loulou Hegobourn. But Gershwin's most ambitious number for the *Scandals* was not a song hit, but a little one-act opera. Though a dismal failure, it paved the way to his future artistic achievements.

For some time Bud De Sylva had discussed with Gershwin the possibility of writing a Negro opera. When White proved surprisingly receptive to the idea of using a twenty-five minute work in his *Scandals,* the collaborators went to work with a will. They completed their opera in five feverish days. When it was tried out at De Sylva's apartment, it made a profound impression on all those present. Ferde Grofé said: "The work struck me as highly original, and representing a new departure in American music." Paul Whiteman, who that year conducted his orchestra in the pit of the *Scandals* and consequently was the opera's conductor, was also excited. This enthusiasm mounted after the *Scandals* tried out in New Haven where a local critic wrote, "This opera will be imitated in a hundred years."

The opera was called *Blue Monday;* for Gershwin it represented a goal toward which he had been groping for several years, his most ambitious effort thus far to enlarge his artistic scope and to extend his musical horizon. The tensions of rehearsals were grueling, since it was difficult to get singers without operatic training to render his music with the exactitude he demanded. An even greater ordeal was to await the verdict of press and public. Before the opening night Gershwin began to suffer from constipation; this malady was to become chronic, and since physicians were unable to put their finger on the source of his trouble, he always referred to it as his "composer's stomach."

Orchestrated by Will Vodery, and with Richard Bold, Lester Allen, Jack McGowan, and Coletta Ryan in the cast, *Blue Monday* was introduced at the Globe Theater on August 29, 1922, the opening night of the *Scandals of 1922*. As the prologue explained, the libretto was about a "woman's intuition gone wrong." In a basement café on Lenox Avenue near 135th Street, Joe and Tom are rivals for Vi's love. Joe decides to visit his mother, and since he is ashamed of such a sentimental gesture, he invents the fiction that he has been called out of town on business. Tom arouses and feeds Vi's suspicions that Joe is having a rendezvous with another woman. In a rage, she shoots Joe, and only then learns the truth.

It was not an impressive libretto. If one were not certain of De Sylva's seriousness of purpose, a suspicion might arise that he was ribbing opera librettos in general. And Gershwin's music was not strong enough to carry the load of a feeble book. Inexperienced as he was in dramatic writing, he produced not an integrated opera but a series of popular songs connected by jazzlike recitatives. Some of the songs are appealing: the "Blue Monday Blues"; the aria, "Has Anybody Seen My Joe"; and the spiritual, "I'm Going To See My Mother." There was a successful attempt at using jazz for humorous effects, as in the entrance of the customers into the saloon. But all this material was not well integrated into the dramatic context, and it appears to have been no more than grafted upon the score to provide interest. The music lacked atmospheric or dramatic interest, while the recitatives were stilted and stiffly contrived.

Many in the audience liked the opera. But George White decided to remove it from the program after the first night because the work's somber theme and drab setting cast a pall over the audience, making it unreceptive for the lighter and gayer numbers that followed. Still a third consideration was a review like that of Charles Darnton's in the *World,* who described it as "the most dismal, stupid and incredible black-face sketch that has probably ever been perpetrated." Most of the other drama critics did not even mention it (no music critic attended). The most positive reaction came from Charles Pike Sawyer on the New York *Post* who said: "It was a little bit of *La Bohème* with the *"Liebestod"* of *Tristan* to close, burlesqued almost beyond recognition, but it was remarkably well sung and acted."

Since that single-night performance at the *Scandals, Blue Monday* has been revived on several occasions. Renamed *135th Street* (the name by which it is now known), it was staged at Carnegie Hall at a concert of Paul Whiteman and his Orchestra on December 29, 1925. The cast included Charles Hart, Blossom Seeley, Jack McGowan, and Benny Fields. Whiteman revived it again in Carnegie Hall in 1936 with Blossom Seeley and Benny Fields, and with a new orchestration by Ferde Grofé. An extract of *135th Street* was also interpolated into the Gershwin screen biography, *Rhapsody in Blue,* and on March 29, 1953, it was performed

over television on the "Omnibus" program, staged by Valerie
Bettis, and with Raun Spearman and Elta Warren in the principal roles.

It cannot be said that rehearings have brought a new
perspective. In 1953, as in 1922, *135th Street* was a work of
an apprentice.

Between 1920 and 1923, Gershwin was involved in
numerous other musical productions besides the *Scandals*. Individual Gershwin songs were heard in *Ed Wynn's Carnival,
The Sweetheart Shop* with Helen Ford, *Dere Mabel,* and the
Broadway Brevities, all in 1920; in 1921, *The Perfect Fool,*
with Ed Wynn, and *A Dangerous Maid,* a "play with songs"
which expired in Philadelphia after a five-weeks out-of-town
tryout; in 1922, in *For Goodness Sake, Spice of 1922, Our
Nell, The French Doll* with Irene Bordoni, and *The Dancing
Girl* for which Sigmund Romberg wrote the bulk of the
score.

Most of the songs in these varied musicals are but the
grist from a highly productive mill. A few deserve attention.
"We're Pals," which Louis Bennison sang to his dog, was a
sentimental bonbon which helped to make *Dere Mabel* the
success it was. "Innocent Ingenue Baby" in *Our Nell* and "Do
It Again," to which Irene Bordoni contributed piquant
French sauce in *The French Doll,* showed a new virtuosity in
staggered accentuation and in rhythmic technique. "No One
Else" in *The Perfect Fool* had striking modulations. "Dancing Shoes" in *A Dangerous Maid* was notable for intriguing
after-beat accents; and "Some Rain Must Fall," from the same
show, for surprising chromaticisms.

There were, then, in scattered Gershwin songs of that
period a search for new effects and an adroitness of technique

which set them sharply apart from most of the other products of Tin Pan Alley. Already—in 1922 and 1923—there were some serious musicians and writers who recognized that something new and significant in popular music was emerging with Gershwin.

Beryl Rubinstein, a concert pianist and member of the faculty of the Cleveland Institute of Music, startled a newspaper interviewer by referring to Gershwin as "a great composer." As quoted in the newspapers on September 6, 1922, Rubinstein said:

> This young fellow has the spark of musical genius which is definite in his serious moods. . . . This young American composer has the fire of originality. . . . With Gershwin's style and seriousness he is not definitely from the popular-music school, but one of the really outstanding figures in the country's musical efforts. . . . I really believe that America will at no distant date honor [him] for his talent . . . and that when we speak of American composers George Gershwin's name will be prominent on our list.

When I interviewed Beryl Rubinstein in 1939 for a book on living musicians I was then preparing, I reminded him of his estimate of Gershwin at a time when the young composer had not written a single serious work. His reply was:

> When I said what I did about Gershwin in 1922 I did not suspect how far he would go. All I knew then was that, in comparison with other popular music of that day, Gershwin's songs represented a unique attempt to bring sound

musical values and rich inventiveness to our popular songs. Gershwin's songs then stuck out from the muck of that period so prominently that you couldn't fail to notice them if you were in the least interested in our music. But I'd be the last to say that I had even a vague idea or hope that the composer of 'Do It Again' would some day write a work like *Porgy and Bess.*

Beryl Rubinstein was not the only one to take notice of Gershwin. In the esoteric literary magazine, *The Dial,* Gilbert Seldes, apostle of the seven lively arts, wrote in the issue of August 1923: "Delicacy, even dreaminess, is a quality he [Gershwin] alone brings into jazz music. And his sense of variation in rhythm, of an oddly placed accent, of emphasis and color, is impeccable."

Nor was recognition confined exclusively to the press. On November 1, 1923, the concert singer Eva Gauthier gave a recital at Aeolian Hall made up of six groups of songs. Five groups were devoted to such composers as Bellini, Purcell, Byrd, Schoenberg, Bliss, Milhaud, Bartók, and Hindemith. One group, the third, endowed her concert with a permanent place in the history of American music, for with the incomparable courage and independence of a true pioneer she devoted it entirely to American popular songs. In this group were Berlin's "Alexander's Ragtime Band," Kern's "The Siren's Song," Walter Donaldson's "Carolina in the Morning," and three songs by Gershwin—"I'll Build a Stairway to Paradise," "Innocent Ingenue Baby" and "Swanee." For this jazz group, Gauthier's regular accompanist, Max Jaffe, yielded his stool to Gershwin. "The singer reappeared, followed by a tall, black-haired young man who was far from possessing the icy aplomb of those to whom playing on the platform of Aeolian Hall is an old story," reported Deems Taylor in the *World*. "He bore under his arm a small bundle of sheet music with lurid black and yellow covers. The audience began to show signs of relaxation; this promised to be amusing. . . . Young Mr. Gershwin began to do mysterious and fascinating rhythmic and contrapuntal stunts with the accompaniment." At one point he made the audience purr with delight at the sly way in which he suddenly introduced a phrase from Rimsky-Korsakov's *Scheherazade* into the "Stairway to Paradise."

Mr. Taylor was impressed by the high musical quality of the songs. "They stood up amazingly well, not only as entertainment but as music. . . . What they did possess was melodic interest and continuity, harmonic appropriateness, well-balanced almost classically severe form, and subtle fascinating rhythms—in short the qualities that any sincere and interesting music possesses." The songs received such an ovation that an encore was required. "Do It Again" was sung, and it inspired such a thunderous acclaim that it had to be repeated.

Thus on the evening of November 1, Gershwin made his first appearance in a major concert hall both as a pianist and as a composer. "I consider this one of the very most important events in American musical history," wrote Carl van Vechten to a friend about the Gauthier recital; but he might well have been speaking of Gershwin's admission to the concert stage. Then Van Vechten ventured a prophecy—"The Philharmonic will be doing it in two years." It must have given him no small satisfaction when, two years later almost to the day, he witnessed the première of Gershwin's Piano

Concerto at Carnegie Hall—not by the Philharmonic, it was true, but by the Philharmonic's rival, the New York Symphony Society under Walter Damrosch.

The Gauthier recital was repeated in Boston toward the end of January. H. T. Parker wrote of his delight in Gershwin's piano playing in the *Evening Transcript.* "He diversified them with cross-rhythms; wove them into a pliant and outspringing counterpoint; set in pauses and accents; sustained cadences; gave character to the measures wherein the singer's voice was still. . . . He is the beginning of the age of sophisticated jazz."

After the Eva Gauthier concert in New York, a party was given to honor Gershwin and Gauthier by Mary Opdycke (now Mrs. John DeWitt Peltz, editor of *Opera News*). This was only one of many instances in which Gershwin now moved among the celebrities of the social world in fashionable homes along Fifth and Park avenues, particularly those of Jules Glaenzer, Mary Hoyt Wiborg, and her sister, Mrs. Sidney Fish.

He first invaded the social world in 1921 when Dorothy Clark, pianist at the Ziegfeld Roof, brought him and Vincent Youmans to Glaenzer's home at 417 Park Avenue. Glaenzer, vice-president of Cartier's on Fifth Avenue, over a period of many years gave fabulous Sunday evening parties, where the great of the world of entertainment met and befriended the social elite.

When Gershwin first appeared at Glaenzer's, he was (in the description of his host) "as naive and as lacking in social graces as you are likely to find in anybody. Why, I had to take him aside and tell him to get the cigar out of his mouth when I introduced him to a young lady. But George learned quickly. In a short time he was as well-poised and as completely at ease on Park Avenue as he was on Broadway."

Gershwin and Glaenzer became good friends, and Gershwin was a frequent visitor to these Sunday evening parties. There he met and came to know Mistinguette, Maurice Chevalier, Georges Carpentier, Charles Chaplin, Lord and Lady Louis Mountbatten, Douglas Fairbanks and Mary Pickford, Beatrice Lillie, Jascha Heifetz, and many others of Broadway and Hollywood, Paris and London, together with brokers and bankers. It was at Glaenzer's, in 1922, that he played a new song, "Do It Again," and had Irene Bordoni come to him with the request that she be allowed to introduce it in her next show. ("I *muss* haf dat dam song," was how she phrased her request!) At Glaenzer's, in 1924, at a party honoring the cast of *Charlot's Revue* of London, which was then appearing on Broadway, he first met Gertrude Lawrence. Once again he was at the piano playing some of his songs when Gertrude Lawrence recognized one of the numbers as a song she had recently performed in London. "Some day, I'd love to meet the man who wrote *that*," she told Glaenzer, and only then discovered that he was the young man at the piano.

Even as his social sphere was expanding so was the circle of intimate friends. There was Bill Daly—William Merrigan Daly, more formally. A shy man with short-cropped hair, large and bewildered eyes behind spectacles, and an academic manner, Daly was a man to command respect. As a boy he had appeared as a piano prodigy and had received a comprehensive musical training. Suddenly he decided to abandon music completely. He then entered Harvard, from which he received his baccalaureate in 1908. After that he worked on *Everybody's Magazine* where, as managing editor, he helped to discover and encourage a young writer named Edna Ferber. In 1914 he conducted a choral concert honoring Paderewski, and made such a good impression that Paderewski urged him to return to music professionally. Paderewski went even further, he recommended Daly to the Chicago Opera for a conductorial post. Unfortunately, the opera company temporarily suspended operations that season before Daly could take on his new job. Instead of working in an opera house, Daly accepted a post as conductor of a Broadway musical comedy, *Hands Up,* in 1915. From then on he conducted many musical comedies (including several by Gershwin), becoming one of the highest paid and one of the most venerated theater conductors of his day.

Daly had first been introduced to Gershwin by Charles Dillingham while Gershwin was still working at Remick's. They did not become friends until a few years later, after working together on the score for *Our Nell* in 1922. From then on, Gershwin often leaned on Daly's friendship and musicianship. Daly had a remarkable musical mentality and an astute musical judgment; he became Gershwin's favorite critic, guide, and advisor through the writing of the first major orchestral works and many of the principal musical-comedy scores. He was Gershwin's favorite orchestrator, and when Gershwin needed a conductor, it was Daly whom he favored for his Broadway scores. In time, Gershwin came to love the man as much as he admired him; in a letter dated August 15, 1931, he described Daly as "the best friend I have."

Among the new faces in the Gershwin circle in the early 1920s was S. N. Behrman—"Berrie" to his friends—who, in 1923, was writing for the New York *Times Book Review* and various magazines. Behrman had been initiated into the theater in his youth when he appeared in a vaudeville sketch

of his own writing. But it was not until 1927 that he emerged
as a leading playwright of social comedy when the Theatre
Guild produced *The Second Man*. Thus Behrman and Gershwin—who were introduced to each other by Samuel Chotzinoff—became friends before either was famous. As each progressed from one triumph to another, he still remained close
to the other.

Gershwin's friends in this period also included Phil
Charig, with whom he had first become acquainted through
his brother Arthur when the family was still living in Washington Heights. Charig appeared in vaudeville as pianist for
Louise Dresser and several others, and in 1920 he started to
write songs. He remained close to the Gershwins until
about 1929. In that time he wrote some successful songs to
Ira Gershwin's lyrics and served as rehearsal pianist for
four Gershwin musicals.

Paul Whiteman, the orchestra leader, and his pianist-
arranger, Ferde Grofé, also moved within the Gershwin orbit.
The son of the director of music education of Denver's public
schools, Paul Whiteman had been trained as a serious musician. He played first violin with various symphony orchestras, including the Denver Symphony. During World War I
he was a bandleader in the Navy, and after the war he led
popular orchestras, experimenting in playing jazz with artistic discipline and through carefully prepared orchestrations. His first success came at the Alexandria Hotel in Los
Angeles, where he and his brother appeared for a year. In
1919 Grofé was engaged as the orchestra's pianist and arranger. Like Whiteman, Grofé had come to jazz by way of
symphonic music, having been violist of the Los Angeles
Symphony for over a decade. One of the first orchestrations
he made for Whiteman, "Whispering," sold a million-and-a-

half records. From then on until 1924, every number played by Whiteman was orchestrated by Grofé. To his task, Grofé brought a consummate technique at instrumentation, an intuitive feeling for jazz colors, and a daring in the use of unusual timbres.

Paul Whiteman and his Orchestra—abetted by Grofé's orchestrations—brought new dignity to jazz. In doing this, the Whiteman orchestra passed from one triumph to another: on records, after signing a two-year contract with Victor; in vaudeville and hotels; at the *Ziegfeld Follies* and the *Scandals*; in the night club at the Palais Royal; even in Europe where an extensive tour of the major capitals was undertaken in the spring of 1923. Paul Whiteman was crowned by the press "the king of jazz."

Gershwin's *Blue Monday*, which Whiteman had conducted for one night at the *Scandals*, had struck a responsive chord with him, for it clarified his own mission in popular music. Like Gershwin, Whiteman had faith in its significance and artistic future. To convince Americans of that significance, he planned an ambitious jazz concert in a serious concert auditorium in which he would present a panorama of America's best popular music. Gershwin's one-act opera had given him an exciting idea for his concert, and his thought was for that composer to write a new piece in a jazz idiom.

T H E *Rhapsody in Blue*

At first Gershwin was not receptive to Whiteman's suggestion that he write a new work in a jazz idiom. He was busy. His latest musical, *Sweet Little Devil,* was about to try out in Boston, and the problems of whipping a show into shape for New York left him little time or thought for anything else. Besides he did not feel that as yet he had the necessary technique to write a major work for orchestra. He put Whiteman off by telling him he would give the matter some thought, but he would give no definite promise.

While he really had no intention of writing anything for the Whiteman concert, he could not help thinking about the project. Musical ideas began to leap into his mind. At a party, while improvising at the piano, he suddenly thought up the core of the broad and flowing melody which he instantly realized could become the spine of the work; that melody was destined to become the basis of the famous slow section of the *Rhapsody in Blue*. Other significant ideas came to him while en route to Boston for the opening of *Sweet Little Devil*—ideas stimulated by the rhythms of the moving train. But these materials remained only fragments, and his plan for a composition amorphous. He pushed the project from his mind.

But one day he read a brief announcement in the New York *Herald Tribune* that he was working on a "symphony" for the Whiteman concert, scheduled for February 12th. That announcement, and the imminence of the concert, galvanized him into action. For the first time he thought seriously of getting down to work. His first plan was to write a symphonic "blues," but this he rejected because he wanted a more ambitious and spacious mold in which to work. If he were to write anything, the composition would have to be sufficiently ample in form and style to give jazz artistic status. Here is the way he put it: "There had been so much chatter about the limitations of jazz, not to speak of the manifest misunderstandings of its function. Jazz, they said, had to be in strict time. It had to cling to dance rhythms. I resolved, if possible, to kill that misconception with one sturdy blow. Inspired by this aim, I set to work composing with unwonted rapidity."

He finally chose the form of the rhapsody because its elastic form allowed him freedom in working out his materials. It was Ira who christened the work *Rhapsody in Blue*, at a social evening at the Lou Paleys. After George played parts of his new work for his friends, he was asked what he planned to call it. George replied he was thinking of *American Rhapsody*. As it happened, Ira had that afternoon been looking at Whistler paintings, "Nocturne in Blue and Green," and "Harmony in Gray and Green," and when George suggested *American Rhapsody* as a possible title, Ira, thinking in terms of color and mood, suddenly asked, "Why not call it *Rhapsody in Blue?*"

It was also Ira who urged George to use a broad melodious middle section for the rhapsody and actually picked out from George's notebook the theme that George subsequently used.

Gershwin completed the Rhapsody in a two-piano version on January 7, 1924. During its composition, Ferde Grofé practically took a lease on Gershwin's apartment at 110th Street and Amsterdam Avenue where the Gershwin family had moved in 1919. It was Grofé's job, as Whiteman's arranger, to orchestrate the work. Since time was running short, the orchestration was done a sheet at a time. As the finished copy of one page left Gershwin, Grofé took it over and went to work. The manuscript of the two-piano copy contains notations in Grofé's hand as to suggested instrumentations, with the names of Whiteman's key performers scrawled in so that Grofé might bear in mind their specific techniques and styles. Grofé's orchestration for piano and jazz band was completed on February 4. Two years later he made a new adaptation, this time for piano and symphony orchestra.

The first complete rehearsal of the *Rhapsody in Blue* took place without any further delay at the Palais Royal night club at noontime. About thirty guests were invited, including Walter Damrosch, W. J. Henderson (the music critic), Edwin Hughes (pianist and teacher), Victor Herbert, Leonard Liebling (editor of the *Musical Courier*), Pitts Sanborn (the music critic), and H. O. Osgood (editor of *Musical America*). Whiteman, in shirt sleeves, brought Gershwin to the guests and introduced him. Liebling and Sanborn had never before heard of Gershwin and had to be told by Osgood who he was and what he had done.

The reaction to this first run of the *Rhapsody in Blue* was varied. Osgood and Hughes were the most enthusiastic. To Hughes "it opened up a new era for American music." Victor Herbert was also deeply impressed and offered Gershwin a valuable suggestion (which was accepted) on how to make the middle melody more effective by preceding it with an extended rising passage ending in a *fermata*. Others were much less excited. Liebling confessed, "I was frankly uncertain whether I liked it or not." And Sanborn said, "I was not enamored of the themes or the workmanship, but the thing certainly had zip and punch."

Whiteman was not discouraged. He was certain that the Rhapsody would be, as he put it, "a knockout success," and his conviction that it was a masterwork could not be shaken by the lukewarm reaction of two venerable music critics. When the rehearsal ended he took some of his guests out to lunch at The Tavern, a restaurant and bar near the Palais Royal, to discuss details of his concert. Liebling and Sanborn helped him draw up a list of critics and notable musicians to be invited.

There was another important run-through of the Rhapsody, but this time without the orchestra. Ernest Hutcheson, the celebrated pianist and teacher, arranged for a select group of musicians to hear Gershwin play the score. This time the praise was unqualified.

Whiteman's concert took place at Aeolian Hall on February 12, 1924. Since the day fell on Lincoln's birthday, the event has since been often described as "the emancipation proclamation of jazz." It cost Whiteman $11,000 to give that performance. Though every seat was occupied and the standing room was more than overcrowded, the deficit was $7,000—and all of it came out of Whiteman's pocket, for no expense had been spared to give the concert in style. The orchestra, which then numbered twenty-three, had been enlarged by nine players, including eight violins, three saxophones; two each of trumpets, trombones, French horns, doublebasses, and pianos; a banjo, and a drum. Since most of the players doubled on other instruments, the orchestra included the following: D-flat and bass clarinets; E-flat soprano, B-flat soprano, E-flat alto, and E-flat baritone saxophones, E-flat flugelhorn, bass tuba, accordion, celesta, flute, oboe, bass oboe, basset horn, and octavion.

A handsome twelve-page program, its covers in decorative purple and gold, had annotations by Gilbert Seldes. The choicest seats in the house had been allocated for the leading musicians in or near New York. Among those present were: John Philip Sousa, Walter Damrosch, Leopold Godowsky, Jascha Heifetz, Fritz Kreisler, John McCormack, Sergei Rachmaninoff, Leopold Stokowski, Moriz Rosenthal, Mischa Elman, and Igor Stravinsky. They rubbed elbows with song writers, song pluggers, vaudevillians, stars of musical comedy, and the rank and file of jazz devotees in what was surely the most polyglot audience to attend a concert at Aeolian Hall.

On the day of the concert, Jules Glaenzer had Gershwin, Whiteman, Zez Confrey, and several others for lunch. Then all of them strolled over to the concert. Gershwin was cool and collected. Whiteman, on the other hand, was all nerves. He could not eat a thing, and on the way to Aeolian Hall kept muttering that he was sick and that he hoped his doctor would be backstage to take care of him.

In his book, *Jazz,** Whiteman recalled:

> Fifteen minutes before the concert was to begin, I yielded to a nervous longing to see for myself what was happening out front, and putting an overcoat over my concert clothes, I slipped around to the entrance of Aeolian Hall. There I gazed upon a picture that should have imparted new vigor to my willing confidence. It was snowing, but men and women were fighting to get into the door, pulling and mauling each other as they sometimes do at a baseball game, or a prize fight, or in the subway. Such was my state of mind by this time that I wondered if I had come to the right entrance. And then I saw Victor Herbert going in. It was the right entrance, sure enough, and the next day the ticket office people said they could have sold out the house ten times over. I went backstage again, more scared than ever. Black fear simply possessed me. I paced the floor, gnawed my thumbs and vowed I'd give $5,000 if we could stop right then and there. Now that the audience had come, perhaps I really had nothing to offer them at all. I even made excuses to keep the curtain from rising on schedule. But finally there was no longer any way of postponing the evil moment. The curtain went up and before I could dash forth, as I was tempted to do, and announce that there wouldn't be any concert, we were in the midst of it.

* *Jazz,* by Paul Whiteman and Margaret McBride. New York: J. H. Sears & Co., 1926.

The program included several sections calculated to present jazz in all its varied facets. As Hugh C. Ernst explained in an introductory address to the audience:

> The experiment is to be purely educational. Mr. Whiteman intends to point out, with the assistance of his orchestra and associates, the tremendous strides which have been made in popular music from the day of discordant Jazz, which sprang into existence about ten years ago from nowhere in particular, to the really melodious music of today. . . . The greatest single factor in the improvement of American music has been the art of scoring. Paul Whiteman's orchestra was the first organization to especially score each selection and play it according to score. Since then practically every modern orchestra has its own arranger or staff of arrangers. . . . Eventually they may evolve an American school which will equal those of foreign origin or which will at least provide a stepping stone which will make it very simple for the masses to understand and therefore enjoy symphony and opera. That is the true purpose of the experiment. If after the concert you decide that the music of today is worthless and harmful, it is your duty to stamp it down. If it is not, then we welcome anyone eager to assist in its development.

The complete program, which included the world première of Victor Herbert's *A Suite of Serenades* as well as Gershwin's *Rhapsody in Blue,* follows:

I. *True Form of Jazz*

(a) Ten years ago—"Livery Stable Blues"
(b) With modern embellishment—
"Mama Loves Papa" .... Baer

II. *Comedy Selections*

(a) Origin of "Yes, We Have No Bananas" ..... Silver
(b) Instrumental comedy—"So This Is Venice" Thomas
    (adapted from *The Carnival of Venice*)

III. *Contrast—Legitimate Scoring vs. Jazzing*

(a) Selection in true form—"Whispering" ... Schoenberg
(b) Same selection in Jazz Treatment

IV. *Recent Compositions with Modern Score*

(a) "Limehouse Blues" .... Braham
(b) "I Love You" .... Archer
(c) "Raggedy Ann" .... Kern

V. *Zez Confrey* (piano)

(a) Medley Popular Airs
(b) "Kitten on the Keys" .... Confrey
(c) "Ice Cream and Art"
(d) "Nickel in the Slot" .... Confrey
    (accompanied by the orchestra)

VI. *Flavoring a Selection with Borrowed Themes*

"Russian Rose" .... Grofé
    (based on "The Volga Boat Song")

VII. *Semi-Symphonic Arrangements of Popular Melodies*

(a) "Alexander's Ragtime Band" .... Berlin
(b) "A Pretty Girl is Like a Melody" .... Berlin
(c) "Orange Blossoms in California" .... Berlin

VIII.   *A Suite of Serenades,* by Victor Herbert

(a) Spanish
(b) Chinese
(c) Cuban
(d) Oriental

IX.   *Adaptation of Standard Selections to Dance Rhythm*

(a) "Pale Moon" .... Logan
(b) "To a Wild Rose" .... MacDowell
(c) "Chansonette" .... Friml

X.   *Rhapsody in Blue,* by George Gershwin

(George Gershwin at the piano accompanied by the orchestra)

XI.   *In the Field of the Classics*

"Pomp and Circumstance" .... Elgar

Up to the *Rhapsody in Blue,* the respective numbers were accorded only a mild reception. Not even the many "flappers" and "cake-eaters"—to whom Whitman was high priest, and jazz a religion—could generate much heat. As the long program progressed, there were even visible signs of growing restlessness and impatience; the sad truth was that the similarity in style and coloring of the various pieces was proving to be a sore trial to the ear.

Even though it came when fatigue and boredom had set in for many in the audience, the *Rhapsody in Blue* changed the climate dramatically. Ross Gorman's opening wail in the clarinet seized the attention of the audience. From then on, the music held its hearers tightly in its grip until the final explosive coda. "Somewhere in the middle of the score I began crying," Whiteman confessed. "When I came to myself I was eleven pages along, and until this day I cannot tell you how I conducted that far."

There was a spontaneous ovation at the end which lasted several minutes. There was no question about the reaction of the audience. As for the more formal jury—the music critics—the best that can be said is that there was a split decision. Some were ecstatic. H. O. Osgood called it "greater than Stravinsky's *The Rite of Spring*." Henry T. Finck considered it "far superior to Schoenberg, Milhaud, and the rest of the futuristic fellows." Gilbert W. Gabriel wrote: "The beginning and the ending of it were stunning; the beginning particularly, with a fluttering tongued drunken whoop of an introduction which had the audience rocking. With all its lag, diffuseness, and syncopated reiterations, here was the day's most pressing contribution. Mr. Gershwin has an irrepressible pack of talents, and there is an element of inevitability about his piece." William J. Henderson described it as "a highly ingenious work, treating the piano in a manner calling for much technical skill and furnishing an orchestral background in which the characteristic antics of the saxophones, trombones, and clarinets were merged in a really skillful piece of orchestration." Deems Taylor reported that the Rhapsody "displayed a latent ability on the part of this young composer to say something of considerable interest in his chosen idiom. . . . His Rhapsody . . . had all the faults one might expect from an experimental work; but it also revealed a genuine melodic gift and a piquant and individual harmonic sense to lend significance to its rhythmic ingenuity. Moreover it is genuine jazz music, not only in its scoring but in its idiom. . . . Mr. Gershwin will bear watching; he may yet bring jazz out of the kitchen." To Olin Downes, the work showed "extraordinary talent, just as it also shows a young composer with aims that go far beyond those of his ilk, struggling with a form of which he is far from being a master. . . . Often Mr. Gershwin's purpose is defeated by technical immaturity, but in spite of that . . . he has expressed himself in a significant and on the whole highly original manner."

Pitts Sanborn and Lawrence Gilman were outright hostile. Sanborn felt that the music "runs off into empty passage work and meaningless repetition." Gilman was even more vigorous in his denunciation. "How trite and feeble and conventional the tunes are, how sentimental and vapid the harmonic treatment, under its guise of fussy and futile counterpoint. . . . Weep over the lifelessness of its melody and harmony, so derivative, so static, so inexpressive. And then recall, for contrast, the rich inventiveness of the rhythm, the saliency and vividness of the orchestra color."

There were those who before February 12 had spoken mockingly of the concert as "Whiteman's Folly." There were others who said of Gershwin's attempt to write a serious rhapsody that "he is breaking his neck trying to starve to death." They were silenced after the echoes of the concert died down. The success of Whiteman's performance was far and beyond anything even Whiteman had dared to hope for. The most serious musicians and critics were discussing it with the discrimination and analytical discernment they brought to all major musical events.

And it was the *Rhapsody in Blue* that gave the concert its significance. It transformed the Whiteman experiment from an idle curiosity to an artistic event of the first magnitude. As Carl van Vechten wrote Gershwin immediately after the première: "The concert, quite as a matter of course, was a riot; you crowned it with what . . . I am forced to regard as the foremost serious effort by an American composer."

The *Rhapsody in Blue* first became known to the world through the blue label recording which Whiteman and his orchestra made for Victor. A million copies were sold. But this was just a trickle compared to the ultimate circulation of the music through various media. On stage, on screen, on records, over the radio, in the concert hall, in the ballet theater, the Rhapsody has achieved a popularity equaled by few serious works of music before or since.

In the concert hall it has outstripped any other single contemporary work for frequency of performance. It has entered the repertory of every major American symphony orchestra and has been directed by the foremost conductors of this generation. In Europe it was introduced as early as 1925, at the Salle de Centaure in Brussels by John Ouwerx. It first came to France in February 1926 in a two-piano version, at a concert of the renowned Société Nationale de Musique in Paris, performed by Giuseppe Benvenuti and Leon Kartum; it arrived in Central Europe in November 1932 at a concert of the Vienna Symphony; and it was introduced in Germany on February 17, 1946, at a symphony concert at the Nuremberg Opera.

The *Rhapsody in Blue* has been heard not only in its original version for piano and orchestra but also in various transcriptions: for piano solo, two pianos, two pianos and orchestra, eight pianos, solo harmonica, an orchestra of harmonicas, a mandolin orchestra, an a capella chorus, and violin and orchestra. It was adapted for the dance: into a Grecian ballet at the Hotel Metropole in London in 1926, into a modernistic ballet two years later by the Ballet Russe of Monte Carlo, and into a tap dance by Jack Donahue.

The Roxy Theater in New York paid Gershwin $10,-
000 to appear for two weeks in May 1930 at its stage show,
with Paul Whiteman and his orchestra, in the Rhapsody. In
the same year the Rhapsody appeared in a motion-picture
revue starring Paul Whiteman, *The King of Jazz;* the sum
paid, $50,000, was without parallel for a musical work for the
screen. In 1946 the Rhapsody title was used for Gershwin's
screen biography.

The royalties from the sale of sheet music, records,
and other subsidiary rights gathered more than a quarter of
a million dollars in a decade. The Rhapsody made Gershwin
a wealthy man. And it spread his fame around the globe. It
also lifted Paul Whiteman to altogether new heights as king
of jazz in the theater, on the screen, in night clubs, and over
the radio. For a long time the question was debated as to
who made whom: whether Gershwin's success was due to
Whiteman or vice versa. The argument is as fruitful as the
one involving the chicken and the egg. Simple decency and
a sense of justice dictate the admission that each owed a profound debt to the other. However, in view of the unwavering
line of Gershwin's musical development, it need not be questioned that he would have arrived at the *Rhapsody in Blue,*
or its equivalent, without the impetus of a Whiteman concert.

Still another controversy deserves comment, the one
involving Grofé's share in the Rhapsody's success. For some
years after the première there was a tendency among some
writers to overestimate Grofé's contribution to the point of insisting that it was to Grofé and not to Gershwin that the lau-
rels belonged. While it is true that some of the impact of the
music came from Grofé's colorful jazz orchestration, it should
always be remembered that an orchestration is but the dress
that adds to a lady's charm. The lady, in this case being the

music, is enticing without ornamental attire. Take the Rhapsody in its varied arrangements, and it remains music of enormous appeal.

Nor should it be assumed, as some have done, that because Grofé did the orchestration that Gershwin was incapable of doing it himself. He had already had some training in instrumentation from Kilenyi; his student books provide testimony that he had acquired enough skill in handling orchestral instruments before 1924 to orchestrate a work like the Rhapsody. But the Rhapsody was written under such pressure to meet the deadline of the concert that the mechanics of the orchestration—like those of orchestrating Gershwin's musical-comedy scores—were assigned to somebody else. Besides, Grofé was Whiteman's arranger, who knew the Whiteman orchestra intimately; even if there had been time for Gershwin to do his own orchestration, it was wise to assign the job to Grofé. That Gershwin knew how to write for the orchestra was definitely proved only a year and a half later when he wrote his Concerto in F for which—as for all subsequent serious works—he did his own orchestration.

The Rhapsody has inspired not only controversies but also tall tales. In his autobiography, *Bad Boy of Music*, George Antheil reveals that the celebrated publishing house of G. Schirmer in New York turned down the Rhapsody because it was "not commercially feasible," thus perpetrating what Antheil described as "the greatest boner in music-publishing history." The simple fact puncturing this story is that Gershwin could not have submitted the Rhapsody to Schirmer's since he was bound by an exclusive contract to Harms.

Another story sometimes repeated by writers on

Gershwin concerns the first complete rehearsal at the Palais Royal. During the beautiful slow section—so goes the tale—Whiteman suddenly stopped conducting and listened to the music in rapt attention. "Goddammit," he is supposed to have said, bearing in mind the numerous revisions to which the composer had subjected his music, "did he think he could improve on *that?*" A pretty story, to be sure—but it never happened.

Perhaps the strangest yarn of all was one reported by Walter Winchell on January 25, 1955. He wrote saying that Gershwin had written an operatic version of *Uncle Tom's Cabin* which was turned down by the Metropolitan Opera. Gershwin then used the overture for the Paul Whiteman concert, calling it *Rhapsody in Blue.* . . . Dismissing for the moment the incontestable fact that a work like the Rhapsody, by its very structure and content, could never have been an overture to an opera or anything else for that matter, the item ignores several salient facts: (1) Gershwin never wrote an opera on *Uncle Tom's Cabin,* a fact that Mr. Winchell could easily have verified if he had taken the trouble; (2) Gershwin never submitted any opera to the Metropolitan that was turned down; and (3) the dates clearly marked in Gershwin's hand on the sketches and the completed manuscript of the Rhapsody, reposing in the Library of Congress, in Washington, D. C., prove beyond a doubt that he wrote the work for the Paul Whiteman concert.

The form of the *Rhapsody in Blue* came from the Hungarian Liszt; the main slow section was derived from the Russian Tchaikovsky; and the harmony sometimes suggests the French Debussy or the Polish Chopin. Yet, like the melting pot that is America, the Rhapsody fused the various foreign elements into a personality wholly American. The Rhapsody is American music in its youth, brashness, restlessness, optimism. It is also Gershwin in the freshness of its rhythmic and melodic ideas, in its vitality and muscular energy, and in its unerring instinct for effect.

The opening measures reveal Gershwin's instinct for effect—the yawp of the clarinet. After a low trill, the clarinet begins a seventeen-note ascent; halfway up there is a pause, and then the clarinet resumes its upward flight with a portamento. Then it reaches out for the first theme. This opening theme establishes the mood for the entire work. It is the musical voice of the turbulent 1920s, an era of iconoclasm, hedonism, defiance of convention, frenetic pursuit of pleasure; an era of flappers and cake-eaters, hip flasks and speakeasies, companionate marriage, and Dorothy Parker wisecracks. It speaks in music for an epoch as vividly as an Offenbach cancan does for the Second French Empire and a Johann Strauss waltz for the Austria of the Hapsburgs.

Once stated, the jaunty opening theme yields immediately to a transition section in the winds which carries a suggestion of the second main theme. This brisk second theme—finally stated in the piano—further conveys the feeling of reckless abandon thus far established. Some pundits have tried to find a similarity between this melodic idea and the one opening Beethoven's Fourth Piano Concerto, but the association is remote. This second theme appears and reappears in the orchestra and is the basis of an extended coda for the piano. The piano then leads with a few ascending chords toward the principal section of the work: the rhapsodic slow movement for strings which has become one of the most frequently quoted and best-known excerpts in serious American music. Whiteman has used it as his permanent signature over the radio and elsewhere; words have been written to it, a version first introduced by Frances Williams; George Gershwin played it on the piano for the wedding ceremony of his sister, Frances, and Leopold Godowsky Jr. at Ira Gershwin's apartment in 1930; and it was performed on the organ at Gershwin's funeral services at Temple Emanu-El.

The full orchestra takes up the song. Then a quick recollection of its opening phrase in fast tempo invokes the final section. After a climactic pronouncement of the opening clarinet theme by full orchestra, the piano wistfully recalls the second theme. The Rhapsody ends abruptly with a brief and dramatic coda.

The *Rhapsody in Blue* is by no means a consistent or integrated masterwork. Some of the things its severest critics have condemned in it are its weak spots. The form is diffuse; the thematic subjects are at times developed awkwardly and without inventiveness; there are lapses in inspiration where repetitions of familiar ideas or ineffectual transitions of scales and chord passages try to fill the gap; there is some naïveté and some amateurishness in the harmonic construction. But the basic melodic and rhythmic material is so fresh and good, and is presented with such verve and spontaneity, that the work as a whole never loses its ability to excite the listener.

FROM BROADWAY

TO PICCADILLY

When the *Rhapsody in Blue* was introduced in Aeolian Hall, the Gershwin musical *Sweet Little Devil* was occupying the nearby Astor Theater. The duality of Gershwin's creative personality was thus pointed up for the first time. Until his death he would always keep one foot in the concert hall and another in the popular theater.

Sweet Little Devil had opened in Boston as *The Perfect Lady* toward the end of 1923 and had come to New York under its new title on January 21, 1924. Its strong suit was neither the book (by Frank Mandel and Laurence Schwab), nor Gershwin's music (which lacked a single winning number), but the performance of its star, Constance Binney. As the simple home girl Virginia, Constance Binney brought to the stage and to her role a personal magnetism and an engaging manner that won the audience completely. Unfortunately the slim story of her rivalry with a Ziegfeld Follies girl for the heart and hand of Tom Nesbitt, a South American engineer, and her ultimate victory, had much less vitality and freshness.

When *Sweet Little Devil* left Broadway after a run of little less than four months, Gershwin was represented on the Great White Way by his last assignment for the *Scandals,* the 1924 edition.

Gershwin left the *Scandals* because the demands it made upon him, from the planning stage of the revue through rehearsals and first performance, left him little time to devote to musical comedies. He asked George White for an increase over the $125.00 a week he was then receiving. When it was denied—as he hoped it would be—he cut his five-year tie with the producer. (That tie was briefly and temporarily renewed in 1927 when White used the *Rhapsody in Blue* for the first-act finale of the *Scandals* as the climax for "The Birth of the Blues" by De Sylva, Brown, and Henderson. Graciously, Gershwin refused any payment for the use of his music.)

Gershwin did not have to wait long for a new association. It came with the new producing firm of Aarons and Freedley, for whom he was to write some of his greatest musical-comedy successes. Alex A. Aarons, of course, was no stranger to Gershwin, having produced *La, La Lucille* in 1919, after which he had become one of Gershwin's most ardent admirers and friends. Neither was Vinton Freedley. Freedley had played a principal role in *Dere Mabel,* in 1920, when Gershwin came to rehearsals to play his song, "We're

Pals," which was incorporated into that production. One year later Freedley played the lead in the ill-fated *A Dangerous Maid,* which never came to Broadway.

It was still another play—Victor Herbert's *Oui Madame,* in 1920—that brought Aarons and Freedley together for the first time. Aarons' father was the producer, and Freedley played a principal role. During the run, the younger Aarons and Freedley became friends and met often to talk about the theater. They dreamed of putting Fred and Adele Astaire—then playing the Winter Garden—into a musical built just for them. It was Alex Aarons who brought this dream to reality in 1922 by producing *For Goodness Sake* (music by Paul Lannin and Will Daly), which starred the Astaires. Two years later Aarons transferred the show to London (still with the Astaires), renamed it *Stop Flirting,* and achieved with it one of the greatest successes of the London season. Incidentally, *Stop Flirting* had a few songs by Gershwin.

Freedley had a small investment in *For Goodness Sake,* and after that he became a full-fledged partner with Aarons in the production of Cosmo Hamilton's *The New Poor.* Aarons and Freedley now planned a smart new Broadway musical for the Astaires, after the completion of their extended run in London. Guy Bolton and Fred Thompson provided them with a suitable book, *Lady Be Good.* Gershwin was engaged to write the music. Today Freedley freely confesses that at the time he did not like the choice of Gershwin since he felt that Gershwin's music was too sophisticated for popular appeal. But Aarons was completely sold on the composer, agreeing wholeheartedly with Bolton when the latter said that "he was beginning to look uncommonly like a genius."

One of the reasons why Aarons was insistent on using Gershwin was that he had already heard one of the songs that would go into the new show. In 1923 Gershwin sketched the first eight bars of an intricate rhythmic number which he played for Aarons in London. The producer, with his natural bent for unusual musical treatments, was enthusiastic to the point where he insisted that Gershwin save it for some future Aarons musical. Gershwin completed his song a few weeks later in New York and put it aside for the time when he could use it in an Aarons production. Thus, before he wrote a single new note for *Lady Be Good*, Gershwin had "Fascinating Rhythm" ready.

In *Lady Be Good*, Fred and Adele Astaire were cast as a brother-and-sister dancing team—Dick and Susie Trevors —who had come upon unhappy days. Unable to pay their rent, they are unceremoniously ejected into the street. The opening scene was one of the best. Out on the sidewalk with their furniture, the Trevors try to make the best of a miserable situation. Susie is meticulous about the arrangement of her furniture around the corner lamppost, upon which she hangs the framed legend, "God Bless Our Home."

There is a way out of their troubles, however, for a rich girl is in love with Dick. Indeed, it is she who, having been spurned, was responsible for their eviction from their home. To save her brother from marrying a girl he does not love, Susie is induced by an unscrupulous lawyer (Walter Catlett) to impersonate a Mexican widow and thus put her hands on an inheritance. The inheritance is as much of a phony as Susie's Mexican act. The difficulties of the Trevors are, nonetheless, happily resolved before the final curtain.

Lady Be Good opened in New York on December 1, 1924, and became Gershwin's first major musical-comedy success. A critic on the *Sun* spoke of it as a "gem" and singled out Gershwin's score for special praise as "brisk, inventive, gay, nervous, delightful." Alan Dale thought that it was only Gershwin's music that "redeemed a quite typical musical comedy." One can understand why these and other critics were taken with Gershwin's score. Never before had he brought such a wealth of original invention to his stage music. The kinesthetic effect of the changing meters in "Fascinating Rhythm," the irresistible appeal of the repeated triplets in cut time in the title song, and the melodic significance accorded to the verses of both songs—all this represented a new sophistication in popular music. Other songs were notable for their personalized lyricism, particularly "So Am I" and "We're Here Because."

But the best song Gershwin wrote for *Lady Be Good* was not in the show when it opened in New York. As "The Man I Love" it has since become one of the Gershwin song classics. But before it finally achieved recognition it had an eventful history. The chorus as it is known today originated as the verse for another song, but Gershwin soon realized that the individual melody of the verse was so strong that it robbed the chorus that followed of any interest. This melody consisted of a six-note blues progression that reappeared throughout with accumulative effect, achieving poignancy through the contrapuntal background of a descending chromatic scale. In rewriting his song, Gershwin now used the verse as the chorus, and prefaced it with a simple but appealing introductory tune.

"The Man I Love" was sung by Adele Astaire in the opening scene of the Philadelphia tryout of *Lady Be Good*. In that setting the song missed aim completely; it was too static. Vinton Freedley insisted that it be dropped from the show, and Gershwin consented.

In 1927 Gershwin removed the song from his shelf and incorporated it into the score he was then writing for *Strike Up the Band* (first version). Once again it was tried out of town, was found wanting, and was deleted.

But the song had admirers. One of them was Otto H. Kahn, to whom Gershwin played it when he planned using it for *Lady Be Good*. Kahn liked the song so much that he decided to invest $10,000 in the musical. Another admirer was Lady Louis Mountbatten, to whom Gershwin presented an autographed copy in New York. When she returned to London, Lady Mountbatten arranged for the Berkeley Square Orchestra to introduce the song in London. It became such a success that—though no printed copies were available in England—it was picked up by many other jazz ensembles in London. Now a hit, the song crossed the Channel and was played by numerous jazz groups in Paris, where it also caught on. American visitors to London and Paris heard the song and, returning home, asked for it. Then singers and orchestras took it up until its acceptance in this country became complete.

Gershwin has explained that the reason it took the song so long to be appreciated is that the melody of the chorus, with its chromatic pitfalls, was not easy to catch; also, when caught, was not easy to sing or whistle or hum without a piano accompaniment.

Lady Be Good set a pattern for several future Gershwin musicals. Sammy Lee staged the ensemble numbers; the two-piano team of Ohman and Arden assisted in the presentation of the Gershwin music; and, most important of all, its lyrics were written by Ira Gershwin. This was the first musical in which Ira wrote all the lyrics for his brother's music. From then on, with some minor exceptions, Ira wrote the words for all of Gershwin's songs. They became the words-and-music team for the most successful of Gershwin's musicals, and in that success Ira played a major role.

Ira had progressed far in plying the trade of lyricist since he had collaborated with George on "The Real American Folk Song" in 1918. His first published lyric was "Waiting for the Sun To Come Out" (music by George) used in *The Sweetheart Shop*, in 1920. In the same year he wrote the lyrics to five of George's songs in *A Dangerous Maid*. Only one year after that Ira was a Broadway success, but this time without the benefit of George's music. He wrote the lyrics for *Two Little Girls in Blue*, music by Vincent Youmans and Paul Lannin, which had an eleven-month run in New York.

The security and self-assurance that attend success were not lacking in Ira. Up to 1924 all of Ira's lyrics appeared under the pseudonym of "Arthur Francis." The mask was removed in that year in *Be Yourself*, a musical whose book was by George S. Kaufman and Marc Connelly, and music by Lewis Gensler and Milton Schwartzwald. It was as "Ira Gershwin" and not as "Arthur Francis" that he now appeared in all the credits, and on the title page of the printed music. And it was as "Ira Gershwin" that he reappeared a few months later in *Lady Be Good*.

Ira revealed new strength in *Lady Be Good;* his was no longer an apprentice hand. A line like "I must win some winsome miss" demonstrates the easy way he now had with a well-turned, well-sounding phrase. A couplet like "this is

tulip weather, so let's put two and two together" pointed to a
natural and charming simplicity. The chorus for "Fascinating
Rhythm" showed a verbal virtuosity in following the lead of
the music in its intricate rhythmic movements.

In 1923, Gershwin paid his first visit to London. He
came to write the music for the *Rainbow Revue,* for which he
received a fee of $1,500 besides the price of his round-trip
passage. The show was a disastrous failure. This was due in
part to the threadbare and frequently insufferably dull material provided by the writers (one of whom was the mystery
writer Edgar Wallace). Gershwin's music, which he himself
regarded as the weakest score he had ever written for the
stage, was hardly more rewarding. Only one of the thirteen
songs, "Yankee Doodle Blues," had vitality and cogency
(in 1925 it was used as a recurring musical theme in John
Howard Lawson's expressionist play *Processional*); the rest
of the songs were pedestrian in style and perfunctory in
technique. But the fiasco was not the exclusive responsibility
of the authors. The leading comedian, chagrined that so much
of his part had been deleted in rehearsal, created a scandal
on opening night by suddenly delivering to the startled audience a violent attack against all the Americans involved in the
production.

From London, Gershwin went by air to Paris to be
Jules Glaenzer's guest at his Paris home near the Bois de
Boulogne. Bud De Sylva was also visiting Glaenzer at the
time, and for the next few days the three made the rounds of
the most famous restaurants and night places. Gershwin fell
in love with the city at first sight; everything about it came to
him as a major discovery. One day while traveling in Glaenzer's car through the Arc de Triomphe and down the Champs-

Élysées, he exclaimed: "Why, this is a city you can write about!" Bud De Sylva answered softly, "Don't look now, George, but it's been done."

Gershwin returned to London one year later with happier results. At the request of Alex A. Aarons he revised the score of *For Goodness Sake* and contributed a few new numbers for its London première as *Stop Flirting*. Besides this, he had a London hit of his own in *Primrose*—to a book by Guy Bolton and George Grossmith with lyrics by Desmond Carter and Ira Gershwin. The cast included the comedian Leslie Henson and Heather Thatcher, favorites of the London stage. *Primrose* deserves a special footnote since it was Gershwin's first musical for which he did some of the orchestrations (three numbers), and the first whose score was published in its entirety. His songs struck a responsive chord with English audiences. "Isn't It Terrible What They Did to Mary Queen of Scots," "Berkeley Square and Kew," and "When Toby Is Out of Town" contain topical suggestions and historical and geographical allusions dear to English hearts. "Four Little Sirens We" carried welcome echoes of Gilbert and Sullivan. The winning lyricism of "Wait a Bit Susie," "Till I Meet Someone Like You," and "Some Far-Away Someone" had the warming quality of English ale, and the smart melodic one-step, "I Make Hay When the Moon Shines," had a captivating pulse. From this point on, Gershwin was almost as great a favorite in Piccadilly as he was on Broadway.

THE HOUSE ON
103RD STREET

In 1925 the Gershwin family bought a five-story white granite house on 103rd Street near Riverside Drive. On the ground floor there was a billiard room which served as a meeting place and general hangout for the young people of the neighborhood. Some were friends of Arthur's or Frances', some were neighbors, a few were total strangers. On the second floor were the living- and dining-rooms where the Gershwin, Wolpin, and Bruskin clans would congregate over cups of tea, or to play poker or pinochle. The next two floors had bedrooms. When Ira married Leonore Strunsky on September 14, 1926, they took over the fourth floor. The fifth floor was George's sanctum. The rooms in which George worked and entertained had a brick fireplace, a grand piano, and comfortable chairs. A study lined with books, music, and a specially designed and built-in cupboard for his manuscripts led to his bedroom.

S. N. Behrman describes a visit to the Gershwin menage: [*]

> For a long time I rang the doorbell but got no answer. Through the screened, curtained door-window, I could see the figures moving inside, and I kept ringing impatiently. No answer. Finally I pushed the door and walked in. Three or four young men I had never seen before were sitting around the hall smoking. . . . I peered in [the billiard room]—there was a game in progress, but I knew none of the players. I asked for George, or his brother, Ira. No one bothered to reply, but one of the young men made a terse gesture in the direction of the upper stories. I went up one flight and there I found a new group. One of them I vaguely recognized from 110th Street and I asked him where George and Ira were. He said they were upstairs. On the third floor I found Arthur . . . who had just come in and didn't know who was in the house, but on the fourth I got my answer to my—by this time agonized—cry. I heard Ira's voice inviting me up to the fifth. . . . 'Where,' I demanded sternly, 'is George?' 'He's taken his old room in the hotel around the corner. He says he's got to have a little privacy.'

When immediate deadlines had to be met George sometimes fled from the frenetic activity that always seemed

[*] *The New Yorker,* May 25, 1929.

to be a part of the Gershwin household, by renting a room in a nearby hotel. He had begun this practice when the family lived on 110th Street and Amsterdam Avenue, which always overflowed with relatives and friends, and continued it at 103rd Street. But since his intimate circle usually followed him to his hotel room and brought with them the tumult and the shouting, his isolation was ephemeral.

Mostly Gershwin could be found on that fifth floor. Here he had his favorite piano, a Steinway (two others were in the family living quarters downstairs), his books, and music, and the precious mementos of his career. The walls were lined with photographs of famous people affectionately inscribed to him, together with his favorite portraits of great composers commissioned by George from Will Cotton. Later on, a framed poster announcing a performance of the Gershwin Concerto in Paris occupied a prominent wall, while some of the composers made way for five lithographs by George Bellows.

Here he did his composing, in spite of distractions of friends buzzing nearby, or the continual hum of activity from the floors below. Probably it was to find more quiet and seclusion that he at this time acquired the habit of working late at night and often until the early hours of dawn. Stripped down to his waist, and puffing continually at a cigar, he would sit at his piano and painstakingly work out his ideas. He always had plenty of ideas, more than he could use. Once when he discovered that he had lost and couldn't find a sketchbook containing material for over forty songs, he remarked placidly that he had too many ideas for other songs to worry unduly about his loss. But working out his material —that was something else again. To find for it the proper mold, to carve it into its most effective design, to seize the precise and inevitable phrase, to bring a new touch—all this required laborious effort on his part. For hours at a stretch he would work on details with the most painstaking fastidiousness.

Sometimes, as he worked at the piano, his father would sit patiently in the hall outside the closed door. If the piano played without interruption, his father's face would beam, for he knew that all went well with George's inspiration. But when there was a prolonged period of silence—or if the playing came by fits and starts—his father was in torment. He knew that at such times George was involved in a bitter creative struggle. On one occasion, George kept on playing a single theme several times, then stopped without progressing to the next idea. The piano was silent for an insufferably long time. Unable to stand the suspense any longer, his father opened the door timidly, pushed his face through the opening, and quickly whistled the fragment of a tune. "Does that help you, George?" he asked.

George would welcome an endless stream of visitors to the fifth floor: interviewers; world-famous musicians eager to meet him and tell him how highly they regarded his music; struggling composers, both serious and the popular, seeking help and advice; men from the concert or theater world come to discuss projects. One of Gershwin's most ingratiating traits was that he would greet a high-school student, seriously interviewing him for the school paper or coming for an autograph, as graciously as he would the music editor of a powerful newspaper. On several occasions he was known to sit down and play the piano zestfully for an audience of one youngster. He would also welcome an unknown musician seeking guidance as warmly as he would one with an established reputation. His door was open to all comers.

He was never out or too busy to those who tried to reach him by telephone. His generosity with his time amounted to outright extravagance, and he remained that way regardless of the increasing pressure of his activities.

On that fifth floor he would entertain his many friends with gay parties, shop talk, and, of course, by playing the piano for hours. But only one part of his social life was lived there. Another and more active part was pursued at the homes of New York society where he was a welcome guest. There he would mingle with powerful figures in many different walks of life, many of whom became very fond of him. Besides those already mentioned, there were Otto H. Kahn (who for a period harbored a hope that Gershwin might become his son-in-law) and Jascha Heifetz. Also there were Mary Hoyt Wiborg, at whose home early in 1925 Gershwin met Igor Stravinsky for the first time; Condé Nast, the magazine publisher, who was Jules Glaenzer's cousin; Jules Glaenzer; the Sidney Fishes; Edsel Ford; the Polish violin virtuoso, Paul Kochanski; Cole Porter; Samuel Chotzinoff, then music critic of the New York *World,* and many others.

He was lionized by these people in New York and Long Island, and he was lionized by English society in London. In *Laughter in the Next Room,** Sir Osbert Sitwell recalled his associations with Gershwin in London:

> He would usually come to have luncheon with us when he visited London. . . . Tall and vigorous, his clearly cut face with its handsome ram's head, the features prominent, but, as it were, streamlined, indicated power, character and talent. I have always understood

---

* *Laughter in the Next Room,* by Sir Osbert Sitwell. Boston: Little, Brown & Co., 1948.

that he was the son of immigrants from Russia or Germany, and was brought up in the poorest quarter of New York; but his manners were notably excellent, his voice was pleasant, and though the force of his personality was plain in his whole air, he was modest in bearing, and I never noticed in him a trace of the arrogance with which he has been credited.

After a repetition of the Eva Gauthier concert in London in 1925, he was honored by Lord and Lady Canisbrooke, who were cousins of King George V. Late one night, in that same year, after a party, the Prince of Wales invited George and the Astaires to Buckingham Palace. The Duke of Kent—then Prince George, son of King George V, who was killed in an airplane crash during World War II— became particularly attached to Gershwin, often invited him to his parties, and even more frequently dropped in at George's apartment in Pall Mall. In the gallery of photographs at Gershwin's apartment on 103rd Street there hung one of the Duke with the inscription: "From George to George." Lord and Lady Mountbatten were also his personal friends.

Gershwin's social life flowed through still another artery during this period. In the early 1920s, and continuing through that decade, he would often meet his Tin Pan Alley friends during the noon hour at the office of Harms at 62 West 45th Street. There were no specific days for such meetings, but it became habitual for Harry Ruby, Phil Charig, Bert Kalmar, Joe Meyer, Bud De Sylva, Vincent Youmans, Irving Caesar, and later on Vernon Duke and Harold Arlen, to congregate there. George appeared several times a week, and the group revolved around him. Since there was a piano there, George often played for his friends his latest creations or works in progress. Irving Caesar was something of the court jester, delighting the group with impromptu parodies and improvised opera arias. Once, while waiting for the others, Bill Daly accompanied Caesar on the piano as the latter hummed the *"Depuis le jour"* aria from the opera *Louise*. When Youmans and Gershwin appeared, they listened to the air with rapt attention, Gershwin exclaiming, "Why, it's wonderful, really wonderful, when did you write it?" He thought it was a new song by Bill Daly, which Daly and Caesar were trying out for the first time. The young composers and lyricists, as well as Gershwin, would sometimes use this social period to discuss new projects with the Harms editor, Dr. Albert Sirmay, and their patron saint, Max Dreyfus. Dreyfus would then take a few of them out to lunch to the Hunting Room at the Hotel Astor where the special Dreyfus table was reserved for them.

It was not unusual for young and inexperienced song writers to come up to Harms to play their unpublished pieces for Gershwin. He saw them all. One of these visitors, in 1925, was Arthur Schwartz, then a practicing lawyer for whom writing songs was still just an amusing diversion. Schwartz had been so overwhelmed by the *Rhapsody in Blue* that he had written a song whose melody quoted some of its material. The lyric, a paean to Gershwin, began with the lines: "O wonderful, wonderful Georgie, What you've done to me!" As he began playing for Gershwin he was seized by the sudden awareness that this was no masterpiece, and he stopped short suddenly, and with embarrassment. Gershwin gently asked him to play some of his other songs, which he did. "I found his reaction the warmest, most encouraging I had yet received," says Schwartz. Later as a successful composer of

Broadway scores and hit songs, Schwartz was a member of Gershwin's intimate circle.

Broadway had three Gershwin musicals in 1925. *Tell Me More* came in mid-April and departed less than a month later. Built around a romance born at a masked ball, *Tell Me More* had one or two appealing elements: Emma Haig's ingratiating portrayal of the heroine who pretends to be a shopgirl to test the genuineness of her beau's affection, and Lou Holtz' own amusing parody, "O So La Mi." But the production as a whole did not jell and failed to please New York. The Gershwin score was also far below par for the course since it did not contain a single number that stood out or is even remembered.

The *Song of the Flame*, which opened on December 30, with Tessa Kosta and Guy Robertson, was described by its producers as a "romantic opera." This musical was also a failure that deserved its fate. It was an effete attempt on the part of Gershwin to invade the province of the operetta dominated by men like Romberg and Friml. The Otto Harbach–Oscar Hammerstein II book made much ado about a peasant uprising in Russia led by Aniuta, a noble-born rebel who came to be known as "The Flame." She falls in love with Prince Volodyn. After each assimilates some of the ideology of the other, they end up in Paris in each other's arms.

The operetta was conceived along spacious lines—with colorful sets and costumes, big scenes, a Russian art chorus, a large *corps de ballet*, and an enlarged orchestra. "There were mobs, riots, balls, and carnivals, both in Paris and Moscow," wrote Percy Hammond. "Picture trod on picture as fast as they came . . . yet . . . the play lacked what

used to be known as 'that something.'" Gershwin's songs
(which were supplemented by several others by Herbert
Stothart) also lacked conviction, particularly in their pseudo-
Slavic flavors. The title song bears a blood relationship to
Friml's "Song of the Vagabonds," while "The Song of the
Cossacks" (perhaps better known as "Don't Forget Me")
sounds like every other Slavic love song in every other Rus-
sian operetta.

In *Song of the Flame* Gershwin had temporarily
parted company with some of the collaborators who had
helped make *Lady Be Good* so good: the producers, Aarons
and Freedley; the lyricist, Ira Gershwin; the authors, Guy
Bolton and Fred Thompson. But the team was happily re-
united in *Tip Toes*, which opened only two days after *The
Song of the Flame*. *Tip Toes* was in the sophisticated manner of *Lady Be Good*. It was good musical comedy, good
Gershwin—and it was a hit. Freedley says that it earned
more money for the Aarons and Freedley combine than any
other Gershwin musical they produced, not excluding *Girl
Crazy* which had a longer run.

"Tip Toes," played by Queenie Smith, is a vivacious
dancer who is used by her brothers as bait to trap a million-
aire in a profitable marriage. They bring her to Miami in a
style befitting a queen. There she finds her prey in Steve, the
glue-king (Allen Kearns). They fall in love, but only when
Steve is convinced she loves him for himself alone, and not
for his millions, are they permanently united.

Such a text is not likely to change the destiny of the
musical theater; but it was studded with smart lines, with
piquant topical allusions, and delightful comic situations.
Best of all it was punctuated with several outstanding Gersh-

win songs. "Bright and gay and good looking . . . [*Tip Toes*] is made altogether captivating by the pretty, rebel, infectious music of George Gershwin, all told the best score he has written in his days in the theater, all told, I think, the best score anyone has written for our town this season." So wrote Alexander Woollcott who added: "It was . . . Gershwin's evening, so sweet and sassy are the melodies he has poured out . . . so fresh and unstinted the gay, young blood of his invention." The cream of the Gershwin crop was "That Certain Feeling," with its subtly insinuating accentuations; the high-voltage rhythms of "Sweet and Low Down"; the wistful tenderness of "Looking for a Boy," which one of England's prominent musicologists, Francis Toye, praised for its Brahmsian personality.

A special word must be said about Ira's lyrics which, in *Tip Toes*, show an advance in technique, assurance, and flexibility over earlier efforts. Ira himself says that he became satisfied with his writing for the first time in this production. Lorenz Hart, himself an ace lyricist and the verbal partner of Richard Rodgers, was so impressed by Ira's skill that he then wrote one of his rare fan letters to a rival lyricist.

> Your lyrics . . . gave me as much pleasure as Mr. George Gershwin's music. . . . I have heard none so good this many a day. . . . It is a great pleasure to live at a time when light amusement in this country is at last losing its brutally cretin aspect. Such delicacies as your jingles prove that songs can be both popular and intelligent. May I take the liberty of saying that your rhymes in *Tip Toes* show a healthy improvement over those in *Lady Be Good*. You have helped a lot to make an evening delightful for me—and I am very grateful.

Ira's rhyming in *Tip Toes* has a new resiliency— "there's a cabaret in this city . . . peps you up like electricity," or "if you need a tonic, and the need is chronic, if you're in a crisis, my advice is." A new simplicity and directness come through the felicitous use of colloquialism ("that certain feeling," which belonged to the jargon of the day). Ira also demonstrated a new and subtle feeling for the comic, though this is to be found in a lyric which unfortunately was deleted from the production, "The Harlem River Chantey."

London also had three Gershwin musicals during this period, all of them hits in varying degrees. *Tell Me More* redeemed itself in London, largely because it was the showcase for two London favorites—Heather Thatcher and Leslie Henson. As we have seen, *Lady Be Good* with the Astaires came to London after a highly successful two-week tryout in Liverpool; it took the town by storm. This was the first Gershwin musical that Aarons and Freedley imported from Broadway to London, and when they followed it with *Tip Toes* they established the tradition of bringing Gershwin musicals from New York to London that continued for several years.

10

THE CONCERTO IN F

Gershwin's shadow fell across Carnegie Hall in 1925 not once but twice. On December 29, 1925, Paul Whiteman and his orchestra gave a concert there including the world première of Grofé's *Mississippi Suite* and the first revival of Gershwin's one-act opera, *Blue Monday*—now rechristened *135th Street*—since that single-night performance in the *Scandals* three and a half years earlier. Gershwin's opera was now given without formal scenery. A few simple props suggested a night club. All the action took place directly in front of the Whiteman Orchestra, and the distraction of watching Whiteman conduct behind the stage action was disturbing. If the Gershwin opera had had inherent vitality and dramatic interest, it surely would have surmounted this handicap; as it was—and in spite of fine performances by Charles Hart, Blossom Seeley, Jack McGowan, and Benny Fields—the opera did not impress the city music critics, who were hearing it for the first time. Perhaps the most favorable reaction came from Olin Downes who found "excellent material" in it, "some good melodies," and "certain dramatic passages." But more characteristic of the general critical response was the report of an unsigned music critic for the *Sun.* "The music . . . with the exception of two clever songs . . . served simply as an unimpressive accompaniment for an old hokum vaudeville skit."

This was not Gershwin's initiation into Carnegie Hall. Three weeks earlier he had appeared there in the dual role of pianist and composer in the world première of his Concerto in F, his first major new serious music since the *Rhapsody in Blue.*

A few months after the première of the *Rhapsody in Blue,* Walter Damrosch, conductor of the New York Symphony Society, had prevailed on its president, Harry Harkness Flagler, to commission Gershwin to write a work for orchestra. Gershwin decided to compose a piano concerto and signed a contract with that organization specifying that he make seven appearances as soloist—in New York, Washington, Philadelphia, and Baltimore.

The story that, after the signing of the contract, Gershwin went out and bought a book to find out what a concerto was is apocryphal. By 1925 Gershwin had had sound training in the sonata form, and he had heard numerous concertos. However, he did make a study of several of the more famous concertos in the repertory to ascertain the approach of the masters to that form.

He began working on his music in July 1925. (At the head of his preliminary sketches appeared the title *New York Concerto*. But he soon abandoned this name for the more formal and less descriptive designation of Concerto in F.) Since he needed a quiet retreat, Ernest Hutcheson provided him with a studio in Chautauqua, New York, where Hutcheson was then conducting a master class in piano. Hutcheson instructed all his pupils that under no circumstance were they to invade Gershwin's privacy until four in the afternoon. At four o'clock sharp, many of the young students would storm into Gershwin's studio to hear him play and sing his music.

The writing of the Concerto took an entire summer; the third movement was completed in late September. The orchestration, which Gershwin now insisted on doing himself, took another four weeks. At the bottom of the last page of the manuscript appears the date when the entire work was completed: November 10.

Soon after its completion, the Concerto was tried out by Gershwin at the Globe Theater. An orchestra of sixty hired musicians was conducted by Bill Daly. The revisions Gershwin made during this trial performance were comparatively slight; they appear on his manuscript.

The official première took place on the afternoon of December 3. The program included Glazunov's Fifth Symphony and Rabaud's *Suite anglais*, both performed before the intermission that preceded the Gershwin Concerto. On the day of his concert, Gershwin appears to have maintained his calm and equilibrium, for at two o'clock that day Phil Charig had to bang on the door of his bathroom to hurry him out of his leisurely bath. But as the moment for his appearance came closer, his nerves began to reveal raw edges. During the intermission, and just before the Concerto, Gershwin paced up and down the artist's room, rubbing his fingers. Damrosch sat by quietly and remarked with a smile, "Just play the Concerto as well as it deserves, George, and you'll come off with flying banners."

Once again, as at Aeolian Hall for the *Rhapsody in Blue,* the auditorium was a strange potpourri of jazz enthusiasts and representatives from Tin Pan Alley, serious musicians, and music-lovers. All seemed enthusiastic over Gershwin's Concerto and participated in a magnificent ovation for the composer at its conclusion. As for the critics, they ranged from excessive enthusiasm to denunciation. Samuel Chotzinoff wrote: "He alone of all those writing the music of today . . . expresses us. He is the present, with all its audacity, impertinence, its feverish delight in its motion, its lapses into rhythmically exotic melancholy. He writes without the smallest hint of self-consciousness. . . . And here is where his genius comes in. George Gershwin is an instinctive artist who has the talent for the right manipulation of the crude material he starts out with that a lifelong study of counterpoint and fugue never can give to the one who is not born with it." W. J. Henderson said: "It has the moods of the contemporaneous dance without their banality. It has lifted their means and their substance. . . . It is interesting and individual . . . and it very frequently reminds one of the frantic efforts of certain moderns. It drops into their language, sometimes, but it has more to say."

In the opposite camp stood Lawrence Gilman to whom the music was "conventional, trite, at its worst a little dull"; Pitts Sanborn who found it fragmentary, uncertain in form, and without an understanding of the requirements of the orchestra; and Olin Downes who regarded it as much less original than the *Rhapsody in Blue*.

Gershwin said of the Concerto's structure that it "is in the sonata form—but. . . ." The "but" is important. The Concerto never follows the traditional patterns of the classical form. The structure is free and elastic; the materials are presented and restated in an unconventional manner.

The very opening of the first movement (*Allegro*) is unorthodox: not an orchestral peroration with basic themes as was habitual with so many classical and romantic masters, but eight measures of mood setting and atmosphere building. An abandoned Charleston motive is shared between kettledrums and woodwinds. The introduction over, three successive ideas emerge. The first is racy, given by the bassoon before the full orchestra takes over; the second is a wistful melody in the piano; the third, a slow, sensual waltz for the strings with filigree treatment by the piano.

In the second movement (*Andante con moto*), an extended song, with the shimmering haze of a Debussy melody, is heard in muted trumpet set against nebulous harmonies of three clarinets. When this sensitive and mysterious introduction ends, an irresponsible jazzy idea is given by the piano against a brisk rhythm in the strings. The second subject is discussed in some detail. A transition in the solo violin leads to a piano cadenza which provocatively suggests the germ of a new melody. This new melody is the heart of the movement, a mobile and sensual song unfolding in the strings. The movement ends with a return of the muted trumpet with which it began, and in the same atmosphere of mystery.

The finale (*Allegro con brio*) is in sharp contrast, erupting like a firecracker, with an outburst of rhythms and orchestral color. The emotions held so long in check are now given release. Principal themes from the preceding two movements are recalled but often changed in details; they are skillfully interjected into the gay and abandoned proceedings. A climax is reached with a stirring restatement in the strings of the second theme of the first movement, and the Concerto ends with a brief coda.

The rich palette of Gershwin's orchestration requires the full symphony orchestra together with a bass drum, snare drum, cymbals, "Charleston stick," xylophone, and bells. Gershwin does not use any saxophones.

The Concerto is a much more astute and a much more musical work than the *Rhapsody in Blue*. The form has less tendency to ramble before arriving at the convenient stopping-off point of a new salient thought; there is less reliance on convenient passage work to fill in gaps. Most of the time Gershwin seems to know where he is heading, and he proceeds toward the new idea with the sure gait of one who knows the lay of the land.

There is greater richness and variety of thought in the Concerto than in the Rhapsody. What we have in the Concerto is not only just one or two good melodies, as was the case with the earlier work, but a gushing of wonderful ideas, refreshing in their contrasting idioms and moods. And, unlike the Rhapsody where a new inviting subject comes almost as a surprise to the composer, most of the ideas in the Concerto are permitted to evolve and develop naturally out of the musical texture. The Concerto is interesting not only for its thematic subjects, but also in the way the material is presented, extended, enlarged, combined, and transformed.

The gamut of moods, feelings, atmosphere is much more elastic in the Concerto. In the larger work we get some of the abandon, wit, satire, and nostalgia of the Rhapsody, but to all this is added something equally vital: the shimmering poetic beauty of the second movement in which jazz is made to plumb new artistic depths. Walter Damrosch underscored this point by saying so felicitously that in the Concerto Gershwin made a lady out of jazz. He wrote in the program notes:

> Various composers have been walking around jazz like a cat around a plate of hot soup, waiting for it to cool off, so that they could enjoy it without burning their tongues, hitherto accustomed only to the more tepid liquid distilled by cooks of the classical school. Lady Jazz, adorned with her intriguing rhythms, has danced her way around the world, even as far as the Eskimos of the North and the Polynesians of the South Sea Islands. But for all her travels and her sweeping popularity, she has encountered no knight who could lift her to a level that would enable her to be received as a respectable member in the musical circles. George Gershwin seems to have accomplished this miracle. He has done it boldly by dressing this extremely independent and up-to-date young lady in the classic garb of a concerto. Yet he has not detracted one whit from her fascinating personality. He is the prince who has taken Cinderella by the hand and openly proclaimed her a princess to the astonished world no doubt to the fury of her envious sisters.

On May 29, 1928, the Concerto in F received its European première in a performance by Dimitri Tiomkin and an orchestra conducted by Vladimir Golschmann. Two years after that, the eminent English conductor Albert Coates compiled a list of fifty of the foremost musical works of our time; only a single American work was included, and that was the Gershwin Concerto. On September 8, 1932, two movements were given at the Second International Festival of Contemporary Music in Venice. Harry Kaufman was the soloist with Fritz Reiner conducting. The correspondent for *Musical America* reported that it was "the only piece to arouse public favor." On October 6, 1939, Serge Koussevitzky included the Concerto in special programs of the Boston Symphony Orchestra honoring American composers.

Like the *Rhapsody in Blue,* the Concerto has become a staple of the contemporary repertory. It is without question the most frequently performed piano concerto written in the last half century, and not only in America but also in Europe. And—though this does not follow as a corollary—it is also one of the best. It was used for a ballet, in Gothenburg, Sweden, in 1954.

"When I die," once said the Peruvian opera singer Marguerite d'Alvarez, in answer to a bitter denunciation of jazz by John Roach Straton, "I want nothing better than that Gershwin's Piano Concerto be played over my grave."

11

Oh Kay, Funny Face,

AND THE PIANO

PRELUDES

There were two important parties celebrating the première of the Concerto. One was given by Jules Glaenzer, at which a golden cigarette case, with the signatures of twenty-eight of Gershwin's friends, was presented to the composer. At the other, the hosts were Dr. and Mrs. Walter Damrosch at their home at 168 West 71st Street. The place swarmed with Gershwin friends and admirers, and the praises gushed as freely as the liquor. Some of the guests there started discussing Gershwin's future as an American composer. The belief was expressed that he should immediately engage in intensive study of theory and composition to fill in the gaps in his training and technique; others countered that such instruction might rob him of his main assets —spontaneity and freshness—and make him studied and self-conscious in his writing. Some suggested that he abandon popular music and dedicate himself completely to serious creation; others felt his popular music was much too good and important in its own right to be discarded.

Gershwin listened to these arguments without comment. He would hear them again and again in the future. If they made any impression on him that evening at the Damrosch's, the fact was not betrayed by his phlegmatic face or quizzical smile. But he often discussed the questions raised at that party. F.P.A. reported in the weekly diary of his column, "The Conning Tower," in the *World*, on January 23, 1926:

> Then G. Gershwin, the composer, came in, and we did talk musique, and about going ahead regardless of advice, this one saying, Do not study, and that one saying, Study; and another saying, Write only jazz melodies, and another saying Write only symphonies and concertos.

Gershwin certainly did not agree with those who felt and said that further study would damage the gifts with which he was born. He said to Ira, "I maintain that a composer needs to understand all the intricacies of counterpoint and orchestration, and be able to create new forms for each advance in his work." He had never actually stopped studying; he never would. After Hambitzer's death, Gershwin took some piano lessons with Herman Wasserman, and received valuable advice and coaching from teachers such as Ernest Hutcheson. Following his formal lessons in theory with Kilenyi in 1922, he thought of studying composition with Ernest Bloch. But Bloch was then in Cleveland, and in 1923 Gershwin turned to Rubin Goldmark, an association of several months' duration that was neither happy nor fruitful for the pupil. There were other teachers after 1926. In or about 1927 he took lessons in counterpoint from Henry Cowell, an American composer then an *enfant terrible* in American music through his development and exploitation of "tone clusters": an unorthodox procedure which called for the use of fists and forearms in playing his piano music. Cowell has written,

> The lessons were to be once a week, but usually something would interfere, so they were nearer once in three weeks. His [Gershwin's] fertile mind leaped all over the place. He was exasperated at the rules—but not because he was incapable of mastering them. With no effort at all he rattled off the almost perfect exercise, but would get side-tracked into something using a juicy ninth and altered chords that he liked better, and would insert these into the Palestrina-style motet. The whole period lasted a little over two years.

After Cowell, there were still other teachers. And less formally, Gershwin was studying all the time by himself, or receiving guidance from various musicians.

As for giving up popular music and concentrating all his energies and efforts on serious composition—this advice made no impression on him at all. Gershwin often confided to his friends that popular music was not only a way of making a handsome living but also a means of artistic expression as necessary to him as the writing of large works. The

Concerto in F—and the accolades it gathered among the in-telligentsia—could not rob him of his zest in writing in a popular idiom for mass consumption.

In 1926 George and Ira Gershwin wrote an excellent production number, "That Lost Barber-Shop Chord," for an intimate revue, *Americana.* Among the other composers who contributed songs were Phil Charig, whose "Sunny Disposish" and "Blowing the Blues Away" had lyrics by Ira. *Americana,* book by J. P. McEvoy, made musical-comedy history on two counts. It introduced Charles Butterworth to the stage; and it seated Helen Morgan for the first time atop an upright piano, from which vantage point she sang a plangent blues number, "Nobody Wants Me," which immediately established her as a leading exponent of torch songs.

Also in 1926 the Gershwins wrote the songs for one of their outstanding musical-comedy successes, *Oh Kay.* It was the first American musical comedy starring Gertrude Lawrence, who had made her Broadway debut in 1924 in *Charlot's Revue,* imported from London. When Aarons and Freedley discussed with her the possibility of coming to New York in a new musical, she was considering a similar offer from Ziegfeld. The information that George Gershwin would write the music was the deciding factor in her acceptance of the Aarons and Freedley contract.

The radiance she always brought to the stage made her presence in *Oh Kay* strongly felt. But putting her in the role of Kay was not the only happy piece of casting. The part of Shorty McGee, a bootlegger, was assigned to Victor Moore—a sad-faced, thin and broken-voiced, helpless little man who had a Chaplinesque way of blending comedy with wistfulness and pathos. Moore had been appearing on the American musical-comedy stage for almost a quarter of a century, but Shorty McGee was one of his greatest personal triumphs up to that time and the first of several unforgettable Milquetoast characters with which he brightened the corners of Broadway for the next decade. Strange to say, he seemed at first so poorly cast as the bootlegger that Vinton Freedley thought of buying out his contract for $10,000 and getting Johnny Dooley as a replacement. But before the shift was made, Victor Moore brought down the house in Philadelphia.

The rest of the memorable cast included Oscar Shaw in the leading male role of Jimmy Winters; Gerald Oliver Smith as the English duke, Kay's brother; and an attractive young lady named Betty Compton who was given a minor role through the influence of the Mayor of New York City, James J. Walker.

The performances of Gertrude Lawrence, Victor Moore, and Oscar Shaw helped to bring out vividly the luster of the scintillating lines and hilarious episodes with which Guy Bolton and P. G. Wodehouse studded a rather perfunctory plot. The story concerned itself with the rather unoriginal theme of bootlegging. An English duke and his sister Kay come to the United States on their yacht. They have been in financial difficulties since World War I, and they are using their yacht for rum-running. Pursued by American prohibition agents, they find an asylum in the palatial home of Jimmy Winter, whose cellar they now use as a secret hiding place for illicit liquor. The liquor is watched over by Shorty McGee, disguised as a butler. Kay and Jimmy fall in love. But they must extricate themselves from varied entanglements and misunderstandings—including the indefatigable pursuit of Jimmy by various blondes—before they can become united.

"It was an event bordering upon the phenomenal," reported Percy Hammond after the première. "Mr. Gershwin's score is a marvel of its kind." Brooks Atkinson was also enthusiastic. "Musical comedy seldom proves more intensely delightful than *Oh Kay*. . . . The distinction . . . is its excellent blending of all the creative arts of musical entertainment."

The Gershwin score was a richer cache of treasure than even that hidden in Jimmy Winter's cellar. To no other musical production up to this time had he been so lavish with his gifts. There was "Someone To Watch Over Me" in his most soaring and beguiling lyric vein, touched with the glow of Gertrude Lawrence's charm; "Clap Yo' Hands," with its fascinating rhythms; "Do, Do, Do," in which Ira Gershwin's infectious use of repeated words throughout the lyric was matched by the capricious feathery touch of the melody. Besides these there were such secondary hits as the title song, "Maybe," and "Fidgety Feet," each of which would have been a shining beacon in any other musical.

In 1927 Aarons and Freedley built a new theater for their productions—the Alvin on West 52nd Street. It was a house that Gershwin had helped build with the profits from *Lady Be Good, Tip Toes,* and *Oh Kay*. What, then, was more appropriate than that it should be opened on November 22 with a new Gershwin musical? This was *Funny Face,* in which Fred and Adele Astaire made their first welcome return in a Gershwin show since *Lady Be Good*. Fred Astaire was cast as Jimmy Reeve, the guardian of Frankie, who was played by Adele. Frankie's pearls are being held by her guardian in a safe and he refuses to part with them. In an effort to retrieve the jewels from her guardian, Frankie enlists the aid of her boy friend, Peter (Allen Kearns). In his effort to penetrate the safe, Peter gets helplessly involved with two comic and blundering thugs, Dugsie and Herbert, who are also after the pearls.

As in *Oh Kay*, it was Victor Moore—as the thug, Herbert—who stole the limelight. The book, originally by Robert Benchley in collaboration with Fred Thompson, called for a lady crook. In this version the show was tried out with disastrous results: It lost about $10,000 a week and received annihilating reviews. Surgery was required. Thirteen Gershwin numbers were eliminated (some of them reappeared in later musicals), and others were substituted to tighten the score. Besides this, on Gershwin's suggestion, Paul Gerard Smith was called in to doctor the book to emphasize comedy. (Robert Benchley bowed out of the picture completely.) During this revision, the producers had the happy idea of recruiting Victor Moore to replace the lady thief. New scenes were rewritten with Victor Moore in mind, and they became the strong points of the production: in one, the two blundering crooks get drunk over a punch bowl with hilarious consequences; in another, Herbert tries to shoot his partner, who accepts his fate with an almost incredible stoicism and resignation. The change was finally achieved in Wilmington, Delaware; almost from the moment Moore took over, the show began doing well. By the time it reached New York it was playing to crowded houses. Among those enchanted by it, and particularly by Gershwin's music, was France's leading composer, Maurice Ravel, then on his first visit to the United States.

The best songs were "'S Wonderful" (the hit of the show), "Let's Kiss and Make Up," and a number that has never received the recognition it deserves (it will probably be revived some day with astonishing results)—"The Babbitt and the Bromide." This last is a patter song with a difference that George always seemed to bring to his writing: an intriguing contrapuntal design runs through the accompaniment of the verse, and the chorus is followed by a delightful instrumental polka. More remarkable still is Ira's lyric—one of his best. This was the only song lyric that Louis Kronenberger saw fit to include in his *An Anthology of Light Verse,* published in 1934.

A Babbitt met a Bromide on the avenue one day,
And held a conversation in their own peculiar way.
They both were solid citizens, they both had been around,
And as they spoke you clearly saw their feet were on the
    ground.

CHORUS

Hello! How are you?
Howsa folks? What's new?
I'm great! That's good!
Ha-ha! Knock wood!
Well, well! What say?
How-ya been? Nice day.
How's tricks? What's new?
That's fine, are you?
Nice weather we are having but it gives me
                such a pain;
I've taken my umbrella, so of course it doesn't
            rain.
Heigh-ho! That's life!
What's new? Howza wife?
Got to run! Oh, my!
Ta, ta. Olive Oil! Good-bye.

"The Babbitt and the Bromide" was last heard in the motion picture, *The Ziegfeld Follies,* released in 1946, sung by Fred Astaire and Gene Kelly.

On December 4, 1926, at the Hotel Roosevelt, Marguerite d'Alvarez, the operatic contralto, stepped in boldly where only Eva Gauthier had previously dared to tread. She sang some Gershwin songs at a serious recital that included French and Spanish art songs. Gershwin participated at this concert, not only by accompanying her in his songs, but also by appearing as a piano soloist. The program opened with a solo-piano arrangement of the *Rhapsody in Blue,* played by Gershwin. Then, after the first group of art songs, he returned for a solo performance, in the world première of his Five Preludes for the piano. This concert was so successful that Marguerite d'Alvarez and George Gershwin went on tour with the same program. They appeared in Buffalo, New York, on December 15, 1926, and in Boston on January 16, 1927. In both cities the *Rhapsody in Blue* was given in a two-piano arrangement, with Isadore Gorn officiating at the second piano in Buffalo, and Edward Hart in Boston.

The Five Preludes was Gershwin's first serious work since the Concerto in F. Three have been published, performed, and recorded. The first prelude, in B-flat major (*Allegretto ben ritmato e deciso*), is a lively rhythmic excursion, utilizing elements of the tango and the Charleston. The second, in C-sharp minor (*Andante con moto e poco rubato*), is the most famous of the set: a poignant three-part blues melody set against an exciting harmony that grows richer as the melody unfolds. Rhythm once again predominates in the third prelude, in E-flat major (*Allegretto ben ritmato e de-*

ciso), an uninhibited outburst of joyous feeling. These three preludes have been orchestrated several times, notably by Lewis Raymond, Gregory Stone, and Roy Bargy. Jascha Heifetz arranged them for violin and piano, and has recorded them in this version for Decca. In addition, the second prelude was transcribed for violin, cello, and piano by Gregory Stone; for saxophone and piano, by Sigurd Rascher; and for trumpet and piano, by Stone.

Of the two remaining preludes, one is a thirty-two bar blues in the style of the Prelude in C-Sharp Minor, and is still in manuscript and never played. The other is a tender melody with a strong narrative quality; it has been transcribed for violin and piano by Samuel Dushkin, and is called *Short Story.*

12

A N   A M E R I C A N

I N   E U R O P E

Early in 1928 Gershwin went to Europe with Ira and Leonore, and Frances Gershwin. It was George's fifth trip abroad and it turned out to be his last. This time he was not going in order to work on some new London production, as he had done heretofore, but to escape temporarily from the continual pressure of Broadway commitments and deadlines. He felt he needed time to think and breathe—perhaps to study with some European master, perhaps to assimilate Europe's musical culture, perhaps to complete a new orchestral work which he had already sketched out.

The first stop was London. They stayed long enough

to see *Oh Kay* on its closing night, which completed its long run with Gertrude Lawrence; to attend a performance of a new London musical, *That's a Good Girl,* for which Ira had written some of the lyrics and Phil Charig some of the music; to participate in a special George Gershwin evening at the Kit-Kat night club; and to revive old friendships with the Duke of Kent, Lord and Lady Mountbatten, and others.

Then on Sunday, March 25, they crossed the Channel to Paris—and stepped into a whirlwind of activity. Six days later the *Rhapsody in Blue* was performed by the Pasdeloup Orchestra under Rhené-Baton at the Théâtre Mogador. It was the last number of a program that included César Franck's Symphony in D Minor, two shorter orchestral works, and Bach's Concerto for Two Pianos and Orchestra. Wiener and Doucet, a two-piano team who had performed the Bach Concerto, returned to divide between them the solo part of the *Rhapsody in Blue.* This singular arrangement was only one of several disturbing factors about that performance. The work had not been properly rehearsed; a stock jazz arrangement was being used; and, since he lacked a full orchestral score, the conductor had to lead from a piano arrangement. The performance was so haphazard that George feared disaster and fled from the auditorium to the bar. From there he was amazed to hear the Parisians acclaiming the work with thunderous enthusiasm and calling to him to take a bow. "How they knew that George was in the audience was a mystery to me," noted Ira in his diary. His appearance inspired another outburst. Deems Taylor, who was in the audience—and who had no idea that George was in Europe—was amazed to see him come to the stage. "You can always count on George to be there when a bow's to be taken," he remarked to a friend. In response to the ovation,

Wiener and Doucet gave a Gershwin encore, the song, "Do, Do, Do."

A few weeks later, at the seasonable opening of the fashionable night club, Les Ambassadeurs, Frances Gershwin began a limited engagement in a program of George's songs. The stage show had been written largely by Cole Porter, who prepared a special routine for Frances. Her rendition of the Gershwin songs was prefaced by a lyric explaining how it felt to be the sister of a famous composer. For her opening-night appearance, George appeared as her accompanist.

On April 16, at the Théâtre des Champs-Élysées, the Gershwins attended the première of a new ballet, the *Rhapsody in Blue*. The choreographer and principal dancer, Anton Dolin, had heard Gershwin play the work at a party attended by the cultural elite of Paris. Then and there he had decided to create a ballet for the music—depicting a struggle between jazz and classical music, with jazz at first succumbing but in the end emerging triumphant. Mme. Vera Neamchinova was Classical Music; Dolin was Jazz.

Six weeks later, on May 29, the European première of Gershwin's Concerto in F took place at the Paris Opéra. Vladimir Golschmann conducted the orchestra, and Dimitri Tiomkin was soloist. This was the first opportunity Gershwin had had to hear another artist play the music. Once again, as at the Pasdeloup concert in March, Gershwin's was the last number. The program included Weber's *Euryanthe* Overture, Liszt's Piano Concerto in A Major (Tiomkin, soloist), and an early work by Aaron Copland, *Cortège macabre*. The Gershwin Concerto received an ovation. It also won over the French critics completely. Arthur Hoerée rhapsodized over its "inexhaustible verve," the "fascination of its flowing melodies," and the composer's "keen feeling for

Gershwin, Pallay, and an unidentified Santa Barbara deubutante, at the El Mirador, in Palm Springs (1930).

a

b

c

a.   Alex Aarons and Gershwin (1926). (*Photo by Keystone View Co., Inc.*)

b.   Koussevitzky and Gershwin (1932).

c.   George Gershwin and Ernest Hutcheson, at Chatauqua (1925). (*Photo by Harold Wagner*)

d.   George Gershwin at the Warburg Farm, Connecticut.

d

a. Gershwin punching bag at 33 Riverside Drive, N. Y. C. (1930).

b. Gershwin at Palm Springs (1930).

c. Will Daly. A camera portrait by George Gershwin.

d. Henry Botkin. A camera portrait by George Gershwin.

e. Kay Swift (1930).

a

b

c

d

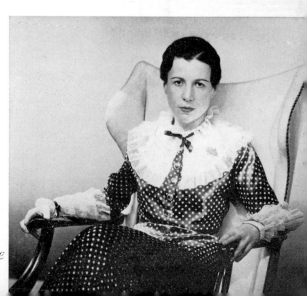

e

George Gershwin, Guy Bolton, and Ira Gershwin in Beverly Hills
(1930).

Ira Gershwin, Leonore Gershwin, George Gershwin, Emerich Kálmán (at George's right), and several others at the Café Sacher in
Vienna (1928).

George Gershwin at work in the living room of his East 72nd Street apartment, N. Y. C.

Left: George Gershwin and Lynn Riggs, in Beverly Hills (1936).
Right: Pirandello, Mamoulian, and George Gershwin (1936).

Above, Ira, Leonore, and George with Mrs. and Mr. Irving Berlin, in Nassau (1933). (*Photo by Jones & Langer*) *Below*, George Gershwin, Harold Arlen, and Lawrence Tibbett, in Beverly Hills (1936).

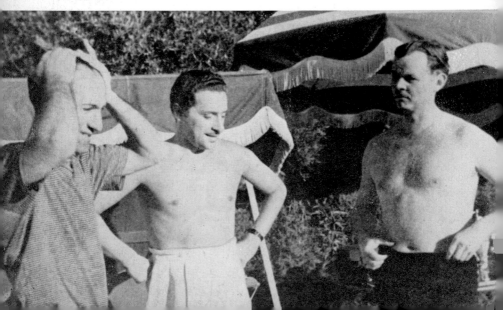

George Gershwin and Jerome Kern.

George Gershwin plays his score for *Shall We Dance?* Seated, *left to right:* Fred Astaire, Ginger Rogers, George Gershwin, Ira Gershwin, and Nathaniel Shilkret. (*Photo by RKO Radio Pictures, Inc.*)

George Gershwin, Du Bose Heyward, and Ira Gershwin just after the Boston première of *Porgy and Bess*.

For Du Bose Heyward
with admiration + affection.
George Gershwin

Du Bose Heyward. A portrait by George Gershwin.

"My Father."
A portrait by George Gershwin (1931). (*Photo by Peter A. Juley & Son*)

Jerome Kern.
A portrait by George Gershwin (1937). (*Photo by Keystone Photo Service*)

"Self-Portrait" (1932). (*Photo by Peter A. Juley & Son*)

Gershwin and his last painting, Arnold Schoenberg. (*Photo by Keystone Photo Service*)

The George Gershwin Collection Exhibition at the Arts Club of Chicago, November 10-25, 1933.

Paul Whiteman, J. Lasky, Ira Gershwin, Marc Connolly, Leonore Gershwin at the christening of the SS *George Gershwin* at San Pedro, California, April 22, 1943.

the orchestra." Émile Vuillermoz wrote: "This very characteristic work made even the most distrustful musicians realize that . . . jazz might perfectly well exert a deep and
beneficent influence in the most exalted spheres." One or
two of the celebrities attending the concert were less ap-
preciative. Serge Diaghilev, the guiding genius of the Ballet
Russe, complained that the Concerto was "good jazz but bad
Liszt." To Serge Prokofiev, one of Russia's foremost composers, the work was not much more than a succession of
many "thirty-two bar choruses."

The Paris holiday consisted of much more than listening to his own music and the welcome applause of French
music-lovers and critics. There was an endless round of visits
and parties at fashionable salons where Gershwin was very
much the man of the hour. Less formally, he paid calls at the
homes of leading musicians in Paris. At Montfort-l'Amaury
he visited Maurice Ravel.

He had met Ravel one year earlier in New York during that composer's first visit to the United States. On Ravel's
fifty-third birthday, March 7, 1928, Eva Gauthier had arranged a birthday party for him. "I asked him what he
wanted for a birthday present," recalls Gauthier, "and his
request was to hear and meet George Gershwin." George
played that night for Ravel to the undisguised delight of the
master. Mme. Gauthier has written: "George that night
surpassed himself, achieving astounding feats in rhythmic intricacies so that even Ravel was dumbfounded." The contact
between Gershwin and Ravel was renewed after that at other
New York parties, including one at Jules Glaenzer's.

When, therefore, Gershwin called on Ravel at his
home in France he came as a friend. Once again Gershwin
played for the master by the hour. Later when Gershwin sug-

gested studying with him, Ravel replied, "Why should you be a second-rate Ravel when you can be a first-rate Gershwin?"

Gershwin also met and played for Darius Milhaud, Francis Poulenc, Georges Auric, and Serge Prokofiev. This time Prokofiev was much more impressed by Gershwin's music, singling out several tunes and embellishments for special praise. He went so far as to predict a successful future for Gershwin as a serious composer—but only if George was prepared to leave "dollars and dinners" alone.

It was a busy life. At the Marbeuf home of the Tiomkins (Mrs. Tiomkin was the famous dancer, Albertina Rasch) Gershwin drank vodka and played the piano till dawn. With the composer Alexandre Tansman he went out to Châtou to spend the day with and play for Rhené-Baton. Yet somehow Gershwin managed to find the time to work on his new orchestral composition, *An American in Paris.* He completed a whole section (the blues) at his apartment in the Hotel Majestic. When the French pianist Mario Braggioti came there to pay his respects, Gershwin joined him in playing the recently completed section much to the pianist's delight for he was an ardent Gershwin fan. (One year later, Braggioti—with his partner Jacques Fray—officiated at two pianos in the London production of *Funny Face.*) Vernon Duke, who also saw the parts that Gershwin had completed, complained that there was too much saccharine in the music. But a distinguished English composer, William Walton, advised Gershwin to disregard Duke's opinion.

One day Leopold Stokowski dropped in at the Hotel Majestic to see Gershwin. He picked up the manuscript on which Gershwin was then working and suggested that he might be interested in directing its première. When Gershwin told him that the première had been promised to Walter Damrosch, Stokowski dropped the manuscript as if it had suddenly become contaminated and discreetly changed the subject.

From Paris, Gershwin went on to Vienna. At the Hotel Bristol he continued to work on his music. He heard some of the provocative musical works of the day, including Křenek's jazz opera *Jonny spielt auf* and Alban Berg's *Lyric Suite,* both of which he enjoyed immensely. The latter work was played for Gershwin at Berg's apartment by an ensemble headed by Rudolf Kolisch. When the performance ended, Gershwin played some of his songs for Berg and the atonalist responded enthusiastically. "How can you possibly like my music," Gershwin asked Berg with surprise, "when you write the kind of music you do?" Berg replied simply: "Music is music."

Emerich Kálmán, the celebrated composer of such Viennese operettas as *The Countess Maritza* and *Sari,* took Gershwin to the world-famous Sacher Café near the Opera, once the rendezvous of the royal family and nobility. When they walked in, the orchestra struck up the *Rhapsody in Blue.* In Vienna, Gershwin also came to know Franz Lehár, composer of *The Merry Widow,* and he visited the aged widow of the Viennese waltz-king, Johann Strauss II. Gershwin listened delightedly to her tales of the great Viennese musician who for half a century had been Vienna's idol. Then he made a discreet exit, after being offered the manuscript of *Die Fledermaus* for an astronomic price.

13

An American in Paris

Gershwin returned from Europe at the end of the summer of 1928. He brought back with him eight bound volumes of Debussy's works, a Musel reed pipe organ, and the manuscript of a part of his symphonic poem, *An American in Paris.*

The piano version was completed on August 1, and the final revisions and complete orchestration were done by November 18. Soon after his return from Europe, Gershwin, in an interview for *Musical America,* furnished a clue to his work:

This new piece . . . is written very freely and is the most modern music I've attempted. The opening part is developed in typical French style, in the manner of Debussy and 'The Six,' though the themes are all original. . . . As in my other orchestral compositions, I've not endeavored to present any definite scene in music. The rhapsody is programmatic only in a general impressionistic way, so that the individual listener can read into the music such episodes as his imagination pictures for him.

While Gershwin disavowed a program, he not only accepted but even bestowed his blessings on the detailed and picturesque narrative provided by Deems Taylor for the program notes of the première performance. That narrative is now celebrated, and it has so felicitously caught the essence and spirit of the music that its reading is indispensable for a full enjoyment of the music.

You are to imagine . . . an American, visiting Paris, swinging down the Champs Élysées on a mild sunny morning in May or June. Being what he is, he starts with preliminaries, and is off at full speed at once, to the tune of the First Walking Theme, a straightforward, diatonic air, designed to convey an impression of Gallic freedom and gaiety.

Our American's ears being open, as well as his eyes, he notes with pleasure the sounds of the city. French taxicabs seem to amuse him particularly, a fact that the orchestra points out in a brief episode introducing four real Paris taxi horns. . . . These have a special theme allotted to them . . . which is announced by the strings whenever they appear in the score.

Having safely eluded the taxis, our American apparently passes the open door of a café where, if one is to believe the trombones, *La Maxixe* [*recte, La Sorella*] is still popular. Exhilarated by the reminder of the gay 1900s, he resumes his stroll through the medium of the Second Walking Theme, which is announced by the clarinetist in French with a strong American accent.

Both themes are now discussed at some length by the instruments, until our tourist happens to pass—something. The composer thought it might be a church, while the commentator held out for the Grand Palais, where the salon holds forth. At all events, our hero does not go in. Instead, as revealed by the English horn, he respectfully slackens his pace until he is safely past.

At this point, the American's itinerary becomes somewhat obscured. It may be that he continues on down the Champs Élysées; it may be that he has turned off—the composer retains an open mind on the subject. However, since what immediately ensues is technically known as a bridge passage, one is reasonably justified in assuming that the Gershwin pen, guided by an unseen hand, has perpetrated a musical pun, and that when the Third Walking Theme makes its eventual appearance our American has crossed the Seine, and is somewhere on the Left Bank. Certainly it is distinctly less Gallic than its predecessors, speaking American with a French intonation, as befits the region of the city where so many Americans forgather. "Walking Theme" may be a misnomer, for despite its vitality the theme is slightly sedentary in character, and becomes progressively more so. Indeed, the end of this section of the work is couched in terms so unmistakably, albeit pleasantly, blurred, as to suggest that the American is on the *Terrasse* of a café, exploring the mysteries of an Anise de Lozo.

And now the orchestra introduces an unhallowed episode. Suffice it to say that a solo violin approaches our hero (in soprano register) and addresses him in the most charming broken English; and his response being inaudible—or at least unintelligible—repeats the remark. The one-sided conversation continues for some little time.

Of course, one hastens to add, it is possible that a grave injustice is being done to both author and protagonist, and that the whole episode is simply a musical transition. The latter interpretation may well be true, for otherwise it is difficult to believe what ensues; our hero becomes homesick. He has the blues; and if the behavior of the orchestra be any criterion, he has them very thoroughly. He realizes suddenly, overwhelmingly, that he does not belong to this place, that he is the most wretched creature in the world, a foreigner. The cool, blue Paris sky, the distant upward sweep of the Eiffel Tower, the bookstalls of the quay, the pattern of the horsechestnut leaves on the white, sunflecked street—what avails all this alien beauty? He is no Baudelaire, longing to be "anywhere out of the world." The world is just what he longs for, the world that he knows best; a world less lovely—sentimental and a little vulgar perhaps—but for all that, home.

However, nostalgia is not a fatal disease—nor, in this instance, of overlong duration. Just in the nick of time the compassionate orchestra rushes another theme to the rescue, two trumpets performing the ceremony of introduction. It is apparent that our hero must have met a compatriot; for this last theme is a noisy, cheerful, self-confident Charleston without a drop of Gallic blood in its veins.

For the moment, Paris is no more; and a voluble, gusty, wise-cracking orchestra proceeds to demonstrate at some length that it's always fair weather when two Americans get together, no matter where. Walking Theme Number Two enters soon thereafter, enthusiastically abetted by Number Three. Paris isn't such a bad place after all: as a matter of fact, it's a grand place! Nice weather, nothing to do till tomorrow. The blues return, but mitigated by the Second Walking Theme—a happy reminiscence rather than homesick yearning—and the orchestra, in a riotous finale, decides to make a night of it. It will be great to get home; but meanwhile, this is Paris!

As Mr. Taylor's programmatic guide suggests, the tone poem is built on a series of basic themes: some are episodic and transitory, others are fully developed. These ideas are presented, enlarged, changed, and brought back in symphonic manner, and within a structure that has the freedom of a rhapsody. In style, it is American to its very tissues and marrow, and just as thoroughly Gershwin in its astute adaptation of such jazz ingredients as the blues and the Charleston. Despite Gershwin's own characterization, the music has nothing of Debussy in it; and the only affinity it has with the "French Six" is not in any stylistic essentials but in its incisive wit, wry tongue-in-the-cheek humor, droll effects, and general insouciance, which are also found in many of the earlier works of Milhaud, Honegger, and Poulenc.

The walking theme that opens the tone poem—heard in strings and oboe—is not in the stately gait of that other famous walking theme, in Mussorgsky's *Pictures at an Exhibition*, but is light and gay. The music is then punctuated with angry taxi horns to suggest the madcap Parisian traffic. A music-hall tune follows in the trombone. As the American continues his walk, a second walking theme appears, more vigorous than the first, in the clarinet. A solo violin represents a transition to the wailing blues melody in muted trumpet. This is succeeded by the Charleston melody for two trumpets. When the blues then returns it is no longer a lament but robust and joyous. The orchestration is for full symphony orchestra with snare drums, bass drum, cymbals, rattle, triangle, two tom-toms, four automobile horns, xylophone, wire brush, wood block, glockenspiel, and celesta.

An American in Paris was introduced on December 13, 1928, by the New York Philharmonic Symphony Society conducted by Walter Damrosch. Franck's Symphony in D Minor and Lekeu's *Adagio for Strings* preceded it; Wagner's "Magic Fire Scene" from *Die Walküre* ended the program.

Once again, as with the Concerto, the critical response was most varied. Samuel Chotzinoff called it "the best piece of modern music since Gershwin's Concerto in F." W. J. Henderson described it as a "frank humoresque," which "freely indulges in unbuttoned humor. . . . It has a rollicking spirit and there is a most engaging candor about some of the ideas, especially the first walking theme, which is aptness incarnate. There is much cleverness in the score, and some rudeness of manner." Lawrence Gilman, never before too sympathetic to Gershwin, now said that the work has the "tang of a new and urgent world, engaging, ardent, unpredictable." Olin Downes found in it a "material gain in workmanship and structure."

So far so good. . . . But there was also loud dissent. Herbert F. Peyser described it as "nauseous claptrap, so dull, patchy, thin, vulgar, long-winded and inane, that the average movie audience would be bored by it. . . . This cheap and silly affair seemed pitifully futile and inept." Oscar Thompson felt that "for those not too deeply concerned with any apparently outmoded niceties of art, it was an amusing occasion," but took pains to point out that while the music was "good fun," it also had "blunt banality" and "ballyhoo vulgarity."

Notwithstanding the adverse opinions, *An American in Paris* has become a fixture in the symphonic repertory both here and abroad. On July 27, 1931, it was performed in Queen's Hall, London, at the fourth concert of the Ninth Festival of the International Society of Contemporary Music. Alfredo Casella conducted. Gershwin's was the only work that day that received an ovation, even though to the English critics it was "innocent but tiresome babble," "banal and silly," and "pretty bad music." At about this time, too, Francis Poulenc—in an interview over La Radiodiffusion Française—singled it out as one of his favorite musical compositions of the twentieth century. The major orchestras of the world have performed it under most of the great conductors of this generation, including Arturo Toscanini.

An American in Paris was several times adapted into ballets, principally in the musical-comedy *Show Girl* and in the motion picture *An American in Paris*. As a mime ballet designed and mounted by Hedley Briggs, who was also the principal dancer, it was interpolated into a revue, *This*

World of Ours, which was presented at the Cambridge Festival Theatre in England in 1932.

After the première performance, Jules Glaenzer honored Gershwin with a party at his home. On that occasion, Gershwin was presented with a brass humidor inscribed with the signatures of his many friends. In making the presentation to Gershwin, Otto H. Kahn made a speech in which he said, in part:

> George Gershwin is a leader of young America in music . . . and, in his art, thoroughly and uncompromisingly American as it is, one of [its] forceful spokesmen. In the rhythm, the melody, the humor, the grace, the rush and sweep and dynamics of his compositions, he expresses the genius of young America. Now, in that genius of young America, there is one note rather conspicuous by its absence. It is the note that sounds a legacy of sorrow, a note that springs from the deepest stirrings of the soul of the race. . . . Now, far be it from me to wish any tragedy to come into the life of this nation for the sake of chastening its soul, or into the life of George Gershwin for the sake of deepening his art. But . . . the 'long drip of human tears,' my dear George! They have great and strange and beautiful power, those human tears. They fertilize the deepest roots of art. I believe in you with full faith and admiration, in your personality, your gifts, in your art, in your future, in your significance, in the field of American music. . . . And just because of that I could wish for you an experience—not too prolonged—of that driving storm and stress of the emotions, of that solitary wrestling with your own soul, of that aloofness . . . which are the most effec-

tive ingredients for the deepening and mellowing . . . of an artist's inner being and spiritual powers.

Like most everybody else at this time, Otto H. Kahn was looking upon Gershwin only as a musical humorist and satirist, even though in certain songs and blues, and in the second piano Prelude, Gershwin had sounded a more poignant note. Unfortunately, Kahn died early in 1934. Had he lived another two years to hear the score of *Porgy and Bess* —and in a province so close to his heart, that of opera—he would have surely realized that even without the influence of personal storm and stress, Gershwin's art was able to achieve that deepening and mellowing he had asked for.

14

T H E   M A N   T H E Y   L O V E D

In her autobiography, *R.S.V.P.*, Elsa Maxwell speaks of a romance between Gershwin and the Countess de Ganny, during his visit to Paris in 1928. Miss Maxwell describes how smitten he was by the lady's beauty and charm, how she was the one woman he wanted to marry, how broken he was to discover suddenly that her intentions toward him were not half so serious as his.

Those who were with Gershwin in Paris at the time, and others with whom he freely shared his most personal thoughts, all claim there is no truth in the story of this frustrated love affair. It is true that he met and was attracted to

the Countess, as he was to a great many women in a great
many places. Neither then, or later, did he ever say he wanted
to marry her. Their whole relationship consisted of nothing
more than a few casual meetings.

Several different people have tried to identify the
"one woman" in Gershwin's life. In most cases each was
thinking of a different woman. There was a schoolteacher in
1918, a pianist in 1919, and a Ziegfeld *Follies* showgirl in
1920 who appealed to him because she was supporting a
sister through school. And there was the glamorous motion-
picture star in the last months of his life to whom he was
powerfully attracted. In between these periods—the beginning and the end of his love life—there were others, many
others: a chorus girl in *Pardon My English;* a sensitive and
well-educated young lady who left him to marry an Albanian
economist; a beautiful and singularly cultured motion-picture actress whom he admired profoundly and whom he
often described as "the intellectual aristocrat of the screen";
several other stars of stage and screen, and several ladies of
impressive social rank. The newspaper columnists and tab-
loid feature writers once had a holiday with a story about a
noted screen star of French origin who presented him with a
gold key to her West Los Angeles estate; while on another
occasion, Walter Winchell linked his name in his column
with that of another motion-picture actress to the consterna-
tion of both Gershwin and the young lady since she was married to somebody else at the time.

At one time or another Gershwin was in love with
most of these women. But when matrimony approached he
always came up with a good reason that satisfied his conscience and explained why marriage had to be avoided. His
reason for not marrying the chorus girl of *Pardon My Eng-*

lish, though he appeared to be thinking of it seriously, was because he heard her play some of his own music on the piano and he knew he could not live with that kind of piano-playing for the rest of his life. He rejected the idea of marriage with one woman because she was older than he and had children; another, because he questioned her morals; a third, because she came from a different social world, that of Park Avenue, while "I'm a guy that will always have the touch of the tenement in me." When he did speak of marriage, which was frequent, it was always a kind of intellectual concept with him. He would say that this and this kind of woman would fit the bill perfectly (usually pointing out a woman who was safely and happily married to one of his friends or relatives). Of the hundreds of women with whom he came into contact, and who were available, nobody seemed able to suit his specifications—usually for one hollow reason or another.

Beautiful women attracted him powerfully, and he found resistance to them either difficult or impossible. But he rarely pursued a woman. In spite of his many and varied amatory experiences he was always a bit shy, a bit prudish, a bit unsure of himself. More than that, he was terribly afraid of rejection. If he never showered his girl friends with expensive gifts or spent a great deal of money on them, it was not out of parsimony (never one of his traits) but out of an instinctive dread of buying affection. One day he naively inquired from a more worldly friend how one goes about the business of "keeping" a woman. When told he would have to furnish and pay for a handsome apartment and then keep her in funds, he made an ugly grimace and never again referred to the unholy subject.

The women who were most dominant in his life were

those who sought him out and made no effort to conceal their feelings about him. And women—usually very beautiful women—were continually seeking him out. There was the time when a stunningly attractive redhead rang his doorbell. She had attended a party on the floor below and was bored; then she heard that George Gershwin lived in the same house and was terribly eager to meet him. She immediately made herself completely at home in Gershwin's apartment. There was also the sexy showgirl who came to demonstrate how well she played the piano. She suddenly leaped from the piano bench to dance around the room, whirling her skirts high enough to reveal her shapely legs. And there was the handsome married lady who lived in Gershwin's house and who repeatedly told her husband that she was visiting the Ira Gershwins. From their apartment she would furtively slip into George's apartment by way of the adjoining terrace. These were three of many similar episodes which crowded Gershwin's life as he became increasingly famous. The women came and went. Like the girl in Dorothy Parker's quatrain, he always got mixed up after the fifth affair.

The simple truth about his love life was that though he always had women, and though he sometimes loved a woman, he never really loved one completely and selflessly. Once, hearing that a girl in whom he was particularly interested had suddenly married somebody else, he remarked to Ira, "I'd be terribly heartbroken if I weren't so damned busy." This reaction is both typical and significant. He never gave himself so completely to a woman that losing her left a vacuum in his life. Some of the girls he loved complained he seemed completely incapable of real sentiment or tenderness; most of the time with them he was so wrapped up in himself and his thoughts that he was only vaguely conscious of their presence. One girl who loved him deeply decided to forget him for good when the most ardent thing he could say to her was that she was good for his nervous stomach.

A reason sometimes given for Gershwin's failure to marry was that he tended to idealize women. He would put a woman on a pedestal, then find that she did not live up to his ideal, and become disillusioned. This sounds reasonable, but it does not tell the whole story. A more convincing explanation lies in the sad fact that his complete absorption with his music and his career made it impossible for him to give himself to a woman in the way a love affair—or a successful marriage—demands. Women found it impossible to penetrate the concrete wall of his creative ego. Gershwin often plagued his friends with questions as to whether or not it was wise for an artist to marry; whether marriage did not put a serious impediment in the way of an artist practicing his art. But he was not really seeking an answer, and often he did not wait for one. He was only looking for an excuse to avoid a permanent relationship.

If there was one woman whom Gershwin esteemed most highly and who filled a major role in his life, she was Kay Swift. A composer of popular songs—by 1930 she had written "Can't We Be Friends," which Libby Holman made famous in the first *Little Show,* and the entire score for the musical, *Fine and Dandy*—Kay had an impressive training in serious music to which she brought a trenchant intellect, a retentive memory, and rare critical discernment. Gershwin admired all these things in her; but he also admired her wit, culture, refinement, social position, *savoir-faire,* and personal charm.

At the time he first met her she was married to a banker, whom she later divorced. One evening in 1925

Gershwin was brought to their home by Marie Rosanoff, the cellist of the Musical Art Quartet. He played the piano for several hours, then leaped nimbly from his bench to announce that he was sailing for England that night. During the next year or so their friendship ripened. Kay had an overwhelming veneration for his genius, and she selflessly and even humbly put her intelligence and training at Gershwin's service. In the years that followed she was often with him when he composed his music: taking down dictation when he asked her to; helping him edit his manuscripts and publications; offering discreet and highly valued criticism; and playing with him two-piano arrangements of his own works or of the music of the masters. She also brought him a sensitive appreciation for the subtle refinements of gracious living and for cultural interests outside of music. She looked after him with a solicitude born out of tenderness, filling his apartment with flowers, always seeing to it that his boutonniere came on time before each of his concerts. Gershwin, in turn, came as close to being completely in love with her as he did with any woman; and he remained devoted to her longer than to any other. He spoke of her in a way few other women inspired him to do. She was the only woman to whom he gave an expensive gift (two precious paintings), the only woman to whom he dedicated one of his works—the piano transcriptions of his songs published by Simon and Schuster.

After Gershwin's death—thanks to her fantastic memory—she was able to rescue from oblivion many songs and ideas he had worked on in her presence and had discarded. Some were used posthumously in the motion picture *The Shocking Miss Pilgrim*. Another treasure house of Gershwin's melodic ideas that Kay Swift painstakingly put down on paper from memory and notebooks, is still untouched, reposing in a safe in the office of Dr. Sirmay at Chappell's.

His music was the be-all and end-all of his existence. He loved to write it, play it, talk about it all the time. He was proud of it when he felt it was good, and did not hesitate to say so. He was in love with his music and he had a lover's expansiveness in extolling the many attractions of his beloved. He talked about himself or his works with an objectivity that made it seem as if he were talking about somebody else. He sometimes alluded to George Gershwin in the third person, as if Gershwin already belonged to the ages, and he were only one of many admirers. This kind of detachment led him to make many ingenuous remarks and responses which have often been quoted to point up his amusing tendency toward self-adulation. When a friend came to him after an all-Gershwin concert to tell him, with breathless enthusiasm, that it was "wonderful," Gershwin asked in all simplicity: "Just wonderful—is that *all?*" He could describe a musical giant like Manuel de Falla as a "Spanish Gershwin." When a hotel manager once called to report a complaint that he was playing the piano too loudly and at too late an hour, he remarked: "Maybe they don't know that *Gershwin* was playing?" From his mother's virtues, he singled out one for special admiration: "She is so modest about *me.*"

The peculiar thing about his egocentricity was that it was never objectionable, and nobody ever resented it. There was such an air of childlike innocence and ingenuousness and quiet self-assurance to him that people were actually won over to his exuberance and enthusiasms. Besides, he had a wonderful gentleness that completely compensated for his self-centered nature. He liked people, was kind and generous to them, and was rarely heard to say anything cruel or malicious about anybody.

To say that Gershwin was egocentric, however, is to give only one side of a complex personality; it is essential to put that egocentricity in proper perspective.

If he was excited about his own music he was also enthusiastic about the good music of other popular composers. Vernon Duke, Vincent Youmans, Johnny Green, Irving Berlin, Jerome Kern, Harold Arlen, Hoagy Carmichael, Arthur Schwartz are a few who knew this well. "It will come as a surprise to many who know . . . the man's excitement over his own work and his enthusiastic appreciation of every contribution he had to make, to learn that he also had a very eager enthusiasm and wholehearted appreciation for what a great many of us were writing," says Harold Arlen. Kay Swift reveals that she once told Gershwin she felt his songs had far greater musical variety and interest than Irving Berlin's. Gershwin immediately went to the piano and for over an hour played Berlin to prove to Kay Swift how much versatility and greatness there was to Berlin's writing. "He's a master," Gershwin kept on saying, "and let's make no mistake about *that*." "And he proved his point," she commented. "Many of the songs he played I knew, but I didn't realize that they were Berlin's."

Gershwin not only often played the music of others with genuine zest and delight but was always ready to provide penetrating criticism when needed. To one composer he would demonstrate how a certain section might be simplified; to another, how a contrasting mood would be beneficial; to a third, how the use of a certain trick or device would solve a specific problem. Gershwin helped and encouraged many composers when they needed it most. Arlen, for example, always remembers the lift he received from Gershwin in 1929 when he had just written his first song "Get Happy," which was used in the finale of the *9:15 Revue*. Gershwin saw the tryout of the show in New Haven and sought out Arlen to tell him that he thought the song made for one of the best production numbers he had seen. "Imagine, the great Gershwin going out of his way to praise a novice that way." From then on Gershwin did what he could to help Arlen's career along.

When Vernon Duke first came to America in the 1920s—he was then still using his original name of Vladimir Dukelsky—he went directly to Gershwin for advice and help. Gershwin listened to his esoteric piano sonatas, then urged him to try writing "real popular tunes, and don't be scared about getting lowbrow." Dukelsky found in Gershwin a ready helping hand in his own efforts to penetrate the popular-music field: indeed, as soon as Duke wrote his first popular songs Gershwin took him down to Max Dreyfus in an effort to get the young composer a publisher. And it was also Gershwin who advised him to adopt the Anglicized name of Vernon Duke.

Ann Ronell came to Gershwin to interview him for her magazine at Radcliffe College. Gershwin heard her play the piano and listened to some of her tunes and was so impressed that he forthwith opened doors for her that led into the theater and radio. This made possible a career in which she became the only woman music director in Hollywood and the composer of many hit songs including "Who's Afraid of the Big Bad Wolf?"

Vincent Youmans' first musical comedy, *Two Little Girls in Blue,* was produced by Alex A. Aarons only after

Gershwin brought the producer the music of the then unknown composer and played it through for him. Oscar Levant, Dana Suesse, Rube Bloom, and Johnny Green are some
others who profited from Gershwin's encouragment and
benefactions. When Arnold Schoenberg, the celebrated modernist of the twelve-tone technique, arrived in America in
1933, Gershwin established a fund so that some young composer might study with Schoenberg at the Malkin School of
Music. Artie Shaw and Xavier Cugat were both unknown and
struggling when Gershwin spoke of them to the right people
at the right time and procured significant engagements for
them. "Even at the time of his death," writes George Antheil,
"I personally know of four American white hopes whom
George was supporting."

One other factor, besides his generosity and enthusiasm for rival composers, must be taken into account in the
discussion of Gershwin's egocentricity. He was also capable
of humility and self-depreciation. He might be the proud
parent boasting of an offspring's commendable traits; but
like many a proud parent he was also painfully conscious
of his offspring's shortcomings, and sometimes to a greater
degree than were his critics. There were many times when
he tended to magnify the shortcomings of his technique out
of all proportion to its importance. On such occasions he un-
derestimated himself profoundly. "There is so much I have
to learn," was a lament he often voiced. To Jerome Kern he
once remarked: "I am a man with a little bit of talent and a
great deal of nerve." (The word he actually used was the
Yiddish expression, *chuzpah*.) When John Kennedy interviewed him for *Collier's*, he said: "What I don't know about
music is enough to keep me occupied for the rest of a nor-
mally long life." He admired musicians with conservatory

training out of all proportion to their significance. He was usually in awe of composers with complex and abstruse techniques, and in their presence he often became as self-conscious as a schoolboy—he who could move with such poise and aplomb among the great of the financial and social world. When composers like Stravinsky, Ravel, or Schoenberg praised him to his face he became as flustered as if he had been the perpetrator of a fraud.

Gershwin was a human dynamo. He rarely walked on the street or the golf course—he had to run. He rarely walked slowly up a flight of stairs, but leaped a few steps at a time. He had more vitality when sick than others did in the full flush of health. Harry Ruby tells an amusing and highly characteristic story about George. In 1931 he took Al Schacht, then the third-base coach of the Washington Senators baseball team and later the jester of the diamond, to visit Gershwin. When they arrived, George was sick in bed with a fever and a cold. Nevertheless he welcomed his visitors eagerly. He could not lie in bed idly. As he spoke to his guests, he picked up sketching paper and pencil and drew a portrait of Ruby which he then inscribed: "I can write music, too. Remember Atlantic City?" When Schacht remarked wistfully, "Some day when you feel better, George, I'd love to hear you play the piano," George jumped out of bed and, sick as he was, played for a full hour, including the complete *Rhapsody in Blue*. "Never in all my many years of sojourn on this sphere," Ruby has said, "have I ever seen anything like it. His vitality and purpose were not in the least bit dimmed by his illness."

He was a man of irrepressible enthusiasms, a man who had an extraordinary zest for living and for enjoying. He loved games of all kinds, and he had the capacity for making everything he indulged in a kind of game. When he found a new diversion he went after it with an incomparable intensity and passion. When it was golf (his game was in the 80s), he played it every free moment he could find, and golf dominated his conversation and thinking all the time. Then it was something else: backgammon, croquet, ping pong, photography, fishing, swimming, horseback riding, roulette. Generally he preferred pastimes that taxed his muscles. He was physically powerful, with the build of an athlete and muscles that knew the discipline of exercise. Besides participating in various sports, he was methodical about doing setting-up exercises at regular intervals. He liked baseball a great deal, but rarely played it for fear of hurting his hands. Once while watching Harry Ruby play ball he remarked sadly, "I couldn't afford to take a chance on my hands the way you do. But then your hands don't matter so much." It took a little time for Ruby to realize that Gershwin really meant no slur on his ability as a pianist but was solely preoccupied with thoughts about himself. Later on Ruby confessed, "He was, of course, right." In baseball, Gershwin satisfied himself by being a spectator, as he did in boxing and wrestling, both of which he loved.

His fine muscular co-ordination that made him such a splendid pianist (and frequently without practicing), and so good an athlete, also made him an excellent dancer. He used feet, body, and hands with the limpid grace of a trained performer. He sometimes gave strikingly effective imitations of Fred Astaire, even in some of his more adroit steps; and during the rehearsals of *Lady Be Good* he gave Astaire a valuable suggestion for an exit step for "Fascinating Rhythm." His gift at mimicry was also apparent at other times. Highly visual, with a detective's keen eye for detail, he would come home from a party and give remarkable imitations of the gestures, vocal inflections, and little personal idiosyncrasies of somebody interesting with whom he had met and talked.

Despite his athletic build and his muscular physique, he suffered most of his life from a chronic constipation which sometimes induced nausea and brought acute gastric pains. He continually consulted physicians after 1923. When they failed to find a cure he sought the help of the psychoanalyst, Dr. Gregory Zilboorg, who attended him for a little over a year between 1934 and 1935. Dr. Zilboorg has said that the source of Gershwin's trouble was a chronic neurosis, though precisely what the source of that neurosis was medical ethics have prevented his elucidating. But Dr. Zilboorg ventured the opinion that Gershwin's ailment was not infrequent with musicians, and it was probably for this reason that Gershwin often spoke of his "composer's stomach." Psychoanalytic treatment helped Gershwin in several ways—it made him somewhat less self-centered and inhibited—but it did not relieve his physical condition, which continued to torment him until the end of his life. He took agar-agar regularly before retiring. Often he recorded in a special notebook the details of the day's diet, hoping thereby to check the origin of one of his attacks. He took to eating yeast and to drinking hot water with lemon juice, and for a time he felt they improved his condition. In 1931, after a long addiction to cigars, he gave up smoking, hoping it would "help my stomach disturbances." That sensitive stomach made him highly fastidious about his eating habits. His meals were unimaginative, to say the least, consisting of various permutations and combinations of cereal, rusk, biscuits, melba toast, Ry-

Krisp, sour cream, fruit salad, cooked fruits. "Nobody believes me when I say I am sick," he would complain end-
lessly. After Gershwin's death, his physicians were unanimous in their agreement that the fatal tumor discovered in
his last days had had no effect on his stomach.

The sick stomach in an athlete's body of steel was only
one of several contradictions about Gershwin. He was the
prude who could slap his sister in public because she had
used the word "darn," while his own private life—well, that
was something else again. Meticulous about adhering to a
Spartan diet during mealtimes, he could, late at night, often
devour a quart of ice cream. In matters that were not of too
much concern to him he could be strongly, obstinately opin-
ionated, resenting differences with his own views; yet in discussions of his music, which was all-important to him, he was
charmingly graceful in accepting unfavorable criticism and
would frequently agree with it instead of offering opposing
arguments. Before a performance of his music before many
thousands he could be as cool as ice; yet he was all nerves at
an unimportant golf tournament. He always made a conscious, even painstaking, attempt to mingle with people in
high places. Yet, once in their presence, he was always his
own simple and disarming self. He once went unshaven to a
party given by an English nobleman, and he dragged along to
a dinner at the Vanderbilt's an arranger who happened to
have been with him that afternoon.

He never put on attitudes or poses for effect, never
assumed grandeur with those less famous than he, nor ever
tried to pretend he was more than he was when he mingled
with the rich or the powerful. In all of his social contacts,
as in his business dealings, he was direct, straightforward,
and unassuming. He never required the services of a busi-

ness representative, never had his own press agent, and never kept a lawyer on a retainer. When he had good cause to sue he usually refused to do so (the exception was when Ziegfeld refused to pay him royalties for *Show Girl*) preferring a financial loss to an ugly squabble in court. He never used friendships to promote anything he wrote; it was always his friends who sought him out for his music. While he enjoyed beautiful surroundings and comfort, he avoided ostentation of all kind. He had no expensive jewelry; except for a second-hand Mercedes Benz in 1927, he never owned a foreign car or a yacht; he never entertained in a baronial manner.

His one indulgence in swank was a beautiful apartment he rented in 1928: a 17th floor penthouse at 33 Riverside Drive. It was furnished modernistically in the then prevailing vogue of blacks and contrasting whites, chromes, severe lines, and indirect lights. The apartment even had a small gymnasium where he could keep his muscles in tone and where, somewhat incongruously, stood a silver-colored upright piano which had been built for him. His Steinway, of course, was in the living-room, together with his favorite books, music, mementos, and *objets d'art*. A terrace, which overlooked the Hudson River, adjoined a second apartment —the home of Ira and Leonore, which they had rented at the same time. For both George and Ira, these two apartments represented their first homes away from their parents: the umbilical cord had finally been cut.

George's house-warming consisted of a festive dinner to which were invited those who had played major roles in his career from its inception. Among them were Max Dreyfus, Eva Gauthier, Paul Whiteman, Ferde Grofé, Fred and Adele Astaire, Walter Damrosch, William Daly and, of course, Ira. The place cards carried quotations from various songs.

From then on, George's apartment usually had the feverish atmosphere of a railroad station. People were always coming and going—sometimes for business, sometimes socially; others hung around so long that they almost became a part of the decorative scheme. The more intimate circle— Arthur Kober, S. N. Behrman, Mischa Levitzki, Vernon Duke, Lillian Hellman, Howard Dietz, Milton Ager, Kay Swift, Samuel Chotzinoff, Oscar Levant—would gather at Ira's place most Sunday afternoons and stay there till long past midnight, vitalizing the air with wit and wisdom, criticism and vitriol, shop talk and violent discussions. During the evening the group would spill over into George's apartment for music. George would play and sing, and at times he and Ira would go through the score of a musical comedy they were then writing. At these parties and gatherings, whether in George's or Ira's apartment, George would be in the spotlight; he was the cynosure; he was the pivot around which all activities rotated. Ira, on the other hand, preferred the background, only too glad to turn over the center of the stage to his more dynamic brother.

It was at 33 Riverside Drive that Oscar Levant "flowered as a buffoon" and developed into a "penthouse beachcomber"—the descriptive phrases, of course, being his own. But Levant and Gershwin had met three years earlier. Levant had been trained in Pittsburgh for the concert stage. After coming to New York in 1921, he made his way as a jazz pianist, and soon joined Ben Bernie's band. Levant became an ardent Gershwin admirer in 1918 when he first heard Gershwin accompany Nora Bayes in Pittsburgh. After coming to New York, Levant's enthusiasm for Gershwin grew as he heard songs like "Do It Again" and "Stairway to Paradise"—quite a contrast to the kinds of songs he was required to play in jazz bands. Early in 1925 he visited a recording studio where Frank Black was about to record the *Rhapsody in Blue* for Brunswick. Black's pianist failed to show up for the session, and Levant took his place, beginning his association with a musical composition that, from then on, would be a staple in his repertory.

Levant met Gershwin through Phil Charig, to whom a mutual friend had confided that Levant was eager to meet the composer. Since Charig at the time was not only Gershwin's friend but also the rehearsal pianist for some of Gershwin's shows, the friend suggested that Charig bring the young man to Gershwin. Charig met Levant in a cafeteria on 43rd Street near Broadway and at once found him to be a brash and rapier-tongued fellow who talked at the top of a shrill voice while rocking in his chair and keeping his feet on the table. Charig brought Levant to Gershwin's home on 103rd Street in 1925. When they arrived, Gershwin was showing Bill Daly some details of the first movement of the Piano Concerto, and the visitors were immediately treated to a preview of the music which was to become so closely identified with Levant's career as concert pianist. So wrapped up was Gershwin with his Concerto that he appeared to Levant, at that first meeting, distant and indifferent. Actually, Gershwin took note of the young man and liked his acid wit and penetrating intelligence, neither of which seemed to suffer from the awe Levant felt on meeting a man he admired so profoundly. Soon after this meeting, Levant became a visitor to 103rd Street; and when Gershwin moved to Riverside Drive, Levant became a more or less permanent fixture there. He brightened many a Gershwin evening with his impudent impersonations of concert pianists, with his spontaneous wit, and his needle-edged comments on music and musicians, friends and enemies.

The George Gershwin apartment on Riverside Drive contained some interesting art. Some of it represented gifts from those close to him. In the bedroom George had a hand-painted screen depicting scenes from *An American in Paris*, the work of his cousin, Henry Botkin, a celebrated artist and art connoisseur. On the arm of a tiered bookcase in the living-room stood a bronze bust which Isamu Noguchi had made of him in 1929. Noguchi described the face as "an exterior of self-assurance verging on conceit, it does not hide the thoughtfulness of a rich and sensitive nature." On the walls were paintings by friends like Max Weber and Maurice Sterne. In 1931 three famous French paintings were added; these included a Derain and a Utrillo, purchased for him in Europe by Botkin. In time Gershwin's collection became such a rich repository of contemporary art that, in 1933, the Chicago Art Club presented it in a show. By the time he died his collection contained more than 140 pieces, including sixty paintings: the work of Kandinsky, Léger, Pascin, Masson, Picasso, Utrillo, Rousseau, Siqueiros, Eilshemius, Benton, Gauguin, Derain, Rouault, Modigliani, together with fine examples of Negro sculpture, precious drawings, water colors, and rare lithographs. Ira estimates that this collection cost his brother about $50,000, but at the time of George's death it was easily worth four or five times that amount. For example, Picasso's "The Absinthe Drinker," for which Gershwin paid $1,500, was bought after his death by J. H. Whitney for the Museum of Modern Art for $15,000.

From the moment he acquired his first painting, Gershwin became passionately interested in art. He would haunt art galleries and the studios of friends and consume what he liked with a voracious appetite. From the beginning he revealed a highly sensitive and personalized taste, preferring the subtle and the complex and the elusive to the obvious and the representational. His favorite was Rouault. "If only I could put Rouault into music," he often said.

The love of art inevitably turned him to easel and brush. In this he was anticipated by Ira who had always shown an aptitude for sketching and drawing and who, upon turning to water colors, showed at once a strong individuality and a sound technique. When George started painting, Botkin helped him set up an easel and gave him some elementary pointers. Botkin says that from his first day at the canvas George showed he was a painter, with a natural feeling for color and design, and a sure instinct and technique. His first completed efforts were a still life ("Black Table") and a "riverscape" ("From the Terrace"). Unlike Ira, who gave up painting after a year or so, George continued until the end of his life. He grew all the time. He never received formal instruction beyond the advice and criticism that Botkin sometimes gave him. His finest works in colors included two self-portraits—one in an opera hat (1932), and another in a checkered sweater (1936)—a portrait of a Negro child (1933), and others of his grandfather (1933), Jerome Kern (1937), and Arnold Schoenberg (1937). Painting became a passion almost as great as music.

Gershwin described himself as "a modern Romantic." Henry Botkin, who was most closely associated with his career in art, has written the following impressions:

> As his painting progressed, he displayed how the specific moods of his musical compositions had given a

vital form and emotional strength to his paintings. The intense, dynamic impulses of his music became the dominating force in his painting. . . . He strove constantly to master the same bold combination of accessories that he possessed as a composer. In his various paintings and especially his portraits he tried for the precise contour that defined the form and constantly concerned itself with composition and color.

His paintings called for no special esthetic theories or psychology. In his many drawings of various degrees of completion—and there are over a hundred—he demonstrated an amazing skill as draughtsman. . . . Besides being an able draughtsman, he possessed a compelling and powerful line and was able to achieve results with the most economical of means. . . .

George had an instinctive sense of art's creative processes and was especially sensitive to rhythm. In quiet and reticent tones he has painted some still lifes and landscapes and though they did not come as easily as the portraits, they show a richness and solidity, together with a considerable amount of assurance. . . . His work was never self-consciously modern and he always avoided distressing mannerisms and surface cleverness. In all his later work he had developed a mastery of his craft and even though he found time to create only small studies, they were never mere exercises but self-contained examples of art.

Just before his death, George planned to hold a one-man show of his art work. That show, embracing thirty-seven paintings (including his maiden efforts) finally did take place at the Marie Harriman Gallery in New York City on December 18, 1937—six months after his death. The noted art critic Henry McBride wrote in review: "He was not yet actually great as a painter, but that was merely because he had not yet had the time—but he was distinctly on the way to that goal. He had all the aptitudes. . . . If the soul be great, all the expressions emanating from that soul must be great."

15

THE OTHER GERSHWIN

Rarely have two collaborators worked together in such complete harmony as did George and Ira Gershwin. Each knew the other's psychological and emotional pattern and was ready to conform to it. Each had not only the sincerest and undivided love for the other but also the highest regard for the other's special talent. Beyond all this, Ira is highly music conscious, even though he cannot read a note of music; and George was equally word conscious. This sympathetic response to and understanding of each other's medium led to a perfect understanding. It was a marriage of true minds.

The strange part about this harmonious partnership is that each member was so different in temperament and personality from the other. Where George was gregarious, a man who flourished at parties and other social affairs and who thrived on movement, activity, and work, Ira is reticent, shy, mild-mannered, somewhat slow-moving. Where women were concerned, George was the man of the world, whereas Ira has had a disarming naïveté. Ira prefers the sedentary life. He is the kind for whom there's no regrettin' when he's settin' biding his time. It requires genuine effort for him to go anywhere or do anything. There were periods at 33 Riverside Drive when he did not descend from his apartment into the street for days at a time.

George had sensitive nerves, and he was given to emotional upheavals and hyperthyroid reactions. Ira is usually even-tempered, placid, soft spoken. George was the idealist, his head in the clouds. Ira is coldly logical and realistic, his feet planted solidly on the ground. George felt he had an artistic mission. Ira regards himself only as a respectable workman, competent and methodical. George loved work, could work anywhere and anytime, and frequently after coming home from a night-long party. To Ira, work is work—certainly less desirable than sprawling on a couch and smoking a series of Montecristo cigars, or spending the day at the races, the evening at poker, or the late and sleepless hours of the night with books and magazines. He once said, "I have a whole day's work ahead of me. I'm going to change the ribbon on my typewriter."

Vernon Duke—who in 1935 wrote the music to Ira's lyrics for the *Ziegfeld Follies*—has described (in *Passport to Paris*) Ira's lackadaisical and easygoing working habits:

> Our work sessions usually began with a family dinner with Ira and Leonore, joined by Fanny Brice or Ellen

Berlin. After a long and copious meal, the company
would repair to the drawing room, which housed the
piano, and hectic conversation would ensue; I, on tenter-
hooks, would be dying to get to the piano and persuade
Leonore and her guests to go elsewhere for their ener-
getic gossip. I would shoot expressive glances at the ever-
placid Ira, who affected not to catch their meaning and
willingly joined in the conversation. After an hour or
so of this, I, totally exasperated, would invade the piano
determinedly and strike a few challenging chords. This
time Ira would heed my desperate call, stretch himself,
emit a series of protracted sighs, say something to the
effect that "one had to work *so-o-o* hard for a living" and
more in that vein, then interrupt himself to intone the
magic word: "However. . . ." This "however" meant that
the eleventh hour had struck and the period of delicious
procrastination was over. Ira, sighing pathetically, would
then produce a small bridge table, various writing and
erasing gadgets, a typewriter and four or five books, which
he seldom consulted—Roget's *Thesaurus,* Webster's dictionary, rhyming dictionary and the like—wipe and ad-
just his glasses, all these preparations at a *molto adagio*
pace, and finally say in a resigned voice: "O.K., Dukie
. . . play that chorus you had last night." After wrestling
with last night's chorus for a half hour, Ira would embark
on an ice-box raiding expedition, with me, fearful of too
long an interruption, in pursuit. There we'd stand in the
kitchen, munching cheese and pickles. Ira obviously delighted with this escapist stratagem, I dutifully pretending to enjoy it too. Another sigh, another "however,"
then back to the piano. At 2 or 3 A.M. Ira would put away

his working utensils and victoriously announce to Lee that he had completed four lines for the new chorus.

Ira provided his brother George with lyrics over a period of thirteen years. It is impossible to overestimate his share in the successes of George's best songs and musical comedies, or in George's development as a composer for the stage. Ira continually provided George with ideas for verses which were able to stimulate the composer's imagination. His dynamic and imaginative concept of what the musical comedy can be was a vital force in opening for George new avenues in his musical writing for the theater. And no one appreciated Ira's talent more strongly than George himself.

It is true that the melody usually came before the lyric. But it is also true—and the fact must be emphasized—that Ira's song ideas, catchy titles, provocative colloquialisms, ingenious verbal and rhythmic patterns were sparks which set aflame the combustible fuel of George's musical imagination. A jingle-like effect such as "Do, do, do what you done, done, done before, baby"—which Ira thought up even before he wrote his lyric—lends itself so naturally to a mobile, skipping melody that George was able to write this song for *Oh Kay* in a single sitting, as soon as Ira presented him with the intriguing first line. George was also stimulated by Ira's trick of transforming words like "passion" into "pash" and "delicious" into "delish" in one lyric, and in another of contracting words like "it's wonderful, it's marvelous" into "'swonderful, 'smarvelous." The song "Sweet and Low Down" is one of several examples in which the lyricist pointed the way for the composer. The digression in the chorus with the lines

Hear those shuffling feet
You can't keep your seat
Professor! start your beat
Come along get in it!

demanded and received an unusual release in the melody
which is one of the high spots of that song.

Their most intensive work was done between the
period when a contract was signed and the deadline. They
would discuss the musical comedy thoroughly: where the
songs and other musical routines were to be placed, what
would be the style and manner of each number. Ira would
come up with various ideas; George would counter with
other suggestions. Once an idea was seized upon, George
would begin working on the music. Ira, who has a keen
musical ear and a phenomenal retentive memory for musical
phrases, memorized the tune. Then he went off by himself
to fit lyrics to the music.

Ira is such a precise, meticulous, and exacting crafts-
man that he is frequently described by his colleagues as "a
jeweler." He works slowly and is rarely satisfied. It takes
him hours to come up with a neat phrase or an agile rhyme;
then it takes him many more hours to change it. When he
produces a line that is seemingly perfect in every detail, he
will say, "This will do. But if I think of something better,
I'll have to revise it." Some time ago when *Lady in the Dark*
—the Moss Hart–Ira Gershwin–Kurt Weill musical—was revived for television, the producers wired him to change one
of the rhymes. Two lines had to do with somebody's mis-
tress, a delicate subject for family consumption. Ira spent a
full day, and experimented with sixty different rhymes, before he was able to substitute two lines that satisfied him.

His preference is always for simple lyrics that employ everyday speech and colloquial phrases such as "I've got a crush on you," or "let's call the whole thing off," rather than the gaudy and often formal language used in operettas and comic operas. He will not stretch for a gag or a funny line, nor will he try to build up comedy with accumulative effect. His preference is for subtle satire and the slow and dry humor that can be found in such lyrics as "The Babbitt and the Bromide," "Bidin' My Time," and "Could You Use Me," and in the series of couplets in "Union Square":

> Down with music by Stravinsky
> Down with shows except by Minsky!

> Happiness will fill our cup,
> When it's Down with ev'rything that's up.

> Down with books by Dostoyevsky
> Down with Boris Thomashefsky!

> Down with Balzac, Down with Zola,
> Down with pianists who play "Nola."

> Down with all the Upper Classes
> Might as well include the Masses.

While there can never be a question about his agility at rhyming—take, for example, the series of four-syllable rhymes in the chorus of "Embraceable You"—he is rarely much concerned with virtuoso rhymes for their own sake. He prefers to have them flow gracefully and fall easily on the ear, as in

> When I'm with you who cares what time it is,
> Or what the place or what the climate is.

He feels strongly that the best lyrics are those that are natural, precise, economical, never distracting the attention of the listener from the music, as in the following:

> In time the Rockies may crumble
> Gibraltar may tumble
> They're only made of clay.
> But our love is here to stay.

Or:

> One look and I forgot the gloom of the past,
> One look and I had found my future at last,
> One look and I had found the world completely new,
>   When love walked in with you.

Such lyrics are deceptively simple; actually they can come only after considerable distillation, refinement, and the most painstaking editing.

16

EXPANDING HORIZONS —

AND THE *Second Rhapsody*

Beyond some individual songs, there was nothing in the three Gershwin musicals produced between 1928 and 1929 to command especial interest. They can be dismissed quickly. *Rosalie* came on January 10, 1928, starring Marilyn Miller as a mythical-kingdom princess who wins the love of an American lieutenant from West Point. This was the first of two musicals which Gershwin wrote for Florenz Ziegfeld. Ziegfeld originally gave the musical assignment for *Rosalie* to Sigmund Romberg, demanding the score in three weeks. Romberg, then busy with *New Moon,* said he could not do the job alone and suggested Gershwin as a collaborator. Together, they finished the music on schedule, Romberg writing eight numbers, and Gershwin seven. The juxtaposition of the names of Romberg and Gershwin tempted Woollcott to suggest that "we shall soon have a novel written by Harold Bell Wright and Ernest Hemingway." The truth is, however, that in the case of *Rosalie* it was "Harold Bell Wright" rather than "Hemingway" who did the more convincing writing; with the possible exception of "How Long Has This Been Going On?" none of the seven Gershwin songs have any significance or interest.

With *Rosalie* launched successfully, Ziegfeld suggested a new project to the Gershwins: a musical version by Anthony McGuire of *East Is West,* a play in which Fay Bainter had a formidable success on Broadway between 1918 and 1920. The idea excited both Gershwins as no other musical had done up till then; they saw it as a sensitive play in which the music would be integral to the stage action and germane to the dramatic context. Without any contracts being signed, Gershwin went to work and had produced about half the score when Ziegfeld suddenly engaged him to work on *Show Girl.* By the time *Show Girl* closed Ziegfeld lost heart in the earlier project.

Out of this uncompleted score came "Embraceable You," which Gershwin used in a later musical; also the only art song Gershwin ever wrote, "In the Mandarin's Orchid Garden." He had planned it as a background to a ballet in *East Is West.* When the musical failed to materialize, he published it as a separate song. It has the delicacy of a Japanese print and some day will find a welcome and permanent place in song recitals. It was introduced at a song recital by Eleanor Marum at the Blackstone Theater in Chicago on November 10, 1929.

With *East Is West* in discard, Gershwin turned to a new musical for Aarons and Freedley: *Treasure Girl*. Produced in November 1928, it proved to be a silly play about a $100,000 treasure buried by Mortimer Grimes on the grounds of his estate during a pirate party. Finders keepers. Ann seeks the fortune, even while she is pursuing and is being pursued by Neil. She gets both her man and the treasure. Not even Gertrude Lawrence as Ann could bring credibility or brightness to these dull proceedings. *Treasure Girl* folded up after sixty-eight performances, leaving behind it, however, a few delightful Gershwin songs: "Oh So Nice," a successful attempt to bring the feeling of the Viennese waltz into fox-trot time; "Feeling I'm Falling"; and a tender blues song, "Where's the Boy," which to this day has not achieved the popularity it deserves.

Gershwin went back to work for Ziegfeld with *Show Girl*, which opened on July 2, 1929, with Ruby Keeler, Clayton, Jackson and Durante, Harriet Hoctor, and Duke Ellington. *Show Girl* was an adaptation by Anthony McGuire of a spicy novel by J. P. McEvoy, tracing the career and loves of Dixie Dugan from the time she crashes an interview with Ziegfeld through her stardom in the *Follies*. The prodigal Ziegfeld hand, which spread splendor with the munificence of an Oriental potentate, succeeded only in transforming a witty, rapidly paced story into a laborious and slow-moving spectacle. There was an elaborate ballet danced by Harriet Hoctor and the Albertina Rasch girls to the music of *An American in Paris*—about which John Mason Brown was tempted to say that the production suddenly "broke out in an Albertina Rasch." Jimmie Durante, happily cast as a property man, sang some of the songs he had previously popularized in night clubs, including "So I Ups to

Him," "I Can Do Without Broadway," and "Who Will Be with You When I'm Far Away" (none of them, of course, by the Gershwins). Ruby Keeler as Dixie Dugan sang and danced to the tantalizing rhythms of "Liza," as her husband Al Jolson ran up and down the aisles singing the refrain to his wife—for several nights an unscheduled, unexpected, and unpaid-for attraction. "Liza" was always one of Gershwin's favorites. He continually played it for friends, frequently with improvised variations. Still another major Gershwin song in that production was "So Are You," in which a beguiling effect is achieved through repeated changes of modality.

But *Show Girl* failed to win admirers or influence audiences. It was one of Ziegfeld's most dismal failures, the only one of his productions to beg for customers at cut-rate counters. Gershwin's association with the fabulous producer ended with that show. It was an unhappy ending. Because he had suffered severe losses in the stock market, Ziegfeld refused to pay Gershwin any royalties and George had to threaten a law suit before he could collect them.

All this while Gershwin had been following familiar grooves in the musical-comedy theater. He was willing to accept and work with the formulas and clichés which had created a tradition. The Gershwin musicals through *Show Girl*—like most of the musicals of that generation—sought to entertain the eye and ear rather than the mentality. A musical-comedy book was merely a convenient excuse for the presentation of song and dance, humor and sentimentality; it was not required to have validity in its own right. Set numbers and routines were interpolated without too much concern for their relevance to the text, their single justification being to amuse or entertain. No one expected a musical comedy to have a basic or significant dramatic idea or to pursue that idea with consistency.

But with *Strike Up the Band,* on January 14, 1930, a new kind of musical came to Times Square. This was no longer just a spectacle for the eye and an opiate for the senses, but a bitter satire on war, enlisting all the resources of good theater.

Strike Up the Band had taken a long and interrupted journey before finally settling on Broadway. It was first launched in 1927, after which it was subjected to drastic overhauling. George S. Kaufman wrote the book of the original 1927 version. Already, then, he was one of the keenest and most trenchant wits of the Broadway stage and one of its ablest technicians. Since 1921 he had collaborated with various writers on sparkling and briskly paced comedies, frequently coated with acid, including *Dulcy, To the Ladies, Merton of the Movies, Beggar on Horseback,* and *Minick.* He had also helped prepare books for standardized musicals. Among them were *Be Yourself,* for which Ira Gershwin wrote some of the lyrics, and *The Coconuts* in which the Four Marx Brothers went helter-skelter through the plot and dialogue with the devastating impact of a bulldozer.

Strike Up the Band was a radical departure from anything Kaufman had thus far written for the musical stage. It assumed that audiences would appreciate a play that, instead of making concessions to girl routines, stock numbers, and synthetic humor, could pursue a subject like war with satiric ferocity. Apparently the idea and its treatment were still too unconventional. When *Strike Up the Band* was tried out in Long Branch, Philadelphia, in September 1927 (with Jimmie Savo and Vivian Hart in the two principal roles) it was a fiasco, and was abandoned.

In 1929 the authors returned to the play. Morrie Ryskind, then still a novice in the theater, was called in as collaborator to contribute his own personal brand of broad humor to Kaufman's text, while making a compromise between Kaufman's ruthless satire and some of the existing traditions of musical comedy. Necessary concessions were made to commercialism, but in spite of this *Strike Up the Band* remained a unique experiment. It brought new dimensions to musical comedy by being one of the first with a pronounced political consciousness. War was the theme, but the text frequently digressed to make a stinging commentary on Babbittry and big business, international relations, secret and open diplomacy, the drawing up of international treaties, and so forth.

With a new cast, headed by Clark and McCullough, *Strike Up the Band* was received with outbursts of enthusiasm by both audiences and critics. As William Bolitho, the brilliant columnist of the New York *World*, remarked with undisguised amazement: "Of all things in the world, here is a bitter . . . satirical attack on war, genuine propaganda at times, sung and danced on Broadway to standing room only." The principal butt for the authors' attack was Horace J. Fletcher, a successful American manufacturer of chocolates, who has a grievance against Washington, D.C., for its refusal to raise the tariff on Swiss chocolates. A sedative administered to him by the doctor induces sleep and dreams. He sees himself at the head of an American army that goes to war with Switzerland over the issue of chocolate. Accidentally, the enemy's secret call to arms is discovered—to be sure, a yodel—and the American troops are able to corner and rout the Swiss army. Fletcher, however, is only hero for a day. The American newspapers uncover the unsavory fact that Fletcher's chocolates use only Grade B milk.

Motivated by an unorthodox book which often made formal musical procedures unserviceable—and stimulated by the stinging acidity of Ira's lines—George Gershwin's music revealed an increasing awareness of the demands of the stage. The resources of musical writing were now used with a new deftness to point up a satiric comment, to emphasize a humorous situation, or to translate nuances of a character or incident into musical terms. A series of descending chords in a nebulous tonality truly suggest that *he* is most certainly not the man in "How About a Man Like Me for a Girl Like You." A deflated descending passage shows up the hollowness of Fletcher when he makes his first entrance. A jazz passage for trumpet in double-time underscores the American in "I'm a Typical Self-Made American." The tart Prokofiev-like dissonances in the "Entrance of the Swiss Army" mercilessly show the army to be bogus. These and other subtle touches throughout the score indicate Gershwin's new ability at musical delineation.

But the Gershwin score—which was published in its entirety—is not only rich in details. A number of individual songs stand out prominently: the purple-mood, minor-mode languor of "Soon," one of Gershwin's most beautiful ballads, which originated as an eight-bar strain in the Act I finale of the original version of *Strike Up the Band;* the fleet-footed witticism of "I'm a Typical Self-Made American" and "The Unofficial Spokesman"; or the caressing charm of "I've Got a Crush on You," which Gershwin originally wrote for *Treasure Girl* but which was used there only out-of-town; it was revived in 1955 in the motion-picture *Three for the Money.*

Passages such as the incidental dream music in both acts—
and the extended finale of the first act in which a résumé of
what has happened recurs both in the text and in the score—
demonstrate Gershwin's new spaciousness in his writing of
stage music.

Outside the theater he was also heading in new di-
rections. On July 8, 1929, he appeared in a new role—as a
symphony conductor. The event took place at a summer concert in Lewisohn Stadium of New York City. He had made
his first appearance at the Stadium on July 27, 1927, when
he was piano soloist in the *Rhapsody in Blue* and the Concerto in F, with Willem van Hoogstraten conducting. Two
years later he returned to the Stadium, this time to conduct
An American in Paris; the rest of the program was conducted
by Van Hoogstraten.

Before making his debut as conductor, Gershwin received some coaching from his one-time teacher, Kilenyi, who
instructed him in the essentials of baton technique and then
had him practice at home with a recording of the tone poem.
One of the largest audiences to attend a Stadium concert,
more than 15,000, came to witness the performance. They
saw him do well. The performance was correct and spirited,
his time-beating was clear and precise, and he showed an
ability to lead the orchestra, instead of being led by it. Considering the fact that this was his first effort with the baton,
Gershwin gave a good account of himself.

In the next few months he acquired more conducting
experience. On November 10, 1929, he was the guest conductor of the Manhattan Symphony, his first indoor appearance as a conductor. Once again he led *An American in
Paris,* while the permanent conductor of the orchestra, Henry

Hadley, led the remainder of the concert. Gershwin led a performance of one of his musicals for the first time when he conducted the Boston première of *Strike Up the Band* on December 25 at the Shubert Theater. His appearances with the baton grew more frequent after that, and he often conducted his music with symphony and radio orchestras as well as many opening-night performances of his musicals.

Fresh contacts opened up still more vistas for him. In 1929 the book-publishing house of Simon and Schuster urged him to put down on paper some of the improvisations and variations with which he had so long been entertaining his friends. Between 1931 and 1932 he made transcriptions of eighteen songs in which, as he explained, he indulged "the desire for complication and variety that every composer feels when he manipulates the same material over and over again." The transcriptions were published together with the original sheet-music versions in *George Gershwin's Song Book* in 1932. The book was reissued in 1941 in a revised edition, and the transcriptions were recorded by Leonid Hambro for Walden Records.

In the fall of 1930 Gershwin received a contract from the Metropolitan Opera Association for an opera to be completed at an unspecified date. The idea for writing an opera engaged his thinking for a long time as he searched for a suitable libretto. His first idea was to find a play about New York's melting pot, but he could find nothing that answered his needs. He then selected *The Dybbuk,* by S. Ansky, a Yiddish play with an old-world Polish setting filled with Chassidic mysticism, lore, and superstition. He began noting down melodic ideas for arias and dances, some filled with religious fervor and Chassidic abandon, others without an identifiable Hebraic origin. He had accumulated quite a storehouse of fragmentary ideas when he received a cable from Italy that the opera rights were not available, having previously been assigned to Lodovico Rocca, the Italian composer.

Still another idea was slowly being fertilized in his mind. One night in 1926, unable to sleep, he reached for a novel on his table, the recently published *Porgy*, by DuBose Heyward. He became so engrossed in the story that he read it through the night. Then, though it was four in the morning, he jumped out of bed to write to the author of his interest in making the novel into an opera. Heyward replied that the idea appealed to him and that he would be glad to discuss it with Gershwin whenever he came north from South Carolina. Soon after this, the Heywards spent a brief vacation in Atlantic City, New Jersey, and Gershwin came down from New York to meet them. The two men paced the boardwalk discussing *Porgy* and agreed that it had the basis for a powerful folk opera. But they both decided to postpone the work for some time. Heyward, at the time, was collaborating with his wife, Dorothy, in adapting the novel for a play to be produced by the Theatre Guild. And Gershwin was occupied by various endeavors. Their ambitious project would have to wait—but the idea of writing an opera on *Porgy* never left Gershwin.

Another contract brought more immediate results. In 1929 he signed an agreement bringing him $70,000 for writing music for a motion picture for Fox. (Ira received $30,000 for the lyrics.) The screen had only recently acquired a voice. In the major upheaval that followed in the industry, a new orientation took place in which emphasis had to be placed on sound as well as sight. Hollywood began to call for musicals, and more musicals. To answer this need, Broadway was combed for its principal composers, and Gershwin was one of the first to be called. He told an interviewer, "I go to work for the talkies like any other amateur, for I know little about them. Because I am inexperienced with films, I am approaching them with humble mind."

He arrived in the screen capital in November 1930, rented a house on Chevy Chase Drive in Beverly Hills which Garbo had previously occupied, and stayed several months. The picture to which he was assigned was *Delicious*, starring Janet Gaynor as a Scottish immigrant and Charles Farrell as a wealthy polo-playing Long Islander. They meet aboard ship en route to New York, and they fall in love. In spite of their social differences, and sundry complications and misunderstandings, they cannot be kept apart. Gershwin devoted seven weeks to writing his score; four songs were used, also a dream sequence for voice and orchestra, and a six-minute orchestral sequence describing the sounds and movements of a city and highlighted by the rhythm of riveting. Only one minute of the six was finally used in the picture, but the entire sequence seemed so good to Gershwin that he decided to use it as the core of a major work for symphony orchestra. "Nearly everybody comes back from California with a Western tan and a pocketful of moving-picture money," he said. "I decided to come back with these things—and a serious composition besides, if the climate would let me. . . . The old artistic soul must every so often be appeased."

Using the tentative title of *Rhapsody in Rivets*, Gershwin began making sketches for his materials in January 1931. The entire work was completed by May 23. On June 26, he tried it out for two-and-a-half hours by conducting it three times with a hired orchestra of fifty-six men, in a studio of the National Broadcasting Company; and at the same time he had a private recording made for his own use and study. "I was more than pleased with the result," he wrote to a friend, "and so were a few of my friends who came. In fact, many of them consider it the best thing I have done." Once again, as had been the case with the Concerto, the revisions after this trial performance were negligible, consisting mainly in details of orchestration. The basic change came in the title. Fearing that the word "rivets" might bring up a disturbing aural image to the listener, besides raising to mind possible programmatic interpretations not intended by the music—Gershwin finally decided to adopt the more abstract name of *Second Rhapsody*.

The idea of "rivets" appears in the opening measures: an incisive rhythmic subject for solo piano which bears a family resemblance to the first principal subject of the *Rhapsody in Blue*. The rivet theme is assumed by the full orchestra, which then embarks upon a rhumba-like melody of its own. Both subjects receive detailed development. A transitory passage in solo piano leads to the broad-flowing blues melody which is the heart of the composition. It appears in the string choir, is taken over by the brass, and then receives extensive elaboration by both the solo piano and the orchestra. The two earlier themes are recalled and embellished before the rhapsody comes to a vigorous close in both piano and orchestra. The work is scored for full orchestra with drums, cymbals, wood block, fly swatter, xylophone, and harp.

Gershwin played his new Rhapsody at a party at Jules Glaenzer's. "Bill Paley, who owns the Columbia Broadcasting System, was there," Gershwin wrote to a friend. "He was so crazy about it that he called me several days later and asked me if I would like to have Toscanini conduct it next season. I said I would like it very much if Toscanini would like to do it."

Nothing came of the plan to have Toscanini introduce the *Second Rhapsody*. Sometime in April of 1931 Gershwin met Toscanini for the first time at Samuel Chotzinoff's. For some time Chotzinoff had been trying to arrange a meeting between these two men, and on this evening Toscanini was Chotzinoff's dinner guest. After dinner Chotzinoff once again suggested to the Maestro that he meet Gershwin. When Toscanini seemed receptive to the idea, Chotzinoff rushed to the telephone and urged Gershwin to come right over. Gershwin appeared with a coterie of his friends, including Oscar Levant. At first Gershwin was considerably flustered to learn from Toscanini that the latter had never heard the *Rhapsody in Blue*. "Can you imagine a man living in the last seven years—being connected with music—and never hearing the *Rhapsody in Blue*," Gershwin wrote to a friend with undisguised astonishment. But after Gershwin played for him not only the *Rhapsody in Blue* but other of his works including the *Second Rhapsody*—and received a warm and affectionate response from the Maestro—he felt much better. Toscanini, however, said nothing of playing the *Second Rhapsody*. About a year and a half later, Gershwin again played for Toscanini, and again at Chotzinoff's, this time at a little informal variety show which Chotzinoff arranged for the Maestro. Once again, Toscanini expressed pleasure at Gershwin's music, and once again he said nothing about playing any of it. Actually he never conducted anything by Gershwin during the composer's lifetime.

The première of the *Second Rhapsody* was given in Boston by the Boston Symphony Orchestra under Serge Koussevitzky on January 29, 1932. Gershwin was the piano soloist. After the concert, Koussevitzky told Gershwin in the artist's room, "You are ten times the genius of X——," mentioning the name of one of the world's most celebrated composers. But the Boston critics were not so enthusiastic. "The *Second Rhapsody*," wrote H. T. Parker in the Boston *Evening Transcript*, "seemed tempered and in degree denatured by reflections and manipulation. It sounded over-often from the study table and the piano rack. . . . The motives . . . lack the arresting and driving qualities of the themes of the First, but the rhythmic, melodic, harmonic, and instrumental expansion is more inventive and skillful. . . . Mr. Gershwin waxes in craftsmanship but at the cost of earlier and irresistible élan." L. A. Sloper said in the *Christian Science Monitor*: "The main musical idea is merely a rhythmic figure of a type easily imagined. The other material of the piece is taken from a grab bag of musical comedy. A great symphony orchestra is not the ideal commentator of Gershwin's music, which belongs essentially to the dance-hall bands." Philip Hale tempered his criticism in the *Herald* with some kind words: "Mr. Gershwin's new rhapsody has not the sweeping irresistible lyric theme that distinguished the preceding rhapsody. No one should cry out against his chief theme, which needs no verbal explanation, for its significance is unmistakable; its character is truly national, as are the dash and recklessness of the better pages. The music has decided individuality."

The New York music critics were much better disposed toward the new work when it was introduced in that city by the visiting Boston Symphony, once again with Gershwin as soloist, on February 7. "Jazzarella, undiminished in gusto and vitality, dances here. . . . The happy few will recognize and value the skill of her evolutions and the subtlety of her guile. . . . Music's most enlivened daughter is, as usual, bringing down the house." Thus wrote Lawrence Gilman. W. J. Henderson said: "Mr. Gershwin is our own product. . . . He does not endeavor to soar into the impalpable. . . . He recognized jazz as a growth from the soil of this country and tries to shape from it artistic forms of music. What he does is indisputably legitimate. . . . The work is spirited, it is full of youth and recklessness, it is America of untrammeled manners and cocktail energy."

There were those who were far less impressed. Olin Downes felt that Gershwin was only copying his own *Rhapsody in Blue,* and with less happy consequences. To the *New Yorker* it was "disappointing in all respects . . . almost totally devoid of ingratiating melody . . . offering nothing but rhythms now grown trite and a reasonably clever though blatant orchestration."

Audiences have not been won over to the *Second Rhapsody,* and it is not hard to see why. The *Second Rhapsody* lacks the wind-swept inspiration of the *Rhapsody in Blue,* its wonderful vitality and spontaneity. While the later composition represents a decided advance in technique, it is mainly contrived where the first rhapsody was inspired.

The European première of the *Second Rhapsody* took place in London on March 20, 1933, at a concert of the London Symphony Orchestra, conducted by Sir Hamilton Harty. To Francis Toye, writing in the *Morning Post,* it seemed to be "spoiled by rhetoric and an effort to be important." Other London critics lamented its "sentimental banalities" and its "clichés."

17

B R O A D W A Y   T R I U M P H S :

Girl Crazy and *Of Thee I Sing*

In 1929 there was produced on Broadway a hilarious lampoon on Tin Pan Alley by George S. Kaufman and Ring Lardner, *June Moon*. In this comedy a meeting takes place in the private office of a music-publishing executive. Suddenly word spreads in that room that George Gershwin is outside. An awed silence fills the room. Then the meeting is disrupted as each one sneaks out of the office to catch a quick glimpse of the great man.

If already in 1929 Gershwin was Mr. Big of Tin Pan Alley, he was to grow bigger and bigger in 1930 and 1931. In these two years he wrote the music for two successive musicals, each in its own way making stage history. For each he wrote the most important and brilliant stage music

of his career; each was a smash hit; and, as if to provide
full testimony to his powers, each was radically different in
approach and in methodology. One was *Girl Crazy,* in the
techniques and traditions of formal musical comedy. The
other—*Of Thee I Sing*—was in the new satirical manner of
Strike Up the Band, with its fresh and unorthodox concept
of the musical theater and its subtlety of detail.

Girl Crazy began a long run at the Alvin Theater
on October 14, 1930. The book, by Bolton and MacGowan,
was no better—or worse—than earlier ones for which Gershwin had supplied the music. The setting is Custerville, Arizona, to which the rich and girl-crazy playboy, Danny
Churchill, comes from New York in Gieber Goldfarb's taxi-
cab. Danny's parents have sent him to Custerville—a town
without women—to keep him out of the fleshpots of the East.
But Danny manages to bring with him the temptations of the
East. He opens a dude ranch with Broadway chorus girls.
By one way or another he manages to get into plenty of
trouble, but he finally mends his ways, after falling in love
with Mollie Gray, the postmistress.

One of the things that made *Girl Crazy* as good as
it was—"a never-ending bubbling of pure joyousness," as
one New York critic described it—was the casting. Ginger
Rogers, fresh from her first screen triumph in *Young Man
of Manhattan,* made her bow on the Broadway stage as
Molly. Allen Kearns, veteran of so many Gershwin musicals,
was cast as Danny; while Willie Howard brought his Yiddish accent, uninhibited comedy, and flair for mimicry to the
part of Gieber Goldfarb. Each of these gave a performance
calculated to steal the limelight. But the limelight belonged
not to any of them, but rather to a young and then still unknown lady whose personality swept through the theater like

a tropical cyclone and whose large brassy voice struck on the consciousness of the listeners like a sledge hammer. She was Ethel Merman in her first appearance in musical comedy. When she stepped on the stage as Kate Fothergill, the wife of the man who ran the gambling room at the dude ranch, dressed in a tight black satin skirt slit to the knee and a low-cut red blouse, and sang "Sam and Delilah" she was a sensation. Then in "I Got Rhythm" she threw her voice across the footlights the way Louis Armstrong does the tones of a trumpet. When, in the second chorus, she held a high C for sixteen bars, while the orchestra continued with the melody, the theater was hers: not only the Alvin Theater, but the musical theater as well.

Before that evening of October 14, Ethel Merman had for years been filling minor and poorly paid engagements in night clubs, at parties, and weddings. A successful engagement at the Brooklyn Paramount Theater was the break that brought her to the attention of Vinton Freedley, then busy with casting problems for *Girl Crazy*. He brought her up to Gershwin's apartment at Riverside Drive for an audition. Merman sang for Gershwin several swing numbers, including "Exactly Like You" and "Little White Lies." "Don't ever go near a teacher," Gershwin told her. "He'll only ruin you." Then Gershwin played for her the three numbers he had in mind for her part in the show. Ethel Merman tells what happened in her autobiography:*

It was the first time I'd met George Gershwin, and if I may say so without seeming sacrilegious, to me it

---

* *Who Could Ask For Anything More*, by Ethel Merman. Copyright 1955 by Ethel Merman Six, reprinted by permission of Doubleday & Company, Inc.

was like meeting God. Imagine the great Gershwin sitting down and playing his songs for [me]. . . . No wonder I was tongue-tied. When he played "I Got Rhythm," he told me, "If there's anything about this you don't like, I'll be happy to change it." There was nothing about that song I didn't like. But that's the kind of guy he was. That I'll never forget. I smiled and nodded, but I didn't say anything. I was thinking how to phrase the music. Gershwin seemed puzzled at my silence. Finally he said again, "If there's anything about these songs you don't like, Miss Merman, I'll be happy to make changes." It wasn't that; it was only that I was so flabbergasted. Through the fog that had wrapped itself around me, I heard myself say, "They'll do very nicely, Mr. Gershwin." There were those who thought that my reply was funny when it was repeated to them, as if I'd given the great Gershwin the old hauteur treatment. I was so drunk with the glory of it all that I could have said anything at all, but whatever I said, I meant it to be grateful and humble. That's for sure.

Ethel Merman was hired for *Girl Crazy* at a salary of $375 a week, and her voice coach, Al Siegel, was engaged to be her piano accompanist on stage. (Siegel fell sick and was able to appear only at the opening-night performance in New York; his place was taken by Roger Edens, now a successful producer at MGM.)

The day after the New York première, Gershwin had a luncheon date with Ethel. Had she seen the reviews? Ethel shook her head. She had gone to bed so late the preceding night and had risen this morning just in time to make her appointment so that she had not had a free moment to read the critics. "They're raves, all of them," Gershwin told her. "You're in with both feet."

The three songs that helped make Merman the triumph she was are among the greatest by Gershwin. That evening of November 14 was one of those rare and fortuitous moments in stage history when the right song and the right singer collided. "I Got Rhythm" is remarkable in its chorus not only for the agility of its changing rhythms but also for the unusual melody made up of a rising and falling five-note phrase from the pentatonic scale. "Sam and Delilah" is a tongue-in-the-cheek Barbary Coast ballad in the style of "Frankie and Johnny," with effective employment of changing tonality and unusual intervallic construction in the melody. "Boy What Love Has Done to Me" shifts from one point of musical interest to another—now in the harmony, now in the melody, now in accentuation, now in dynamics— with the deftness and versatility of Fred Astaire passing from one intricate routine to another.

Other songs were equally exciting. "Bidin' My Time," sung by a quartet of rubes who drifted in and out of the production during scene changes, is in the subtle satiric vein of "Sam and Delilah." Here was not only a refreshing take-off on Western ballads, but also on Tin Pan Alley through the wry and skillful interpolations of the titles (and at times melodic reminders) of several songs popular in 1930. And the dry and casual humor of Ira's lines provided a perfect foil for Gershwin's tune:

> Next year, next year
> Somethin's bound to happen,
> This year, this year,
> I'll just keep on nappin'.

"Embraceable You," the hit song of the production (and written two years earlier for *East Is West*) belongs to the half dozen or so of Gershwin song classics in which his melodic writing is most expressive. In a similarly tender vein is the sentimental ballad "But Not for Me"; strange to say, Willie Howard used it to exhibit his adeptness at imitating famous performers of the day—but not before it had been poignantly introduced by Ginger Rogers. On the other hand, "Could You Use Me" is more refreshing for its lyric than the melody. Lines like these are characteristic:

> There's a chap I know in Mexico
> Who's as strong as he can be,
> Eating nails and drinking Texaco
> > He is the type for me.

> There is one in California
> More romantic far than you
> When he sings hot-cha-cha-chornia
> > I often think he'll do.

Some mention should be made of the orchestra in the pit and of its share in the performance of Gershwin's music. That ensemble was surely the kind about which jazz enthusiasts dream, for it included Benny Goodman, Glenn Miller, Red Nichols, and Gene Krupa!

The strength of the *Girl Crazy* score lay in individual songs; in *Of Thee I Sing* the individual songs are of lesser significance. Especially noteworthy are the numerous details which show Gershwin emerging as an outstanding musical satirist and as a composer who consciously and adroitly adapted sound to sight, tone to words, and musical means to stage action. Gershwin interpreted the nuances of the satirical play with the sensitivity and appropriateness he had merely suggested in *Strike Up the Band*. In none of his musicals before this had score, book, and lyrics been so inextricably combined into a single unity.

Gershwin had a brilliant book and some of the most brilliant lyrics of Ira's career to work with. The authors were the same who had produced *Strike Up the Band*. Book and lyrics were filled with laughter and mockery; wisdom was couched with wit; gentle irony sometimes developed into outright malice. As George reported to one of his friends, "Ira and I have never been connected with a show of which we were prouder."

In *Strike Up the Band* the focal point for attack had been war and international diplomacy. In *Of Thee I Sing* it was a presidential campaign and the local political scene. In a smoke-filled hotel room the political bosses decide to run Wintergreen for the Presidency, with Throttlebottom as his running mate. Wintergreen is a blustery, brash kind of fellow (played with the necessary élan and gusto by William Gaxton). Throttlebottom, on the other hand, is a meek, sad little man with a high-pitched voice that is always breaking, and a spirit that is always broken; he, to be sure, was played by Victor Moore in the most poignant characterization of his long career. The campaign issue is "Love." A Miss White House is chosen in an Atlantic City beauty contest to become the First Lady; she is Diana Devereux.

> If a girl is sexy
> She may be Mrs. Prexy.
>
> The prize is consequential
> Pres-i-dential.

Love sweeps the country—and Wintergreen—into the White House. But Wintergreen upsets the applecart by falling in love with homespun Mary Turner because:

> Some girls can bake a pie
>   Made up of prunes and quinces
> Some girls, an oyster fry;
>   Others are good at blintzes;
> Some lovely girls have done
>   Wonders with turkey stuffin's—
> But I have found the one
>   Who really can make corn muffins.

Wintergreen marries Mary. An international incident develops when it is discovered that the spurned Diana Devereux is of French descent, "the illegitimate daughter of the illegitimate son of an illegitimate nephew of Napoleon." America and France are about to break diplomatic relations; there is even a movement afoot to impeach the President. Then Mary announces, "My husband is in a delicate condition. He is about to become a father." Throttlebottom points out that the United States has never yet impeached an expectant President—and thus Wintergreen is saved. The complicated situation is unraveled by nobody but Throttlebottom himself when he accepts Diana as his own wife.

The general outline, however, is only the frame for the detail work in which a wide gamut of subjects is mercilessly exposed and ridiculed. The devices and the often absurd maneuvers by which political bosses select candidates for the highest office in the land, the vacuity of campaign issues, the ballyhoo and circus showmanship accompanying presidential campaigns, the often strange goings on in the hallowed halls of the Senate, the often confused judicial proceedings of the Supreme Court, the obscurity surrounding the Vice President—all this is grist for the mill of a satirist, of an American Gilbert and Sullivan. And the authors make the most of their opportunities. They combine political rallies with a wrestling match. They have the Senate debate over granting a (long overdue) pension to Paul Revere's horse, Jenny; and, upon learning to their surprise that Jenny is dead, the members of the Senate stand in reverence to her memory. The authors insist upon having the Supreme Court decide the sex of Mary's child—or, rather, children, since she has twins—before she can give birth, the vote being strictly along party lines.

The portrait of the Vice President—the man nobody knows—is particularly trenchant. He does not want to run because his mother might find out; once elected, he cannot join the Public Library in Washington because he cannot provide two references; the only way he can gain admission into the White House is by joining a conducted tour; even the man who nominated him does not recognize him or remember his name. . . . Victor Moore brought a touch of pathos as well as ridicule to this sad little creature.

In *Of Thee I Sing* the play's the thing, and for its sake the old threadbare formulas of musical comedy were once and for all abandoned. It became, instead, a play with music, and the music is as vital to the text as dialogue and lyrics. Musical devices become the means by which the skillful composer achieved not only a desired effect but underscored some stage business and provided a provocative comment on a character or situation.

Early in the play there is a five-minute political torchlight parade, with all the trimmings. The illuminated signs read: "Even Your Dog Loves Wintergreen" and "A Vote for Wintergreen is a Vote for Wintergreen," and so forth. A chant is sounded, "Wintergreen for President," filled with provocative musical quotations from "Hail, Hail the Gang's All Here," "Tammany," "A Hot Time in the Old Town Tonight," and "Stars and Stripes Forever." At one moment in the melody there is a faint suggestion of the Irish and the Jews—for Wintergreen loves them both. Thus stage action and music become indivisible.

As the play progressed, the music continued to stress and point up each situation; always Gershwin managed to find the proper musical equivalent for the stage shenanigans. Wintergreen goes on his campaign tour with a theme song that begins like a solemn hymn (even as do the words) and suddenly lapses into maudlin Tin Pan Alley sentiment: "Of thee I sing—*baby*." Patriotic songs and Tin Pan Alley are thus felled with a single blow. The Senate scene (which opens with startling informality with some "vamp till ready" chords) makes a mockery of the pretenses of grand opera; also in the quasi-operatic vein are the recitatives which are sprinkled judiciously throughout the play. A droll effect is achieved when the judges of the Supreme Court count themselves off to the tones of the whole-tone scale. Viennese-waltz sentimentality is just right for "I'm About to Become a Mother," while there is an appropriate recollection of the Salvation Army in "Posterity Is Just Around the Corner."

After opening in Boston, *Of Thee I Sing* came to New York on December 26, 1931. It was hailed with hosannas. In Boston, H. T. Parker called it a "most significant addition to the theater," and "one of the drollest satirical operettas of all time." In New York, Brooks Atkinson wrote that it "substituted for the doddering musical-comedy plot a taut and lethal satire of national politics, and George Gershwin has compounded a score that sings in many voices, simmers with ideas, and tells the story more resourcefully than the book. . . . It has very nearly succeeded in liberating the musical-comedy stage from the mawkish and feeble-minded formula that has long been considered inevitable. It is funnier than the government, and not nearly so dangerous." George Jean Nathan hailed it as a "landmark in American satirical musical comedy" which "set a fresh pattern for the American musical stage."

The greatest salute of all came on May 2, 1932, from the Pulitzer Prize committee at Columbia University. With remarkable courage it shattered tradition by making *Of Thee I Sing* the first musical comedy to win the Pulitzer Prize. "This award may seem unusual," read the citation, "but the play is unusual. . . . Its effect on the stage promises to be very considerable, because musical plays are always popular, and by injecting satire and point into them, a very large public is reached." There is only one cause for regret in the award: no mention was made of the part played by Gershwin's music in the over-all success of the play. The Pulitzer Prize judges felt at the time that they were not authorized to make an award to the composer of a musical play. However, eighteen years later, they decided music could be included in their award and Richard Rodgers received it for *South Pacific.*

Another distinction earned by *Of Thee I Sing* was that it became the first American musical comedy whose text was published in book form. It was selected by George Jean Nathan for a series on the contemporary drama of which he was editor: *The Theater of Today Dramatic Li-*

brary. As Nathan has disclosed, it outsold all other previous titles. The play reads well—the best lines still have sting on the printed page, and many of the uproarious situations are still mirth-provoking. But as one reads the text one realizes how much was added by the comments, asides, and finger-pointing of the score.

Of Thee I Sing enjoyed the longest run of any Gershwin musical: 441 performances. After that it went on an extended road tour, returning to Broadway on May 15, 1933, for a new engagement. This tour was supplemented by another throughout the whole country over a period of almost eight months by a second company starring Oscar Shaw, Harriet Lake (now better known as Ann Sothern), and Donald Meek, which opened in Chicago early in 1933. This was the only Gershwin musical to have two productions running simultaneously.

Twenty years later, on May 5, 1952—on the eve of a new Presidential campaign—*Of Thee I Sing* was revived at the Ziegfeld Theater with Jack Carson as Wintergreen and Paul Hartman as Throttlebottom. With a slightly modernized text to bridge the gap of the intervening years but with no change of music, *Of Thee I Sing* was still able to arouse the critics to enthusiasm. But the critical approbation could not bring audiences into the theater. Despite the sacrifices made by the cast—and by Billy Rose, the owner of the Ziegfeld Theater—to keep the play running, it had to close for lack of patronage. It is hard to guess why it was such a failure in 1952. It was still a very funny play; its satire still had plenty of edge; the music sounded even better and more adventurous than before. Possibly in the musical theater of the 1950s, *Of Thee I Sing* had lost its capacity to startle, surprise, and electrify audiences through the unorthodoxy of its procedures because it has so often been imitated not only on the stage but even on the screen. Possibly in the changed political climate—aftermath of four terms of the Roosevelt Administration and a world war—audiences no longer were able to respond favorably to this kind of political satire.

18

T H E *Cuban Overture*

Early in 1932 Gershwin went to Cuba for a holiday. No sooner did word get around that he was a visitor than a rhumba band appeared under his window to serenade him with Cuban music.

Gershwin heard much Cuban music by native performers during his visit and was continually fascinated by the rhythms of the Cuban dances and by native percussion instruments. He decided then and there to write a work in which these rhythms and instruments would be combined with his own thematic ideas.

First he planned to go to Europe, but these plans

were abruptly frustrated by the death of his father on May 14. The poignant loss of one for whom he had always had such affection and tenderness made it impossible for him to consider a vacation at this time. Instead he went to work on his new composition. He wrote it in about three weeks, completing it in July. Orchestration took him eight days between August 1 and August 9. He called it *Rhumba*.

The overture is in three sections. A provocative rhythm, partly rhumba, partly habanera, opens the work. The first theme, of Cuban identity, makes its appearance in the strings. A three-part contrapuntal episode then leads to the second theme, which is soon combined contrapuntally with fragments of the first theme. A solo-clarinet cadenza leads to the middle section, which is mostly a gradually developed canon in a melancholy vein. This canon is in two voices and is unusual in that (unlike traditional canons) it has a harmonic background. After a climax is built out of the ostinato theme of the canon, the finale makes its appearance. This finale uses themes of previous sections but treated in a stretto-like manner. The composition ends with a dynamic and exciting rhumba in which native Cuban instruments of percussion are used. In his conductor's score Gershwin specified that these instruments be placed in a row in front of the conductor's stand: first the cuban stick, then the bondo, the gourd, and the maracas.

The première of *Rhumba* took place at the Lewisohn Stadium on August 16, 1932, Albert Coates conducting. Gershwin himself did not think the work was heard to best advantage that evening, since its percussive effects and tone colors were weakened or completely lost in an open-air stadium. A few critics, however, liked it. The *Musical Courier* said it was "a highly effective vehicle for Mr. Gershwin's gifts," and Pitts Sanborn considered it fresh and spontaneous, superior in rhythmic inventiveness to Ravel's *Bolero*.

"I really believe," Gershwin wrote to a friend the morning after the concert, "that last night was the most exciting I ever had. First, because the Philharmonic Orchestra played an entire program of my music [this was the first time that an all-Gershwin program was given anywhere], and second, because the all-time record for the Stadium Concerts was broken. I have just gotten the figures: 17,845 people paid to get in, and just 5,000 were at the closed gates trying to fight their way in—unsuccessfully." When future attendance records were broken at the Stadium—as happened in 1937 and again in 1941—it was always for an all-Gershwin concert.

This first all-Gershwin concert opened with "Strike Up the Band," conducted by William Daly. The Concerto in F followed, with Levant as soloist, and Daly conducting. (This was not Levant's first appearance at the Stadium; one year earlier he had made his debut there with the *Rhapsody in Blue*.) Albert Coates then conducted *An American in Paris*. After the *Rhapsody in Blue* (Gershwin as soloist, and Daly conducting), Coates returned to conduct the *Second Rhapsody* and the world première of *Rhumba*. The program ended with four Gershwin songs orchestrated and conducted by Daly: "Fascinating Rhythm," "The Man I Love," "Liza," and "I Got Rhythm."

The following winter, on November 1, *Rhumba* was performed for the first time in an indoor auditorium—the Metropolitan Opera House. The occasion was a benefit concert of the Musicians Symphony Orchestra. It was for this concert that Gershwin changed the title of his new work to the one by which it is now known, *Cuban Overture*. He explained: "When people read *Rhumba* they expect the 'Peanut Vendor' or a like piece of music. *Cuban Overture* gives a more just idea of the character and intent of the music." That concert was divided between César Franck and Gershwin. Franck's Symphony in D Minor was led by Sandor Harmati in the first half of the program. In the second, Daly conducted the Concerto in F (Gershwin, soloist) and his own transcription of four Gershwin songs; Gershwin conducted *An American in Paris* and *Cuban Overture*. This performance, with Gershwin seated at the piano, and with many of his intimate friends seated in the first row, has been caught permanently in a painting by Siqueiros.

This concert, incidentally, was the immediate cause of one of the severest attacks leveled against Gershwin's music. During the rehearsal of the four Gershwin songs, for which Daly had written the connecting transition passages besides orchestrating the whole, the trumpeter played a part of one of the transitions that puzzled Daly. He asked, "Did I write that there?" This question led one of the violists in the orchestra, William Lincoln Langley, to infer that Daly had had quite a hand in *all* of Gershwin's compositions. He wrote an article entitled "The Gershwin Myth" for the *American Spectator* (December 1932), a four-page monthly founded and edited by George Jean Nathan. Langley found that all of Gershwin's serious music was full of "blatant orchestrations" and "transparent anachronisms"; he called the Concerto "disgusting" and ended up by inferring that others—men like Grofé and Daly—did much of Gershwin's composing for him. "As for *An American in Paris*, the genial Daly was constantly in rehearsal attendance, both as repititeur and adviser, and any member of the orchestra could testify that he knew far more about the score than Gershwin.

The point is that no previous claimant of honors in symphonic composition has ever presented so much argument and controversy as to whether his work was his own or not."

Daly rushed to set Langley straight, in a letter to the New York *Times* (January 15, 1933): "I thank Mr. Langley for the compliment, but I neither wrote nor orchestrated the *American.* . . . I have never written one note of any of his compositions, or so much as orchestrated one whole bar of his symphonic works."

19

YOUNG MAN

WITH A PIANO

In 1933 George Gershwin moved from 33 Riverside Drive to new, more spacious, and more elegant quarters at 132 East 72nd Street. Ira and Leonore moved to an apartment across the street. The collaborators—formerly joined by a terrace—were now connected by a private telephone which enabled them to consult each other at any time of the day or night.

George's apartment was one befitting a man who was now a giant figure in American popular music, earning over $100,000 a year. It was a fourteen-room duplex, equipped with gymnasium, art studio, paneled reception room, English den, trunk room, a sleeping porch with jalousies, and a glass bar. The high-ceilinged living-room was a veritable art museum, with its collection of great paintings together with several examples of his own work, notably his portrait of his father. His study had a special desk which he had designed and had built for his work. It was wide enough to hold comfortably his large manuscript paper (printed expressly for him, with his name in the left corner) and had special drop-leafs, panels, a built-in pencil sharpener, and all sorts of compartments and racks for pencils, rulers, erasers, and so forth. (After George's death Ira presented this desk—and the four executors of the Rose Gershwin Estate, the manuscripts and sketchbooks of his serious works —to the Library of Congress in Washington, D.C., where they can now be seen.) The entire apartment was handsomely furnished along restrained modern lines and colors— by "one of our best decorators," as George always took pains to point out to a first-time visitor. He had by now outgrown the severe and formal modernity of the Riverside Drive place, and his apartment was filled with the traditional pieces which he liked.

The Sunday convocations of the Gershwin circle at 33 Riverside Drive now became Saturday night jamborees at George's new apartment. The scene and time might change; the proceedings, never. Here, as before, and wherever else George might be, the focal point of interest and activity was George playing his own music. It was something to hear. He had a beautiful singing tone, a sensitive touch, a sure instinct for rhythmic effect, and a glittering but precise technique. His use of the pedals was tellingly effective. The right and left hands were remarkably independent of each other, as he kept two different rhythms flowing evenly.

He had a unique way of using his thumb to bring out the color of a brass instrument. Chords were produced with a percussive, steel-like precision that was magnetizing. Serge Koussevitzky once described as "incredible" Gershwin's "sweeping brilliance, virtuosity, and rhythmic precision. . . . His dynamic influence on the orchestra and audience was electrifying." Other celebrated musicians—Fritz Kreisler, Efrem Zimbalist, Leopold Godowsky, Josef Hofmann, Leopold Auer, Jascha Heifetz, Maurice Ravel—could listen to him by the hour. Even those who did not know a chord from a glissando were held spellbound. The pity of it is that not more of that playing was permanently caught by the modern machine. Between 1916 and 1925, Gershwin made numerous piano rolls for Perfection, Universal, Standard, and Duo-Art which are now both obsolete and unavailable. And he made several recordings: the *Rhapsody in Blue*, which he played with the Paul Whiteman Orchestra for Victor; and an English Columbia record of the slow section of the *Rhapsody in Blue* and the three Preludes which is out of circulation. In the 1930s Gershwin made records of some of his songs, and some of these have been preserved in special reissues on long-playing records. (See Appendix 8.)

He was at his best, however, in the intimacy of a living-room—either his own or that of others—surrounded by his admirers and friends, and communicating to them through his music. He was always playing the piano at the slightest pretext (George S. Kaufman once remarked, "I'd bet on George any time—in a hundred yard dash to the piano"), because there were few things he liked to do more. "I have never seen a man happier, more bursting with the sheer joy of living than George was when he was playing his songs," recalls Bennett Cerf. "He would improvise and

introduce subtle variations and chuckle with childlike delight when his audiences exclaimed over them." His friends
used to say that an evening with Gershwin was always a
Gershwin evening; that Gershwin's music simply had to live
—just as long as Gershwin was around.

He was not long at a gathering before he drifted to
the piano, running his fingers casually across the keys the
way some men caress the hair of a beautiful woman, and then
slipped onto the stool and began playing for his own delight,
He would keep right on playing for the rest of the evening.
Before long, everybody's attention in the room would be fo-
cused on him, and every other activity stopped dead. It was
after a series of such impromptu concerts that Oscar Levant
was tempted to ask him acidly: "Tell me, George, if you had
to do it all over again—would you still fall in love with yourself?"

Combined with an extraordinary pianism was a no
less remarkable gift at improvisation. The modernist, Henry
Cowell, who at one time taught Gershwin counterpoint, says:
"He improvised on the piano with such security and facility
that it sounded like a written-down and memorized piece."
No two Gershwin performances were ever the same. He
would begin by throwing out the melody of one of his songs,
then catch the melody of another. "He would draw out a
lovely melody out of the keyboard like a golden thread,"
wrote Rouben Mamoulian, "then he would play with it and
juggle it, twist it and toss it around mischievously, weave it
into unexpected intricate patterns, tie it in knots and untie
it, and hurl it into a cascade of ever-changing rhythms and
counterpoints." His rhythms had the irresistible drive of a
bulldozer. At other times his poignant lyricism acquired the

delicate movement of a ballet dancer. Then he would pick up momentum. His imagination would roam without restriction. The left hand would produce novel harmonic colors. A canonic passage would suddenly leap into the pattern; an ingenious counterpoint would bring new dimensions to a stated idea. The melody in the right hand would plunge into an unexpected modulation and be off toward a new direction. New ideas would emerge; they, too, would grow and change like some living organism. This was no longer interpretation but creation. "As I watched him," wrote Koussevitzky, "I caught myself thinking, in a dream state, that this was a delusion, the enchantment of this extraordinary being too great to be real."

At the piano Gershwin not only made music; he was part of the music. He would perform a kind of restrained dance in which every part of his body participated. His face would become eloquently expressive. He would achieve a kind of exaltation as if he were suddenly the audience and not the performer or composer. Mamoulian put it well when he said: "George at the piano was George happy . . . like a gay sorcerer celebrating his Sabbath."

On the rare occasions that George yielded the piano stool to a rival composer, the newcomer would frequently fall into the swing of things by playing more Gershwin. Once Richard Rodgers found himself performing Gershwin, and the humor of the situation struck him midway in his performance. He stopped short and remarked, "Hell, I'll never earn a dime *this* way." There was a time when Gershwin invited a composer-friend to play his latest hit. George S. Kaufman commented, "If Gershwin wants to hear it, it's only because the song was stolen from him."

The Gershwin gatherings at East 72nd Street gave

Kaufman and Moss Hart the idea for the character of Sam
Frankel in *Merrily We Roll Along* (1934). Sam was a popular composer who played his own music at the slightest
provocation. And these gatherings were also in Moss Hart's
mind when, a year later, he wrote the book for Cole Porter's
Jubilee. There the celebrated hostess Eva Standing (by another name, Elsa Maxwell) provides a shocking novelty at
one of her parties: the presence of George Gershwin—but
without his playing the piano.

20

SOME BROADWAY

FAILURES — SOME SUCCESS

ELSEWHERE

If *Porgy and Bess* is regarded as an opera and not as a musical comedy, then Gershwin's last two musicals on Broadway came in 1933. Both were failures.

Pardon My English, which opened on January 20, was from the beginning a sorry misadventure for all concerned. Alex Aarons had signed Jack Buchanan and Lyda Roberti to exclusive contracts, guaranteeing the former $3,000 a week for eight weeks, and the latter $1,000 a week for a similar period. Aarons needed a show for them and—as he told his partner, Vinton Freedley—needed it quickly. Herbert Fields concocted a book involving a pair of actors who are confused with swindlers, and in which a kleptomaniac marries the daughter of the chief of police. Into this frame Fields fitted, as best he could, as strange and varied an assortment of accents as has been heard at one time on the American musical-comedy stage, involving Jack Buchanan (British), Lyda Roberti (Hungarian), Jack Pearl (German), and George Givot (Greek). Some of the gags were the kind that Jack ("Vas you dere, Sharlie") Pearl had popularized on his radio program as a modern Baron Munchausen: "I traveled to America on a ship with nine hundred chefs—it was a Cook's tour." The book fell flat on its face. Gershwin's score —one of the weakest in many years—provided little support. *Pardon My English* had to close in about a month, involving the producers in a deficit exceeding $75,000. Freedley fled to Panama to escape his creditors and stayed away for several months. The bitterness aroused by this disaster had one permanent result: it broke up the producing partnership of Aarons and Freedley. For Aarons this meant the end of his career on Broadway. He left for Hollywood, where he died a decade later. Just before his death he was associated with the impending Gershwin screen biography, *Rhapsody in Blue*. The circle had closed—Aarons ended as he had begun —with Gershwin's music. Freedley, on the other hand, did not delay in passing on to new victories, as producer of several smash-hit Cole Porter musicals, beginning with *Anything Goes* in 1934.

In this same year of 1933 many of those who had helped make *Of Thee I Sing* the historic occasion it was in the theater joined forces for a sequel entitled *Let 'Em Eat Cake*. Once again George S. Kaufman and Morrie Ryskind wrote the book; Ira, the lyrics; George, the music. Once again Sam H. Harris was the producer, and the principals in the cast were William Gaxton as Wintergreen, Lois Moran as Mary, and Victor Moore as Throttlebottom.

In *Let 'Em Eat Cake* Wintergreen and Throttlebottom run for election and are defeated. Wintergreen then heads a revolution to overthrow the government, recruiting an army with the aid of Union Square's Kruger (Philip Loeb). The revolution succeeds, and a dictatorship of the proletariat is set up. In the end, a critical international dispute is settled with a baseball game between nine members of the Supreme Court and nine foreign representatives of the League of Nations. Throttlebottom is the umpire. One of his unhappy decisions sends him to the guillotine which has been imported from France for this occasion. He is saved at the zero hour by Mary Wintergreen's quick thinking; he even becomes, at last, President, when the republic is restored.

There was much that was bright and witty and stinging: many needle-edged lines, many amusing episodes, some brilliant lyrics. A song like "Union Square" had the pungent flavor of the recipe used so successfully in *Of Thee I Sing*. Other moments also brought back to mind the high spots of the earlier play, as, for example, the opening scene, the Union League Scene, and "Comes the Revolution."

On the positive side was one of Gershwin's important songs—"Mine." This uses a vocal counterpoint for the main melody (a practice subsequently employed so effectively by Frank Loesser in "Baby, It's Cold Outside" and by Irving Berlin in "You're Just in Love"). The vocal counterpoint consisted of an amusing aside by the chorus:

> The point they're making in the song
> Is that they more than get along;

And he is not ashamed to say
She made him what he is today.

But a musical dish in which a left-wing revolution is successful was an unsavory meal, even in 1933. The picture of a dictatorship in America, a blue-shirt army, and Throttlebottom preparing to meet his doom at the guillotine hardly added spice to it. "Their hatreds have triumphed over their sense of humor," remarked Brooks Atkinson. *Newsweek* called the play "strained, dull, and dreary." *Let 'Em Eat Cake* failed to reach its hundredth performance on Broadway, and it did just as badly on a brief road tour.

The song "Mine" was originally written as an exercise for one of Gershwin's lessons with Joseph Schillinger. Schillinger, who died in 1943, was Gershwin's last teacher. A mutual friend—the composer-violinist, Joseph Achron—first told Gershwin of Schillinger's original theories of composition and suggested that Gershwin might profit from studying them. Gershwin began these studies with Schillinger in 1932 and continued on and off for almost four years.

The entire subject of Schillinger's influence on Gershwin has inspired so many claims and counterclaims, particularly since the composer's death, that it demands clarification.

Schillinger was a theorist who evolved a new approach to musical composition through the application of scientific methods. Feeling that all great works of music were constructed according to exact principles, Schillinger systematized the procedures of the great composers of the past and present. He also analyzed all the possibilities in melody, harmony, rhythm, orchestration and form, and in all known musical styles. Thus he evolved a system of exact techniques and procedures for the writing of music in any style and for any combination. Composition was reduced to mathematical formulas; effective creation was made possible through the application of these formulas and systematic patterns, and through use of graphs and slide rules. Schillinger once showed how a polyphonic composition in the style of Bach could be manufactured by tracing on graph paper the fluctuations of a business curve in the New York *Times*, and then translating the units of the graph into proportionate values in melodic and harmonic intervals. The text of his theories and their application was published posthumously in a two-volume edition: *The Schillinger System of Musical Composition* (1946). Among some popular composers and arrangers it has become something of a Bible. Courses in the Schillinger method have been given in several leading universities and conservatories.

Some excessive claims have been made, first by Schillinger himself, and after his death by the Schillinger Society, as to the influence of this method on Gershwin. In the preface to one of his texts, *Kaleidophone* (1940), Schillinger wrote:

> When the late George Gershwin . . . met me for the first time he was at a dead end of creative musical experiences. He felt his resources, not his abilities, were completely exhausted. . . . When we met, Gershwin said, "Here is my problem. I have written about seven hundred songs. I can't write anything any more. I am repeating myself. Can you help me?" I replied in the affirmative, and a day later Gershwin became a sort of

Alice in Wonderland. Later on he became acquainted with some of the material in this book by playing them through. "You don't have to compose music any more—it's all here," he remarked.

None of the close friends or associates who were continually with Gershwin during and after 1932 and who—since he was an open book about his creative processes and any problems confronting them—have every reason to know his most intimate reactions to his own work, can recall a single incident or remark to substantiate Schillinger's contention that, in 1932, Gershwin was "at a dead end of creative musical experience." Gershwin was such a fount of both musical ideas and enthusiasms all the time that it is impossible to conceive of his ever suffering creative sterility or fatigue at any time.

Schillinger, and the Schillinger Society, have maintained that whatever Gershwin wrote after 1932—particularly *Porgy and Bess*—was according to Schillinger processes. Schillinger himself communicated to this writer on October 20, 1942, this assertion: *"Porgy and Bess was written entirely under my supervision; it took a year and a half, at the rate of three lessons a week (which at the time consumed four-and-a-half hours)."*

These are the facts: Gershwin seized upon the Schillinger method with the delight of a precocious child coming upon a complicated network of electric trains. He always loved games of all sorts, and the Schillinger method became a kind of game with him. He was fascinated by the idea of composing by formula and was both startled and delighted to find that it worked well—to a certain degree. His keen and alert mind was stimulated by the intellectual processes involved. For a brief period he spoke continually to his friends and fellow-musicians about Schillinger, with the excitement of a man discovering a new world.

There is no doubt that Gershwin derived much stimulation from his lessons and exercises and that to a certain extent he strengthened his own technique with them. It is also true that he occasionally applied the Schillinger method to his own musical writing. This application can be found in sporadic scale passages (used as thematic material) in the *Cuban Overture,* in the *Variations on I Got Rhythm,* in passing choral incidents and in some of the storm music in *Porgy and Bess.* During the orchestration of his opera, Gershwin sought out and profited from Schillinger's advice.

But Gershwin discovered that though the Schillinger formulas might reinforce his technique they could never be a substitute for inspiration. His music after 1932 was written along the more formal and traditional creative procedures. Ira Gershwin made this emphatic point in a letter to *Newsweek* (October 23, 1946), in response to an article in which the Schillinger claims about Gershwin in general, and *Porgy and Bess* in particular, were put forward. "If the writer of the article wishes to give the impression that *Porgy and Bess* wouldn't have had quite the same value or integrity or acclaim if George hadn't studied say 'Rhythmic Groups Resulting from the Interference of Several Synchronized Periodicities,' with Schillinger, he is musically uninformed. Lessons like these unquestionably broaden musical horizons, but they don't inspire an opera like *Porgy and Bess.*

The year of 1934 was crowded with activity.

It began with an exhaustive tour of one-night stands with the Leo Reisman Orchestra, conducted by Charles Previn and with James Melton as soloist, in programs made up principally of Gershwin's music. Harry Askin, who had been company manager for *Miss 1917* and who had brought Gershwin to Max Dreyfus, was in charge. Previn had also had a long association with Gershwin, for he had been in the orchestra pit of *La, La Lucille* and later had been the conductor for *Of Thee I Sing;* he had also conducted Ira Gershwin's first musical-comedy success, *Two Little Girls in Blue.*

The tour opened in Boston on the afternoon of January 14, and ended at the Academy of Music, in Brooklyn, New York, on the evening of February 10. In a little less than a month, the company traveled 12,000 miles and performed in twenty-eight cities in as many days, going as far north as Toronto, as far south as Richmond, and as far west as Omaha. Gershwin conducted *An American in Paris* and was the piano soloist in the Concerto, the *Rhapsody in Blue,* and in a work written expressly for the tour, the *Variations on I Got Rhythm.* There were two groups of Gershwin songs, together with two groups of songs by other composers. After the formal program, long though it was, came another improvised one, with Gershwin playing numbers repeated by the audience.

The entire route provided testimony to the immense appeal of Gershwin's music, not only through the enthusiasm of audiences everywhere but also through the box-office receipts. With a top of $2.75, the tour grossed over $66,000, averaging approximately $4,000 gross for most of the concerts. It would have done even better if the itinerary had not included seven stops that were too small to support such an expensive undertaking. These stops, and the long jumps between concerts, were responsible for creating a deficit for the entire project, despite the almost universally sold-out audito-

riums. Gershwin, who had been persuaded to be a partner in
the tour, received nothing except his fare and hotel expenses,
and had to contribute $5,000 to the deficit.

The tour demonstrated something else, too: Gershwin's remarkable stamina and physical indestructibility, notwithstanding his own tendency to regard himself as a sick
man. He took in stride not only the ordeal of continual travel
but also the more formidable demands made upon him by
twenty-eight concert appearances in twenty-nine days in an
exhausting program. Seeing him after the Brooklyn concert,
friends were amazed to discover that the exhilaration and
excitement he had brought to the tour at its inception had
not lost much of their edge for him. There was, to be sure, a
certain amount of fatigue, though not too much of that. But
there was nothing jaded or effete about him now that he had
come to the end of the long road. It was felt by many then
that he would have been ready and willing—he might even
have relished—continuing the tour the next morning with another twenty-eight one-night stands.

The *Variations on I Got Rhythm*—whose world première took place at the Boston concert on January 14—was
written mostly during a vacation in Palm Beach in December
1933, where Gershwin was a guest of Emil Mosbacher. It
was completed in New York on January 6, 1934. The work
represented an effort on his part to put on paper and formal-
ize some of the more salient ideas he had so often developed
for his friends while improvising for them on "I Got
Rhythm." While the *Variations*, as it now stands, does not
have the combustible heat and spontaneity that made Gershwin's extemporizations so exciting, it does provide the present generation with at least a glimpse at his powers of improvisation.

The work is scored for full symphony orchestra, E-flat and B-flat saxophones, banjo, and Chinese gong. It opens with a four-note ascending phrase from the first measure of the "I Got Rhythm" chorus given by the solo clarinet. The theme is passed on to solo piano, then to full orchestra. At last the solo piano presents the song (chorus only) in its entirety. The variations that follow demonstrate Gershwin's remarkable progress in the science of developing and altering a stated theme. He changes not only its basic structure, melodically and rhythmically, but also its mood and feeling. The first variation is a release of animal energy; in the second, the theme suddenly becomes a melancholy dirge. In other variations the melody grows muscular and aggressive; or it is as festive as a New Orleans Mardi Gras, with the orchestration a veritable pyrotechnical display of fireworks and the piano a glittering cascade of whirling figures; or it is a poignant and deep-throated blues melody.

With the ambitious tour over, Gershwin did not wait long to embark on still another project. On February 19 he inaugurated a sponsored radio program. For the next few months "Music by Gershwin" (with "The Man I Love" as the theme song) presented him over WJZ every Monday and Friday evening from 7:30 to 7:45 in the varied role of genial master of ceremonies, conductor, composer, and pianist. For this chore he received $2,000 a week.

This radio series was not his first appearance before a radio microphone. His radio debut had taken place on the Ever-Ready Hour over WEAF on December 14, 1926, when he played some of his songs and a part of his Concerto (without orchestra). Following this he had been a guest performer on various programs: the Rudy Vallee program, the Ted

Weems show, the American Telephone and Telegraph radio hour, and as a soloist under Walter Damrosch. But "Music by Gershwin" was his first radio show, and he made the most of the opportunities it offered him to play his music, conduct it, and talk about it. Much to Gershwin's credit, and characteristic of the man, he also used these programs as a forum for the presentation of some of the best popular music of other composers, and more important still he frequently gave a hearing to unknown composers. Among those who were still comparatively unknown when Gershwin introduced them on the air were Harold Arlen, Rube Bloom, Dana Suesse, and Oscar Levant. The following October Gershwin returned to the radio for a second series: this time he had a weekly half-hour program, every Sunday at 6:00 P.M. over WABC.

In some ways Gershwin found his radio duties more taxing and exacting than his road tour. As he explained, when he traveled with the orchestra he had only a single program to give. Since it had been carefully rehearsed beforehand, all he had to do was go through the motions. But a regular once-a-week or twice-a-week stint over the radio meant the continual preparation of new programs and never ceasing rehearsals as well as the mass of details involved in selecting songs by other composers and guest artists.

Nevertheless, in the midst of all this he found both the time and energy to begin working intensively on his greatest serious composition, the opera *Porgy and Bess*.

21

Porgy and Bess

The idea of writing an opera continued to haunt Gershwin, and he knew he would have no peace of mind until he did it. He had long since decided that his text would be DuBose Heyward's *Porgy*, but it had been several years since he had discussed the project with the author. But on March 29, 1932, he suddenly wrote to Heyward: "In thinking of ideas for compositions, I came back to the one that I had several years ago—namely *Porgy*—and the thought of setting it to music. It is still the most outstanding play that I know about colored people." Heyward replied by re-affirming his interest in the opera.

But even now Gershwin kept on postponing the actual writing, for there were various commitments he had to fulfill. He probably would have delayed the opera indefinitely —always choosing some assignment that needed doing right *now*, and pushing off *Porgy* further into the future—if his hand had not suddenly been forced. One day in 1933 Heyward called him to say that the Theatre Guild was pressing him for permission to allow Jerome Kern and Oscar Hammerstein II (the authors of *Show Boat*) to adapt *Porgy* into a musical for Al Jolson. It seems that Jolson, too, had long expressed an interest in the play for himself, and had even used a part of it for one of his broadcasts. Gershwin told Heyward that he was reluctant to stand in the way of Heyward's accepting a deal that gave every indication of becoming a tremendous box-office attraction and that his own opera could easily wait a few years more. Heyward countered by insisting that he was not interested in money; he wanted *Porgy* to become a folk opera not a musical comedy. "I want you to tell me if you are really going to write that opera—and *soon*," Heyward continued. "If you are, I'm going to turn the Guild down definitely." Gershwin thought a moment, then said he would begin working without any more delays. And he kept his word.

There now ensued a lively and continuous exchange of correspondence between Heyward and Gershwin as they discussed how the Dorothy and DuBose Heyward play could be made into a suitable opera. Almost half had to be cut away, while drastic revisions had to be made in the dialogue to make it acceptable for the operatic stage; besides there was the additional task of writing lyrics for the songs.

Heyward has written:

> At the outset we were faced by a difficult problem. I was firm in my refusal to leave the South and live in

New York. Gershwin was bound for the duration of his contract to the microphone at Radio City. The matter of effecting a happy union between words and music across a thousand miles of Atlantic seaboard baffled us for a moment. The solution came naturally when we associated Ira Gershwin with us. Frequently we evolved a system by which, between my visits North, or George's dash to Charleston, I could send scenes and lyrics. Then the brothers Gershwin, after their extraordinary fashion, would get at the piano, pound, wrangle, sweat, burst into weird snatches of song, and eventually emerge with a polished lyric.

The following exchange is typical of their correspondence over a period of many months as the libretto began taking shape:

Follywood,
Folly Beach,
So. Ga.
Feb. 6, 34

DEAR GEORGE:

I know you will be eager to see more of the script, so I am sending the next two scenes herewith. I have about completed the next scene also, but it is not yet typed, and I want to do a little more work on it.

Act 2, Scene 1 may still seem a little long to you, but I have reduced it from 39 pages in the talking script to 18 for the opera, and it is strong on humor and action. Let me know how you feel about it and if you think it needs more lyrics.

Act 2, Scene 2 ought to be good. I have cut out the conventional Negro vaudeville stuff that was in the original play and incorporated material that is authentic and plenty "hot" as well. I have discovered for the first time a type of secular dance that is done there that is straight from the African phallic dance, and that is undoubtedly a complete survival. Also I have seen that native band of harmonics, combs, etc. It will make an extraordinary introduction to the primitive scene of passion between Crown and Bess.

I think maybe the composition on the lyrics I have done better wait until we get together. I have in mind something for them but I cannot well suggest it by writing, especially the boat song. But don't let that stop you, if you feel moved with ideas of your own. . . .

Affectionate greetings and all good wishes from us all.

Sincerely,
DuBose

26 February 1934

DEAR DuBose:

I received your Second Act's script and think it is fine. I really think you are doing a magnificent job with the new libretto and I hope I can match it musically.

I have begun composing music for the First Act and I am starting with the songs and spirituals first.

I am hoping you will find some time to come up North and live at my apartment—if it is convenient for you—so we can work together on some of the spirituals for Scene 2, Act 1. . . .

Hoping you and your wife and child are 100% well and looking forward to seeing you soon, I am,

> As ever,
> GEORGE G.

Folly Beach, S.C.
March 2, 1934

DEAR GEORGE:

I was very glad to hear from you. . . .

As for the script from now on, I am sort of at a deadlock. The storm scene must stand about as is with very few cuts in dialogue. Musically it must be done when we are together. It must carry itself on the big scene when Crown sings against a spiritual, and I can't do the lyrics until I get your ideas as to time. Then I am doing a lyric for Porgy just before the curtain as he gets ready to drive out for Bess. Have you any thoughts about any of this last section of the play?

8 March 1934

DEAR DuBOSE:

I was happy to get your letter with the 3rd Scene of Act II enclosed. I think it is a very interesting and touching scene, although a bit on the long side. However, I see one or two places that do not seem terribly important to the action and which could be cut. You must make sure that the opera is not too long as I am a great believer in not giving people too much of a good thing and I am sure you agree with this. . . .

I would like to write the song that opens the 2nd Act, sung by Jake with the fish nets, but I don't know the rhythm you had in mind—especially for the answers of the chorus, so I would appreciate it if you would put dots and dashes over the lyric and send it to me. . . .

I am looking forward to seeing you next month. Hoping you and your family are well, I am,

Sincerely,
GEORGE

The Metropolitan Opera still hoped to have an opera by Gershwin, and it was interested in *Porgy*. Otto H. Kahn even proposed giving Gershwin a bonus of $5,000 if he signed a contract with the Metropolitan Opera. While Gershwin was flattered by the offer and grateful for it, he felt any arrangement with the Metropolitan over *Porgy* would be highly impractical. He did not relish having his opera performed three or four times for one or two seasons and then being thrown into discard—the fate of most new operas performed there. He wanted *Porgy* to reach a large audience of Americans, rather than a limited opera public. Most important of all, he felt strongly that this opera should be performed by a cast made up mostly of Negroes, and this, of course, was out of the question at the Metropolitan.

When, therefore, contracts were signed for *Porgy* it was with the Theatre Guild, which had produced the play. The signing took place on October 26, 1933. "It's going to be a labor of love," Gershwin wrote a friend as soon as the deal was consummated, "and I expect quite a few labor pains with it."

In December 1933 Gershwin went to Charleston to discuss with Heyward further details of the opera and to get the "feel" of the city which was the locale and setting of the opera. "I would like to see the town," he said, "and

hear some spirituals, and perhaps go to a colored café or two
if there are any." Two weeks later, on his way back to New
York from Florida, he once again paid a brief visit to Charleston.

But a much more extended stay in South Carolina was
possible during the summer of 1934. Then Gershwin and his
cousin Henry Botkin—who was at the time painting Negro
subjects—entrained for the South, preceded by a car
filled with baggage and art equipment. They settled on Folly
Island, a small barrier island ten miles from Charleston, and
occupied a screen-porched shack near the waterfront. It was a
primitive existence. Their rooms were crude, with an old iron
bed, a small wash basin, and decaying furniture. Their drinking water had to be brought in from Charleston. Gershwin's
room had an old-fashioned upright piano. There they lived—
under a scorching sun—through July and August. They visited numerous plantations, churches, and other Negro places
in an avid search for musical materials and subjects for painting.

DuBose Heyward has vividly described the impact
that this visit made on Gershwin:

> James Island with its large population of primitive
> Gullah Negroes lay adjacent, and furnished us with a
> laboratory in which to test our theories, as well as an
> inexhaustible source of folk material. But the interesting
> discovery to me, as we sat listening to their spirituals, or
> watched a group shuffling before a cabin or country store,
> was that to George it was more like a homecoming than
> an exploration. The quality in him which had produced
> the *Rhapsody in Blue* in the most sophisticated city in
> America, found its counterpart in the impulse behind the

music and bodily rhythms of the simple Negro peasant of the South.

The Gullah Negro prides himself on what he calls "shouting." This is a complicated rhythmic pattern beaten out by feet and hands as an accompaniment to the spirituals, and is undoubtedly of African survival. I shall never forget the night when, at a Negro meeting on a remote sea island, George started "shouting" with them. And eventually to their huge delight stole the show from their champion "shouter." I think that he is probably the only white man in America who could have done that.*

Another night, as we were about to enter a dilapidated cabin that had been taken as a meeting house by a group of Negro Holy Rollers, George caught my arm and held me. The sound that had arrested him was the one to which, through long familiarity, I attached no special importance. But now, listening to it with him, and noticing the excitement, I began to catch its extraordinary quality. It consisted of perhaps a dozen voices raised in loud rhythmic prayer. The odd thing about it was that while each had started at a different time, upon a different theme, they formed a clearly defined rhythmic pattern, and that this, with the actual words lost, and the inevitable pounding of the rhythm, produced an effect almost terrifying in its primitive intensity. Inspired by the extraordinary effect, George wrote six simultaneous prayers producing a terrifying primitive invocation to God in the face of the hurricane.

---

* In the spring of 1938, after Gershwin's death, Kay Swift visited Folly Island and spoke to the Negroes there about Gershwin. Many remembered his visit vividly, and spoke with renewed excitement of the way he was able to join them in their "shouts" and become one of them.

The opera occupied Gershwin about twenty months. Most of the actual composition was done in about eleven months and was completed in mid-April 1935. While some of the orchestration for the first act had been done in September 1934, that task consumed about eight months in 1935. Part of the orchestration was done in Palm Beach in February of that year; part, at Mosbacher's home in White Plains that spring; part, at Ocean Beach on Fire Island (off Long Island) where Ira and Leonore Gershwin rented a house with Moss Hart during the summer; part, in New York City the same summer. The actual date of completion—it appears at the end of the last page of the manuscript—was September 2, 1935, but revisions continued throughout the rehearsal period and even up to opening night. During the exacting and all-consuming labor of putting his opera down on paper, Gershwin was continually assisted by Kay Swift, Joseph Schillinger, and Stephan Zoltai, a copyist.

Then it was completed: seven hundred neat and compact pages of written music (560 pages of the published vocal score), which would require four-and-a-half hours if performed as written. The name *Porgy and Bess* was on the title page. Gershwin had decided that to call the opera *Porgy* would create an inevitable confusion between the play and his opera and that a title like *Porgy and Bess* was in the operatic tradition of *Tristan und Isolde* and *Pelléas et Mélisande*.

Rouben Mamoulian, who had directed the original stage production of *Porgy* for the Theatre Guild, was chosen to direct the opera as well. He was in Hollywood when he signed his contract, and at that time he had not even seen or heard a note of the music. But on his first evening in New York he visited Gershwin's apartment and there heard the complete score. He recalls:

It was rather amusing how all three of us [George, Ira, Mamoulian] were trying to be nonchalant and poised that evening, yet we were trembling with excitement. The brothers handed me a tall highball and put me in a comfortable leather armchair. George sat down at the piano while Ira stood over him like a guardian angel. George's hands went up in the air about to strike the shining keys. Halfway down he changed his mind, turned to me, and said, "Of course, Rouben, you must understand, it's very difficult to play this score. As a matter of fact it's really impossible! Can you play Wagner on the piano? Well this is like Wagner!" I assured George that I understood. Up went his nervous hands again and the next second I was listening to the opening "piano music" in the opera. I found it so exciting, so full of color and so provocative in its rhythms that after this first piano section was over, I jumped out of my armchair and interrupted George to tell him how much I liked it. Both brothers were as happy as children to hear words of praise, though heavens knows, they should have been used to them by then. When my explosion was over and they went back to the piano, they both blissfully closed their eyes before they continued with the lovely "Summertime" song. George played with the most beatific smile on his face. He seemed to float on the waves of his own music with the Southern sun shining on him. Ira sang—he threw his head back with abandon, his eyes closed, and sang like a nightingale. In the middle of the song George couldn't bear it any longer and took over the singing from him. To describe George's face as he sang "Summertime" is something beyond my capacity as a writer. "Nirvana" might be the word. So it went on. George was the orchestra and played the parts. Ira sang the other half. Ira was also frequently the "audience." It was touching to see how he, while singing, would become so overwhelmed with admiration for his brother, that he would look from him to me with half-open eyes and pantomime with a soft gesture of the hand, as if saying, "*He* did it. Isn't it wonderful. Isn't *he* wonderful?" George would frequently take his eyes away from the score and watch me covertly and my reaction to the music, while pretending he wasn't really doing it at all. It was very late into the night before we finished with the opera. . . . We all felt exultantly happy. The next morning both George and Ira had completely lost their voices. For two days they couldn't talk; they only whispered. I shall never forget that evening—the enthusiasm of the two brothers about the music, their anxiety to do it justice, their joy at its being appreciated and with it all their touching devotion for each other. It is one of those rare tender memories one so cherishes in life.

The state of euphoria in which Gershwin played his score for Mamoulian was one into which he invariably succumbed whenever he played or listened to his opera. In the Arthur Schwartz–Howard Dietz revue *At Home Abroad,* in which Beatrice Lillie was starred in 1935, Gershwin appeared as a marionette who sang to the tune of "I Got Rhythm": "I wrote *Porgy*—who could ask for anything more?" This scene reflected rather than satirized Gershwin's reaction to his own opera. Its writing had been, as he had anticipated, a labor of love, and to it he brought an exhilaration and excitement unique even for him. Once the opera was written, he never quite ceased to wonder at the miracle that *he* had been its composer. He knew it was his greatest work. While he was partial to each of his earlier serious compositions, this was the first one that satisfied him completely. He never stopped loving each and every bar; never wavered in the conviction that he had produced a work of art. After the first rehearsal (which, like most first rehearsals, had gone rather badly) he telephoned Mamoulian to tell him how "thrilled" and "delighted" he was. "I always knew that *Porgy and Bess* was wonderful," he told Mamoulian with his directness and ingenuousness, "but I never thought I'd feel the way I feel now. I tell you, after listening to that rehearsal today I think the music is so marvelous I really don't believe I wrote it."

He was so completely absorbed with his opera, so convinced of its significance, that he expected everybody else to be similarly affected. Mamoulian tells of a revealing incident at Lindy's (a Broadway restaurant frequented mostly by theater people) right after one of the rehearsals. During the meal, Mamoulian whistled a snatch from Rimsky-Korsakov. Gershwin was immediately upset. "How can you be humming some Russian melody when you have just been rehearsing *my* music all day?" he asked with obvious pique. But the depression disappeared and his face lit up as a thought came to him. "I know why you hummed that Russian music —it's because *my* parents came from Russia."

During the rehearsal period he thought, breathed, dreamed, and played *Porgy and Bess* all the time; nothing and nobody else was of even secondary interest. At one point during the rehearsals—when the music was beginning to drive everybody to distraction—Gershwin suggested to Mamoulian and several others connected with the production that they all go out to Long Island for a week-end "to forget completely about *Porgy and Bess*." The suggestion was wel-

comed warmly. When they returned from this three-day excursion, Mamoulian was asked what they did all the time. He
answered wearily: "Can't you guess? From morning to night,
for the three days, George was at the piano, playing the music
from *Porgy*."

The Theatre Guild had also immediately contracted
Alexander Smallens as conductor, Alexander Steinert as the
coach for the singers, and Serge Soudekeine as scenic
designer. The grueling process of selecting a cast followed.
Assembling a practically all-Negro cast presented formidable
limitations, since few Negroes had extensive opera-house experience and new singers had to be discovered. Hundreds of
auditions followed, and out of them came the two principals,
Todd Duncan and Anne Brown. Duncan was teaching music
courses at Howard University in Washington, D.C., when
he was sent to Gershwin by a mutual friend to audition for
the role of Porgy. Duncan sang for Gershwin highly classical
arias like Sacchi's *"Lungi dal caro bene."* His manner was
stiff, but his voice had such beautiful texture and was pro-
jected so easily and fluidly that Gershwin arranged a second
audition with the producers present, and he was instantly engaged. Anne Brown came to Gershwin without benefit of any
introduction. She came to his apartment one day asking to
be heard, since she had been told that Gershwin was looking
for a Bess. She sang both spirituals and pieces from the classical repertory. She, too, revealed her inexperience in her self-
consciousness, but she sang well enough for Gershwin to realize at once that his search for a Bess had ended.
The choice of John W. Bubbles as Sportin' Life also
represented an act of discovery on the part of Gershwin, even
though Bubbles, as the partner of Buck, was a tap dancer

with a long and successful career in vaudeville. But Bubbles as an opera singer was something else again, particularly since he could not read a note of music and seemed incapable of learning to sing with any degree of accuracy as to pitch, tempo, or rhythm. For example, he simply could not learn how to sing the slow triplets in "It Ain't Necessarily So" the way Gershwin wanted; finally Steinert hit upon the happy idea of tap-dancing the rhythm for him, and only then did Bubbles understand what was wanted from him. Training Bubbles in other songs and in the recitatives was an ordeal to try the patience of a saint. There was one day when Gershwin lost his temper and wanted to fire him, and was only restrained from doing so by Mamoulian. However, the effort expended on Bubbles paid off rich dividends. His character-ization of Sportin' Life was one of the freshest and most un-forgettable performances of the production, both in the way he used his restless dancing feet and in his personal manner of half-chanting his part. Gershwin often spoke of him affec-tionately as "my Bubbles" with the justifiable pride of a Pygmalion who has fashioned his Galatea.

One of the many problems Gershwin had to solve was the fact that many of the singers in the cast, having had training in serious music, were intent on covering up any Ne-groid qualities in their singing and speech. Gershwin, on the other hand, was insistent on accentuating the Negro inflec-tion in music and diction. With his protruding full lips and whining voice he seemed more Negro than many members of the cast as he stood on the stage and sang for them the music the way he wanted it to sound.

It was not all trial and pain, however. Other moments of the rehearsals came when the genius of the opera shone with a blinding light to dazzle all those present. Todd Duncan describes such a moment:

> One day we were in the midst of hard work in Serena's Prayer Scene, he [Gershwin] walked in and immediately disappeared into the back of the dark theater where he quietly took his seat. The director, Mamoulian, was working like mad with the actors, setting the entrances, positions, the music, and the action. This is a very quiet scene, one of profound religious fervor. We singers were very tired, tired enough fortunately to set up the exact atmosphere for the prayer. It must have been our tenth consecutive trial. . . . Miss Elzy [Serena] went down on her knees. Two seconds of silence intervened that seemed like hours, and presently there rose the most glorious tones and wails with accompanying amens and hallelujahs for our sick Bess that I ever hope to experience. This particular scene should have normally moved into the scene of the Street Cries, but it did not. It stopped there. The piano accompaniment ceased, every actor (and there were sixty-five of them) had come out of his rest position, sitting at the edge of his seat and Rouben Mamoulian was standing before us quietly moving his inevitable cigar from one side of his mouth to the other, his face lighted to sheer delight in realization, and then, George Gershwin, like a ghost from the dark rows of the Guild Theater appeared before the footlights. He simply could not stand it.

As the rehearsals continued, heading toward the fateful première, cuts had to be made in order to compress the opera within the prescribed limits of a normal evening at the theater. These cuts hurt Gershwin, who loved every note; but, showman that he was, he accepted them willingly and often insisted on them. Slices were taken out of the opening scene —the sinuous dance and chant of the Negroes that precedes "Summertime," from Maria's reading in the second act, and from the last scene trio. After the Boston opening, Porgy's effective "Buzzard Song" and other of his passages in the third act were removed at Gershwin's suggestion. "If we don't," he told Ira, "you won't have a Porgy by the time we reach New York. No one can sing that much eight perform-ances a week."

And then the opera was ready. About a week before its première in Boston, a final run-through of the entire score —but without action, sets, scenery, or costumes—was made at Carnegie Hall before a handful of Gershwin's most inti-mate friends and closest associates. "In some ways," recalls Henry Botkin, "I think it was the most beautiful performance of *Porgy and Bess* I ever heard. Without the distractions of the stage, the music itself became a profound and moving experience that stirred everybody listening to it to the very depths of their being."

Porgy and Bess opened at the Colonial Theater in Bos-ton on September 30, 1935, with the following cast: Todd Duncan, Porgy; Anne Brown, Bess; Ruby Elzy, Serena; John W. Bubbles, Sportin' Life; Ford L. Buck, Mingo; Abbie Mitchell, Clara; Edward Matthews, Jake; Georgette Harvey, Maria; Helen Dowdy, Lily; Henry Davis, Robbins; Warren Coleman, Crown; J. Rosamond Johnson, Frazier; and the Eva Jessye Choir.

The audience began early to demonstrate its enthusi-asm and by the time the opera ended the ovation reached such proportions that the shouts and cries lasted over fifteen minutes. When George Gershwin, Rouben Mamoulian, and Alexander Smallens appeared on the stage—and were embraced by the principals in the cast—pandemonium was let loose in the theater. The excitement infected all of those present. S. N. Behrman was beside himself. "It's immense," he said. "It should be played in every country of the world—except Hitler's Germany—it doesn't deserve it." When Sigmund Spaeth approached George Gershwin he had tears in his eyes. "Hey, look," Gershwin remarked to a friend, "we've got the old doc crying." Serge Koussevitzky, who almost never descended from his cloistered refuge in the Jamaica Plain section of Boston (except when he had to conduct the concerts of the Boston Symphony Orchestra) was also present. "It's a great advance in American opera," he said, "and one of the greatest." J. Rosamond Johnson told Gershwin simply, "You're the Abraham Lincoln of Negro music." Eva Gauthier a few days earlier had given Gershwin the birthday gift of a score of Monteverdi's *Orfeo* inscribed, "the first opera ever written to the composer of the latest opera"; and she, with Cole Porter, Irving Berlin, and Roland Hayes expressed unqualified enthusiasm. Gershwin's own reaction to his opera might have been expected, "It sounded exactly as I thought it would sound when I wrote it."

There was a virtually unanimous acclaim in the Boston newspapers. Moses Smith wrote in the *Transcript*: "It is unique. Is there another American composer for the lyric stage who exhibits at once such eclecticism and individuality? . . . He has traveled a long way from Tin Pan Alley to this opera. He must now be accepted as a serious composer." The drama critic for the same paper, Edwin F. Melvin, said: "The composer has put together something that has dramatic intensity and power, with songs, dances, and racial humors that seem to spring naturally from the place and the people. . . . Opera as it is set forth in *Porgy and Bess* can become a cause for popular rejoicing." Elinor Hughes wrote in the *Herald*: "It was an interesting, often striking event. . . . *Porgy and Bess* is a folk opera, American opera, and at the same time it is the play, fortified and enlarged." In the *Christian Science Monitor,* L. A. Sloper regarded it "easily as Gershwin's most important contribution to music."

Two weeks later, on the evening of October 10, *Porgy and Bess* came to New York, to the Alvin Theater. Once again the audience—a virtual Who's Who of Broadway, Tin Pan Alley, Hollywood, and Carnegie Hall—was heatedly demonstrative. But the critics the next day were divided in their judgment. Generally speaking, it was the leading drama critics who gave a strongly positive verdict. Brooks Atkinson wrote, "Mr. Gershwin has contributed something glorious to the spirit of Heyward's community legend." John Mason Brown said, "Unless my untrained ears deceive me it contains some of the loveliest music he has written. Its idiom is the idiom of spirituals and of Harlem. But he crossed them so that . . . it succeeds at most times in being compellingly dramatic."

The music critics were far less impressed than their dramatic colleagues. Olin Downes liked some of the parts, but the whole left him cold. "It does not utilize all the resources of the operatic composer or pierce very often to the depths of the pathetic drama. . . . The style is at one moment of opera and another of operetta or sheer Broadway entertainment." Lawrence Gilman, on the other hand, felt that the individual parts were deficits. "Perhaps it is needlessly

Draconian to begrudge Mr. Gershwin the song hits which he has scattered through the score and which will doubtless enhance his fame and popularity. Yet they mar it. They are cardinal weaknesses. They are the blemishes upon its musical integrity. Listening to such sure-fire rubbish as the duet between Porgy and Bess, 'You Is My Woman Now' . . . you wonder how the composer . . . could stoop to such easy and such needless conquests." Virgil Thomson described the opera as a "fake" in *Modern Music* (November-December 1935); "It is crooked folklore and halfway opera, a strong but crippled work. . . . *Porgy* is falsely conceived and rather clumsily executed." To Paul Rosenfeld, in *Discoveries of a Music Critic,** the opera was "an aggrandized musical show. . . . The score sustains no mood. There is neither a progressive nor an enduring tension to it. The individual numbers spurt from a flat level, and ending, leave one largely where they picked one up. Nor do they communicate a reality. . . . It would seem as if Gershwin knew chiefly stage Negroes and that he very incompletely felt the drama of the two protagonists." Even Samuel Chotzinoff—always ready to accept everything Gershwin wrote—had reservations: "As entertainment it is hybrid, fluctuating constantly between music drama, musical comedy, and operetta. . . . The score contains pages of beautiful and original music but the interruptions of the facile and the inconsequential are too frequent to give to the work the true aspect of homogeneity."

There were always gala parties after important Gershwin premières, and there was one after *Porgy and Bess*—at the home of Condé Nast at 1040 Park Avenue. The entire cast was present to repeat highlights from the opera, and Paul

---

* *Discoveries of a Music Critic*, by Paul Rosenfeld. New York: Harcourt, Brace & Co., 1936.

Whiteman brought his orchestra to perform the *Rhapsody in Blue* with Gershwin at the piano. A large silver tray, engraved with one hundred and fifty signatures of George's closest friends and most ardent admirers, was presented to the composer (it now decorates a coffee table in Ira Gershwin's living room).

The half-hearted response of New York's music critics did not shake Gershwin's own enthusiasm and complete faith. He returned frequently to the Alvin Theater—sometimes as often as four times a week—and stood in the back listening. Nor did he experience serious disappointment that *Porgy and Bess* had the comparatively unimpressive run of 124 performances. He looked upon it this way: if, say, an opera like *Die Meistersinger* was given about six times a season at the Metropolitan Opera, then the 124 performances of *Porgy and Bess* represented a run of over twenty years for a great opera house.

It had cost about $17,000 a week to keep *Porgy and Bess* running, and the box office lagged far behind this figure both in New York and during a three-month tour that followed the New York closing. George, Ira, and DuBose Heyward lost the $5,000 investment each had made in the production. George earned $10,000 in royalties, but he had spent more than that in copyist fees. DuBose and Dorothy Heyward divided $8,000, and Ira received $2,000.

During the three-month tour, Alexander Steinert took over the baton from Smallens as the company played in Detroit, Pittsburgh, Chicago, and Washington, D.C. During the run in the nation's capital, *Porgy and Bess* helped to shape social history. For the first time in a century racial barriers were dropped at the National Theater for performances of the opera, and Negroes were accorded their rights as American citizens to attend performances without the indignity of segregation.

Gershwin revealed and clarified his methods and approaches in writing his folk opera in the New York *Times:*

> When I first began work on the music I decided against the use of original folk material because I wanted the music to be all of one piece. Therefore I wrote my own spirituals and folk songs. But they are still folk music—and therefore, being in operatic form, *Porgy and Bess* becomes a folk opera.
>
> However, because *Porgy and Bess* deals with Negro life in America it brings to the operatic form elements that have never before appeared in opera and I have adapted my method to utilize the drama, the humor, the superstition, the religious fervor, the dancing, and the irrepressible high spirits of the race. If, in doing this, I have created a new form which combines opera with the theater, this new form has come quite naturally out of the material. . . .
>
> It is my idea that opera should be entertaining— that it should contain all the elements of entertainment. Therefore, when I chose *Porgy and Bess,* a tale of Charleston Negroes, for a subject, I made sure that it would enable me to write light as well as serious music and that it would enable me to include humor as well as tragedy— in fact, all the elements of entertainment for the eye as well as the ear, because the Negroes, as a race, have all these qualities inherent in them. They are ideal for my purpose because they express themselves not only by the spoken word but quite naturally by song and dance.

Humor is an important part of American life, and an American opera without humor could not possibly run the gamut of American expression. In *Porgy and Bess* there are ample opportunities for humorous songs and dances. This humor is natural humor—not "gags" superimposed upon the story, but humor flowing from the story itself. For instance, the character of Sportin' Life, instead of being a sinister dope-peddler, is a humorous dancing villain, who is likable and believable and at the same time evil. . . .

I have written my music to be an integral part of the story. It is true that I have written songs for *Porgy and Bess*. I am not ashamed of writing songs at any time so long as they are good songs. In *Porgy and Bess* I realized I was writing an opera for the theater and without songs it could be neither of the theater nor entertaining, from my point of view.

But songs are entirely within the operatic tradition. . . . Of course, the songs in *Porgy and Bess* are only a part of the whole. The recitative I have tried to make as close to the Negro inflection in speech as possible, and I believe my song writing apprenticeship has served invaluably in this respect, because the song writers of America have the best conception of how to set words to music so that the music gives added expression to the words. I have used sustained symphonic music to unify entire scenes, and I prepared myself for that task by further study in counterpoint and modern harmony.

In the lyrics for *Porgy and Bess* I believe that Mr. Heyward and my brother, Ira, have achieved a fine synchronization of diversified moods—Mr. Heyward writing most of the native material and Ira doing most of the

sophisticated songs. . . . There is the prayer in the storm
scene written by Mr. Heyward; and in contrast there is
Ira's song for Sportin' Life in the picnic scene. Then
there is Mr. Heyward's lullaby that opens the opera; and,
again, Ira's song for Sportin' Life in the last act, "There's
a Boat That's Leavin' Soon for New York."

All of these are, I believe, lines that come naturally
from the Negro. They make for folk music. Thus *Porgy
and Bess* becomes a folk opera—opera for the theater,
with drama, humor, song, and dance.

It is the folk element that is the strong suit of the
opera,* rather than the outpouring of unforgettable songs and
duets. Like another great national opera—Mussorgsky's *Boris
Godunov*—the chief protagonist is no single character, not
Porgy or Bess in the Gershwin opera nor the Tsar Boris
in Mussorgsky's. Mussorgsky's masterwork is first and foremost a mighty drama of the Russian people, particularly of
the lower strata of Russian society. Gershwin's opera is an
epic of Negroes, mostly a picture of the lower depths of Negro life. The tragic love of Porgy and Bess is incidental to the
humor and pathos, the emotional turbulence, the psychological and social maladjustments, the naïveté and childlike ter-
ror, the violence and tenderness of the much-abused Negro
in a Southern city.

To portray this people in all the varied facets of its
personality, Gershwin made extensive use of musical
materials basic to the Negro people. His recitatives are
molded after the inflections of Negro speech. His songs are
grounded either in Negro folk music or in those American

* For a detailed plot of *Porgy and Bess,* together with its principal
numbers, see Appendix 1.

popular idioms that sprang out of Negro backgrounds. His street cries simulate those of Negro vendors in Charleston. His choral pages are deeply rooted in spirituals and "shouts."

So completely did Gershwin assimilate and absorb all the elements of Negro song and dance into his own writing that, without quoting a single line from outside sources, he was able to produce a musical art basically Negro in physiognomy and spirit, basically expressive of the heart and soul of an entire race. The pages that stir one most profoundly, and which bring to the opera its artistic importance, are those most deeply rooted in Negro folk culture: the wake scene beginning with the lament, "He's a-gone, gone, gone," and continuing through the stirring choral, "Overflow, Overflow" to Bess' ecstatic spiritual, "Oh the train is at the station"; the ecstatic "shout" of Serena in her prayer for Bess' recovery; the piquant street cries of the honey man, crab man, and strawberry woman; Jake's work song, "It take a long pull to get there"; the moving choral exhortation to Clara on the death of her husband, "Oh Lawd, Oh My Jesus, Rise Up An' Follow Him Home"; and the final hymn, "Oh Lawd, I'm on My Way."

The transmutation of Negro musical idioms and styles into a powerful and moving art was one indication of Gershwin's growth as a composer. Another was his new ability in tone-painting, in translating into musical terms many different moods and backgrounds. The opening prelude, with its brilliant picture of the helter-skelter turmoil of life in Catfish Row is in marked contrast to the eloquent portrait of a serene Catfish Row early at dawn in the prelude to Act II, scene 3. The dramatic writing in the Kittiwah scene, in the hurricane music, and in the scene in Serena's room during the storm is balanced by the tender lyricism of his love music in duets like "Bess, You Is My Woman Now" and "I Loves You, Porgy."

But it is in the many subtle details of his writing that Gershwin proves most conclusively his new-found mastery as a composer for the serious stage and his formidable development as a creative artist. One cannot fail to note how he uses vocal glissandi to heighten the tragedy of the wake scene; how he interpolates the ejaculation "huh" into the work song "It take a long pull to get there" to suggest the physical effort of rowing a boat; how dramatically telling is his juxtaposition of the spoken dialogue of the detective with the answers sung in the trio in Act III, scene 2; how the use of spoken dialogue for the white folk and sung recitatives for the Negro provides subtle contrast between the races; how he continually alternates chords and ostinato rhythmic patterns to keep the play moving; how skillfully he either gives warning of a later song or subsequently refers to it with an orchestral recollection; how he breaks up the accents in "My Man's Gone Now" to intensify the pathos (not unlike the way Beethoven did in the closing measures of the funeral march of the *Eroica*); and how effective is the use of the broken monotone in the closing lines of "A Woman Is a Sometime Thing." If one notices these details, the shattering impact of the whole becomes understandable.

Writing Negro music so strongly flavored with folk ingredients was certainly the logical goal for Gershwin. The man who wrote *Porgy and Bess* grew out of the boy who had acquired a vivid and unforgettable musical experience from hearing a Negro band in Harlem; out of the young man whose first effort to outgrow the limitations of a song was to write a one-act Negro opera; out of the successful composer whose best writing was in the Negro idioms of the blues and ragtime; the white man who could compete successfully with Negroes in their competitive "shouts" in Charleston. But *Porgy and Bess* was Gershwin's inevitable achievement for still another reason: it represents, at last, the meeting point for the two divergent paths he had all his life been pursuing —those of serious and popular music. The serious musician is found at his best in the musically distinguished tone-speech, in the powerful antiphonal choruses, in the expressive dissonances and chromaticisms, in the brilliant orchestration, in the effective atmospheric writing, in the skillful use of counterpoint in the duets and particularly in the last-scene trio. The popular composer emerges in the jazz background of several choruses like that in Act II, scene 1, "Woman to Lady"; in the two songs of Sportin' Life, "It Ain't Necessarily So," and "There's a Boat That's Leavin' Soon for New York"; and in Crown's sacrilegious blues ditty, "A Red-Headed Woman Makes a Choochoo Jump Its Track." Yet there is no feeling of contradiction, no sense of incongruity, in this mingling of the serious and the popular, for the popular is as basic to Gershwin's design as the serious, with its own specific artistic function.

Neither George Gershwin nor DuBose Heyward lived to see vindicated their faith in *Porgy and Bess,* nor did they reap their rewards for the sacrifice they made in writing it. Gershwin died two years after the première. DuBose Heyward succumbed to a heart attack in Tryon, North Carolina, three years after Gershwin's death.

By 1937, the year of Gershwin's death, some of the songs from the opera had achieved considerable popularity, particularly "Summertime," "I Got Plenty o' Nuttin'," and "It Ain't Necessarily So." The opera itself, however, had fallen into that oblivion which sooner or later seems to await so many American operas. Indeed, in its editorial to Gershwin upon his death, the New York *Times* said: *"Porgy and Bess . . .* is utterly innocent of elemental tragedy or of real dramatic import." Gershwin, consequently, had no way of knowing that the opera he loved so dearly and which he knew was his crowning achievement would survive him.

For Heyward, at least, there were one or two clues. One of these came soon after Gershwin's death when the David Bispham silver medal was bestowed on *Porgy and Bess* "for distinguished contribution to native American opera." Another clue came in Los Angeles on February 4, 1938, when Merle Armitage revived the opera. The cast was made up mostly of the original members, with one major exception: Avon Long replaced Bubbles as Sportin' Life. George Gershwin himself had discovered Avon Long at the Ubangi night club in Harlem and had picked him out as a possible understudy or replacement for Bubbles. When Bubbles demanded from Armitage too high a fee for his appearances in the opera's revival, Alexander Steinert, the conductor of the revival, remembered Gershwin's choice of Long and suggested that he be engaged. Once again Mamoulian was the stage director.

In Los Angeles, and after that in Pasadena, *Porgy and Bess* was an outstanding box-office success and one of the major artistic events in California that year. "It won," reported a correspondent for *Musical America*, "the emphatic approbation of a star-sprinkled first-night audience." Unfortunately, when the opera came to San Francisco it had to engage in a losing battle with the elements. Just before the opera opened there, San Francisco had been ravaged by one of its worst floods in many years, which isolated all the outlying districts from the heart of the city. Attendance was so poor that the opera had to close down before the end of its run.

Awareness of the greatness of *Porgy and Bess* did not come until after the death of DuBose Heyward. Late in 1940 Cheryl Crawford, who had been casting director for the Theatre Guild when it first presented *Porgy and Bess*, once again revived the opera, with some basic and significant changes. The over-all production was more subdued in color, sound, and movement than Mamoulian's. Parts of the opera were cut to speed up the action, and some of the recitatives gave way to spoken dialogue. The result did not change the artistic value of the work, but it did extend its popular appeal. *Porgy and Bess* in this new presentation proved itself to be grand entertainment as well as grand art.

The cast was virtually the same as that seen in the Los Angeles revival. It opened in Maplewood, New Jersey, in October 1941, and Virgil Thomson, then the music critic of the New York *Herald Tribune*, attended. He now found that *Porgy and Bess* was "a beautiful piece of music and a deeply moving play for the lyric theater. Its melodic invention is abundant and pretty distinguished. . . . The score has both musical distinction and popular appeal." Thus one major New York music critic had the courage to reverse himself. Others followed his lead when the production hit the Majestic Theater in New York on January 22, 1942. Olin Downes now conceded that "in his own way and according to his own lights, Gershwin has taken a substantial step, and advanced the cause of native opera." The New York music critics recanted as a unit, too—the Music Critics Circle singled out the opera as the most significant musical revival of that year.

Audiences responded in kind. *Porgy and Bess* became a hit. It stayed on Broadway for eight months, enjoying the longest run of any stage revival up to then in the history of the New York stage. Then the company went on tour. In spite of restrictions imposed on travel by the war, it appeared in twenty-six cities—three of these being one-night stands. In several cities new box-office records were established. When the opera returned to New York for a limited engagement of two weeks at the New York City Center on February 4, 1943, the run was sold out.

Europe, too, began to acclaim the opera.

The European première took place at the Danish Royal Opera in Copenhagen on March 27, 1943, in dramatic circumstances. Denmark was then occupied by the Nazis, and it was no secret that the Nazis did not look with favor upon the presentation of an American opera. The performance took place, nevertheless, in a Danish translation by Holger Bech, and with a Danish cast that included Einar Norby as Porgy, Else Brems as Bess, Franz Andersson as Crown, and Paul Wiedemann as Sportin' Life. Johan Hye-Knudsen conducted, and the stage director was Paul Kanneworff. It was given twenty-two times that year, always to sold-out houses; a cordon of Danish police surrounded the opera house to protect it from Nazi interference. But when the Gestapo threatened to bomb the opera house if another performance was given, *Porgy and Bess* was withdrawn from the repertory. After that, and throughout the war, the opera became a symbol of Danish resistance to the Nazi invaders. Each time the Nazis boastfully sent their victory communiqués over the Danish radio, the secret Danish underground cut in with a recording of "It Ain't Necessarily So." The song became to the Danes as much a symbol of ultimate victory as Churchill's V sign and the first four notes of Beethoven's Fifth Symphony.

Porgy and Bess returned to the Danish Royal Opera in 1945 with the same cast that had introduced it there. Between then and 1952 the opera was given forty-nine times, always to capacity houses. For a few of these performances Todd Duncan and Anne Brown appeared as guests in the title roles.

Porgy and Bess was introduced in Sweden, at the Lyriska Teatern in Gothenburg, on February 10, 1948, where it was given fifty-five performances. On April 1, 1949, it came to the Oscarsteatern in Stockholm, and on March 19, 1952, to the Stadsteatern in Malmö. Anne Brown appeared as Bess in Stockholm, and Evy Tibell in the other two cities; Bernhard Sönnerstedt was Porgy.

Meanwhile, on May 14, 1945, *Porgy and Bess* was performed in Moscow by the Stanislavsky Players, with staging by Konstanin Popov and under the musical direction of Prof. A. Khessin. "The audience, which included famous musicians, greeted the performance enthusiastically," was a report to the New York *Times*. This enthusiasm is all the more remarkable when it is realized that the accompaniment used for the production was a piano and drum instead of a symphony orchestra. Shostakovich, one of the most celebrated of Soviet composers, called it "magnificent" and did not hesitate to compare it favorably to the great Russian folk operas of Borodin, Rimsky-Korsakov, and Mussorgsky.

A few weeks later, in June, *Porgy and Bess* was given at the annual Zurich Festival in Switzerland, at the Stadttheater. Veteran European opera singers were recruited: Desider

Kovacs (Porgy), Claire Cordy (Bess), Karl Pistorius (Robbins), Andreas Bohm (Crown), and Laslo Csaby (Sportin' Life). Victor Reinshagen conducted. Josef Kisch, eminent Swiss critic, described the opera as "a miracle of technique, transcribing the sounds of life into the precinct of music. It is astonishing how this work succeeds in reflecting the emotional, the naïve, and the realistic elements of the stage action." Willi Reich, another eminent European critic, called the event "an honor to the Zurich Municipal Theater and a triumph for Gershwin's inspired work."

The enthusiasm aroused by this performance was not forgotten. Five years later, in the fall of 1950, *Porgy and Bess* entered the regular seasonal repertory of the Zurich Stadttheater. Of the principals in the earlier Zurich production, only Andreas Bohm returned. Manfred Jungwirth and Emmy Funk were brought in from Vienna to play Porgy and Bess respectively. "It scored a resounding success," reported Horace Sutton in the New York *Times*.

The Zurich performance, as well as those in the Soviet Union, were with white performers in blackface, and in a German translation by Dr. Ralph Benatzsky. Katherine Harvey, the only American appearing in the second Zurich presentation, said that "they treat *Porgy* as an opera, and it comes out slower, more melodious, and more serious." Alexander Smallens, who attended this same Zurich performance, found it too slow and humorless by American standards. Besides, the Negro vernacular of Charleston was completely lost in the German translation in which it was presented.

The triumph of *Porgy and Bess* abroad became complete when Europe had the opportunity to see and know the opera as America did, with a Negro cast. This happened in

1952 when the Blevins Davis–Robert Breen production was sent to Europe with the support and blessings of the United States Department of State.

Before that production went to Europe, however, it opened in Dallas, Texas, on June 9, 1952, before a brilliant audience that included Ira and Leonore Gershwin. Much that had been deleted from the score in earlier performances was restored, particularly some of the finer choral passages and the "Buzzard Song," the latter now being placed in the third act for better balance. The entire presentation was vitalized by the imaginative settings of Wolfgang Roth, the costumes of Jed Mace, and a swiftly paced and vividly dramatic staging by Robert Breen that emphasized sound as well as sight values. There was also a new freshness of approach to other details, particularly to the choral singing and the performance of the minor roles.

The Dallas cast had new leads: William Warfield (Porgy), Leontyne Price (Bess), Lorenzo Fuller (Sportin' Life), John McCurry (Crown), Helen Thigpen (Serena), and Helen Colbert (Clara). In later performances of the same production there were some changes. Cab Calloway stepped into the dancing shoes of Sportin' Life; William Warfield withdrew to allow LaVern Hutcherson, Leslie Scott, and Irving Barnes to share the role of Porgy; and Urylee Leonardos alternated with Leontyne Price as Bess. Georgia Burke, Helen Dowdy, Ray Yeates, Joseph Crawford, Joseph James, and Catherine Ayers—as well as conductor Alexander Smallens and the Eva Jessye Choir—were carry-overs from the original 1935 production.

When this production reached New York, Brooks Atkinson wrote that it was the best that the opera had thus far received, "and it was magnificent. . . . It is all Gershwin and all gold. . . . They all sing and act as though they believed in the validity of what they are doing. The performance is not so much uninhibited as powerfully sincere, expressing the tempestuousness of the music with conviction . . . [giving] *Porgy and Bess* a sustained exultation it has not had in recent productions. This is what a theater classic ought to be—alive in every fiber, full of passion for a theme."

With a gross of over $100,000 for its two-week run, *Porgy and Bess* became, as the Dallas *Times-Herald* reported, "the box-office champion in the history of summer musical shows in Dallas. . . . One test of *Porgy and Bess'* power: For the first time, the large majority of each audience remained in their seats applauding past every curtain call."

During the next few weeks, the production visited Chicago, Pittsburgh, and finally Washington, D.C., where it played before President Truman and other high dignitaries of the United States government and of foreign legations.

Then the State Department sent the opera on its mission of good-will to Europe, at a cost of $150,000, to prove that American art could be vigorous and significant and that the Negro in America was not always the object of humiliation and oppression. What happened after that exceeded the wildest hopes of those who had proposed and supported the tour. *Porgy and Bess* made artistic and political headlines.

The first stop was Vienna where, on September 7, 1952, it gave the first of five performances at the Volksoper. Tickets were at such a premium that they could only be bought on the black market, at several times face value. A distinguished audience that included the American Ambassador, the Austrian President and Chancellor, and representatives from the foreign embassies gave the opera a tumultuous ovation. A city that had seen so much opera history created at first hand—and where an American opera had always been regarded either with condescension or outright hostility— called *Porgy and Bess* "sensational," "a great event," and an "unqualified masterwork." The *Wiener Kurier* reported that "the applause and jubilation of the unique company reached proportions hitherto given only to the most beloved artists of the State Opera." One critic said that no new foreign opera had been received this way by Vienna since the Austrian première of *Cavalleria Rusticana* in 1902.

Then the company went on to Berlin to participate in the Cultural Festival there. Though the audience did not understand a word of what was being said on the stage, the reaction at the première was so stormy that the company had to take more curtain calls (twenty-one) than any other modern opera in over a quarter of a century. The audience kept shouting out its enthusiasm to individual members of the company. Reporting from Berlin to the New York *Times*, Jack Raymond wrote, "It is impossible to exaggerate the tremendous outburst of popular acclaim it received from the people of Berlin night after night." *Der Tag* called the presentation a "triumph. . . . None of us has ever seen anything like it—and it is probable that we never will again." H. H. Stuckenschmidt, probably one of Germany's most distinguished musical scholars, did not hesitate to call the opera "a masterpiece."

The excitement in Vienna and Berlin was repeated in Paris and London. In London, three days after the première, the Stoll Theatre was sold out for three months, and the opera had to stay on for almost half a year. The *Daily Herald* blazed the headline that "It Was Worth Waiting 17 Years for *Porgy*." In Paris the limited engagement threw all other musical and dramatic events into a shade. *Porgy and Bess* had to return to the French capital the following season for a ten-week run, the longest of any American production in France.

Washington sat up and took notice. President Eisenhower wrote to Blevins Davis on March 30, 1953:

> I have heard reports of the extraordinary success that met your . . . trip. I cannot emphasize too strongly how serious and enduring the value of this work seems to me. You and your distinguished company are making a real contribution to the kind of understanding between peoples that alone can bring mutual respect and trust. You are, in a real sense, ambassadors of the arts."

After the company returned to the United States early in 1953 to begin an extended engagement at the Ziegfeld Theater in New York on March 10—and after that to undertake a tour of nineteen cities that began on December 1 in Philadelphia and ended the following September in Montreal —the State Department dispatched *Porgy and Bess* on another foreign jaunt. This time the tour began on September 22 in Venice, at the Festival of Contemporary Music, of which it was the highlight. For the first time in a half-dozen years, box-holders at the historic La Fenice opera house threw flowers onto the stage. In December, after a ten-week stay in Paris, the company went eastward, opening in Zagreb, Yugoslavia, on December 11, and appearing in Belgrade five days later. "All Yugoslavia is singing," was a cabled report to the New York *Times*. "The workers and the peasants are singing. The Communist officials, the man in the street, the students, all are singing the songs of George Gershwin and the praises of the cast of the folk opera. . . . When the curtain rang down for the final performance, the packed house stayed for twenty minutes." There were more than twenty curtain calls. In Egypt—Alexandria on December 31; Cairo, the following January 7—the opera and its performers made so many friends that when the company left each of these two cities there were thousands of Egyptians to see them off at the railroad stations. The same excitement was aroused in Athens, Tel Aviv, Casablanca, and Barcelona, between January 17 and February 5. *"Porgy and Bess* brought laughter and tears to sophisticated Athenians" reads still another cabled report to the New York *Times*. An Israeli newspaper described the performance as "an artistic event of first-class importance." The eight performances in Tel Aviv were sold out even before the company arrived; twenty thousand applications for seats had to be turned down. A critic for the *Diari de Barcelona* wrote: "In all truth it may be said that a greater perfection in unity than that achieved by the American artists is not possible."

Then *Porgy and Bess* swung back to Italy. After a stopover at Naples at the venerable San Carlo, on February 15 it came to the stage of the world's most celebrated and historic opera house—La Scala in Milan on February 22. Milan was not the end of the road by any means. The company subsequently played in Florence, Rome, Marseille, Switzerland, Belgium, and the Netherlands; on July 8, 1955, it started a four-month tour of South America at the Teatro Municipal in Rio de Janeiro; on October 12, 1955 it began a two-week engagement in Mexico City; and before the year ended it made a history-making appearance in the Soviet Union. But La Scala was surely the climax of the entire tour. This was the first time an American company had been invited to appear in the theater; the first time that an opera by an Amer-

ican-born composer was performed within those hallowed
halls; the first time that a single opera held that stage for an
entire week. Among those who witnessed this historic event
were Leonore Gershwin, who had accompanied the production on its entire Near East tour, and Dorothy Heyward, who
had flown from New York just for this performance. "Music
lovers went wild tonight in the staid La Scala Opera House,"
reported the New York *Herald Tribune*. "Italian opera fans
who jammed the famous opera house forgot their traditional
reserve and loudly cheered the performance. . . . At the
conclusion of the performance, the American cast received an
eight-minute ovation." The Italian critics were unanimous in
their praises of both the opera and its performance. In
L'Unita Rubens Tedeschi placed the opera "among the mas-
terworks of the lyric theater."

On February 24, a George Gershwin exhibition was
inaugurated at La Scala, sponsored jointly by the theater and
the United States Information Service. Made up of information, photographs, manuscripts, and other documents rele-
vant to Gershwin's career, the exhibition drew huge throngs
whose curiosity and interest in the American composer had
been aroused and stimulated by the phenomenal success of
his opera.

22

BEVERLY HILLS

When the complete 560-page vocal and piano score of *Porgy and Bess* was issued in 1935, it bore the imprint of a new publishing house: the Gershwin Publishing Company, at whose head still sat Max Dreyfus. Gershwin was inordinately proud of the fact that the company bore his name, and he reacted with an almost childlike glee to the handsome office outfitted with two Steinway pianos for him.

Many changes had taken place in the music-publishing industry to bring about the emergence of the Gershwin Publishing Company. Up to 1927 Gershwin's music was published by Harms, which had discovered him and which was run by Max Dreyfus and his brother, Louis. In 1927, beginning with *Funny Face,* the New World Publishing Company was founded as a subsidiary of Harms to issue Gershwin's music. In 1929, when the motion-picture screen began to talk, Hollywood started frantically scooping up all the properties it could lay its hands on for the making of talking films. In the scramble, Warner Brothers entered into a giant deal, estimated at $10,000,000, to buy out three leading New York song publishers: Harms, Witmark, and Remick.

The Gershwin Publishing Company was started by Dreyfus in 1935 as a subsidiary of Chappell and Company, which he headed, expressly for the *Porgy and Bess* music. As originally published, this music appeared in the difficult piano version Gershwin had prepared before his final orchestration. He firmly told his editor, Dr. Sirmay, that he wanted it to be printed as he wrote it, instead of in popular arrangements. Only later on, when some of the songs became popular, did he allow them to appear in simplified piano versions. The Gershwin Publishing Company also issued the principal songs from the scores Gershwin wrote for the motion pictures.

With the publication of his opera out of the way, and with the opera itself running smoothly at the Alvin Theater, Gershwin decided to take a deserved and badly needed rest. He had not been too well. The chronic constipation had still not been relieved and—despite all the exhilaration and excitement attending the writing and the production of his opera—his spirit was low at times. "I can't eat, I can't sleep, I can't fall in love," he complained to friends. Kay Swift prevailed on him to go to Dr. Gregory Zilboorg for psychoanalytic treatment in 1934. He did not complete his analysis since he finally felt—as with all the other treatments physicians had been prescribing for him for years—that he was not being helped.

A holiday was another attempt to relieve the tensions and anxieties. Late in November 1935 he went on a four-week trip to Mexico, in the company of Dr. Zilboorg, Edward Warburg, and Marshall Field. There he heard considerable Mexican music, but little of it made much of an impression on him. He was much more excited by Mexican art. One of the highlights of his vacation was a visit to the outstanding painter Diego Rivera. Gershwin planned to ask Rivera to paint his portrait but instead ended up by sketching Rivera. He returned to New York in mid-December on the *Santa Paula* to be greeted at the gangplank by the entire cast of *Porgy and Bess* and the Charleston Orphan Band playing his music. The trip had refreshed him considerably.

His plans for the immediate future touched neither Broadway nor Carnegie Hall, but Hollywood. He had been signed by RKO to write the music for a new Fred Astaire–Ginger Rogers musical, and he had considerable misgivings about the assignment. Fred Astaire and Ginger Rogers had been paired as a dance team in a succession of striking screen triumphs, including *Top Hat* and *Follow the Fleet,* both with music by Irving Berlin, and *Swingtime,* with a Jerome Kern score that included "The Way You Look To-night," which won the award of the Motion Picture Academy. The conviction was strong with Gershwin that anything Astaire and Rogers might do henceforth, and anything he might write for them, could be only anticlimactic.

His fears were without foundation. As it turned out, his new Astaire-Rogers picture, *Shall We Dance,* was described by Frank S. Nugent in the New York *Times* as "one of the best things the screen's première dance team has done, a zestful prancing, sophisticated musical." The story followed familiar grooves. Astaire was cast as Peter F. Peters, who dances in the Russian Ballet under the name of Petrov; Ginger Rogers is a ballroom dancer, Linda Keene. They meet, fall in love, accidentally take the same liner to America, confront many unpleasant situations arising from the mistaken notion of the American press that they are married, and finally end up that way. During the progress of this perfunctory plot, Astaire is given an opportunity to do an intriguing engine-room dance to the sounds and movements of the ship's machinery; to join Ginger Rogers in a roller-skating dance on the Central Park Mall; and to do a routine that alternated an *entrechat* with a tap dance. Gershwin's score was a gold mine: "Let's Call the Whole Thing Off," "They Can't Take That Away from Me" (which in 1949 returned to the screen in *The Barkleys of Broadway*), "Slap That Bass," "They All Laughed," and the title song.

One chore completed, Gershwin went to work on another for RKO. The star was once again Fred Astaire, but this time he was paired with a new dancing partner—Joan Fontaine. In this new film, *A Damsel in Distress*, to a story by P. G. Wodehouse, Astaire is a matinee idol who, though actually shy and retiring, is publicized by his press agent as a lady-killer. Somehow the hero gets the idea that Lady Alyce, of English nobility, is in love with him. The initial distaste of the matinee idol and Lady Alyce for each other is succeeded by love. As was customary with Astaire films, dance routines were emphasized. Here the best numbers included an eccentric dance at a country fair with the help of carnival paraphernalia. And Howard Barnes wrote in the New York *Herald Tribune* that those routines would not "have been half so good without the splendid Gershwin melodies." The best of those melodies were: "Nice Work If You Can Get It," "The Jolly Tar and the Milkmaid," and "A Foggy Day."

The three Gershwins—George, with Ira and Leonore —rented a palatial home, with swimming pool and tennis court, in Beverly Hills, on 1019 North Roxbury Drive. The elite of Hollywood—movie magnates, top directors, film stars —opened their doors to them. For George, life in Hollywood consisted of an interminable round of evening parties and dinners. During the day, when he was not working, he enjoyed taking long, brisk hikes accompanied by his wire-haired terrier, Tony; or playing a hard game of tennis with friends, after a vigorous warm-up volley with his factotum, Paul. He was surrounded by many old and close friends: Oscar Levant, Harold Arlen, Yip Harburg, Moss Hart, George Pallay, Alexander Steinert, Lillian Hellman, Arthur Kober, Bert Kalmar, Edward G. Robinson, and Harry Ruby, among others. And new friends supplemented the old. Among those whom he liked particularly was the celebrated modernist composer and theorist, Arnold Schoenberg, who lived nearby and who came once a week to play tennis.

As he stayed on in Hollywood through 1936 and into 1937 George grew increasingly restive. Despite the many attractions of California, it did not appeal to him strongly. The climate, and the lackadaisical, easygoing existence it encouraged, might suit Ira's more placid nature, but it irritated George, who preferred the frenetic whirlwind activity of New York. He missed poignantly the music, the art, and some of the friends he had left behind. Besides, he found working for the motion pictures distasteful. The producers could not or would not understand or accept his fresh and new approaches to screen music. He was continually upset by their efforts to give his songs Gargantuan settings and elaborate orchestrations, when he was now seeking simplicity and economy. Hackneyed musical procedures were a sore trial, and he was continually beset by artistic frustrations. He chafed under his assignments and was impatient to get back to writing music for stage productions and, particularly, serious compositions, now that he had found new creative strength within himself through his opera. He spoke of writing some choral music along original lines, and he planned to make a trip abroad to hear the leading choral groups of Europe perform native folk music. He thought of writing a string quartet, a symphony, a ballet, and—to be sure—another opera. As far as the opera was concerned, he had already contacted Lynn Riggs (whose folk play, *Green Grow the Lilacs,* had already been produced by the Theatre Guild. It later became the source of the Rodgers and Hammerstein musical play, *Oklahoma.*) Riggs was writing a libretto for George called *The Lights of Leamy.*

Despite his many friends and his active social life, Gershwin was suddenly beginning to feel terribly alone. For the first time, his fame and success did not provide the answer to his every need. He began to talk continually of getting married—for the time being there was no specific woman in his mind—and with a kind of fierce desperateness. Once he sat down and wrote letters to a few of his old girl friends inviting them to come out to California to visit him. When not one of them came, his feeling of aloneness grew more chilling than ever.

Then he fell in love—or thought he did. At a gala Hollywood party he met Paulette Goddard, then married to Charlie Chaplin. He was instantly drawn to her powerfully, and when he came home from the party he was convinced she was the woman he would marry, even though she was then married to somebody else. He was deaf to the advice of his closest friends who tried to convince him that such a marriage would not work out for him. A turbulent love affair during the next few weeks absorbed him completely. Just before his fatal illness he continually spoke to her of possible marriage; her refusal to leave Chaplin was a blow that shook him to his very roots. His restlessness and loneliness were intensified. The news that Bill Daly, one of his dearest friends, had suddenly died of a heart attack on December 4, 1936, at the premature age of forty-nine, further increased his mounting despondency.

Little things began to annoy him out of all proportion to their importance. He began to grow sensitive about the way he was losing his hair. He purchased a machine as large as a refrigerator in which a hose connected a motor pump to a metal cask. The cask was to be adjusted to the scalp of the head. For half an hour each day, he subjected himself to rigorous scalp treatment which brought a rush of blood to his head through electric suction; at the end of each treatment his scalp was so callous that it could not feel anything if a pin were stuck into it. What effect this treatment had upon his then dormant brain tumor is hard to say, but it certainly could not have been salutary.

New assignments came. Samuel Goldwyn signed him and Ira to write the songs for a lavish screen revue to be called *The Goldwyn Follies,* for which George Balanchine, the celebrated ballet-master of the Ballet Russe de Monte Carlo, was brought to Hollywood to plan the choreography. But the one-time zest and excitement George always brought to new assignments were not there any longer. He was slipping into periods of melancholia. One day he asked Alexander Steinert, "I am thirty-eight, famous, and rich, but profoundly unhappy. Why?" He said he wanted to get away from everybody for a while. The only hitch was that he also could not stand being by himself for any length of time.

Yet he looked remarkably well. His face was a healthy bronze; his eyes were keen and alive. His strong athletic body had lost none of its power or resiliency. His doctors, finding nothing physically wrong with him, insisted he was suffering from no more than a temporary attack of nerves that would surely pass.

But before long there were portents that something was seriously wrong.

23

JOURNEY'S END

On February 11, 1937, Gershwin appeared with the Los Angeles Philharmonic in an all-Gershwin program. While playing the Concerto in F, his mind went suddenly blank. For a fraction of a minute he lost consciousness and missed a few bars. Then, in complete control of himself and his senses, he continued the performance as if nothing had happened. Later he said that during the blackness he had the curious sensation of smelling burned rubber.

He had a repetition of the same experience—the temporary mental blackout and the smell of burned rubber—the following April, while sitting in a barber-shop chair in Beverly Hills.

However, until June he gave no visible evidence of

being seriously ill. In that month he began to grow somewhat listless. Some mornings he would wake up in a befuddled state, physically washed out, slightly dazed mentally. During the day there were moments when he found himself swaying. At times he suffered agonizing headaches.

On one or two occasions he was found sitting in his bedroom, the shades drawn to keep out the light that seemed to annoy him. His head was bent low; his eyes glazed. When questioned he said he did not know how long he had been sitting there and that his body seemed so sapped of vitality that he was unable to move. It took a concerted effort for him to get up and go downstairs. He was, of course, under the continual surveillance of his physician, Dr. Gabriel Segall (Garbo's doctor), but repeated examinations showed him to be in sound physical condition.

With each passing day he grew increasingly jumpy, irritable, and restless. One evening at dinner he was so upset by a political conversation about Nazi Germany and Hitler that he fled from the table after making a bitter and cutting remark. He sought refuge in his bedroom, where he complained of a splitting headache and ragged nerves. He went to bed and stayed there a day or two, unable to summon the energy to leave it.

Some of his intimate friends felt that all George was suffering from was a hateful association with the motion-picture industry and that he was eager to escape his commitments and return to New York. Others insisted that he was reacting to physical and mental fatigue. For a while, the latter had reason to believe they were right. On June 12 George went on a brief holiday to Coronado with his agent and friend, Arthur Lyons, and he seemed suddenly to revert to his one-time good spirits.

But on Sunday, June 20, after a dinner at the Irving Berlins', he complained to Leonore of a blinding headache. Two days later he had a luncheon engagement with Paulette Goddard, George Pallay, and Constance Collier. His general listlessness and his lack of interest in his friends convinced them that something was basically wrong. Leonore consulted the physicians, who suggested a thorough and immediate physical check-up for George at the Cedars of Lebanon Hospital. George entered the hospital the following day, on Wednesday the 23rd, and stayed there until Saturday the 26th. The very comprehensive three-day tests revealed nothing; the physicians insisted that he was a perfect specimen of health. They had taken into account the possibility of a brain tumor, but there was simply no symptom to substantiate this suspicion. A spinal test, which might have provided definitive proof, had been vehemently rejected by George as too excrutiatingly painful.

It was at this point, on June 27, that Walter Winchell announced on his radio program (and repeated the following morning in his syndicated column) that Gershwin was seriously ill. An avalanche of inquiries descended on the Gershwin household at 1019 North Roxbury Drive and on his mother's apartment at 25 Central Park West in New York City. Everybody was told that Winchell had greatly exaggerated the situation, that the recent hospital tests had proved that there was nothing organically wrong with George, and that quiet and rest would surely prove beneficial. George's mother told reporters in New York that she had recently seen George in California and that he had looked remarkably fit but that he was terribly nostalgic for New York.

Nevertheless, George was now placed under daily treatments with the psychoanalyst, Dr. Ernest Simmel; and a male nurse, Paul Levy, was engaged to be with him all the time. Despite his daily visits to his physician, George's condition was becoming more alarming all the time. Late one night he and Ira were returning from a party at Samuel Goldwyn's, and before they could step into the house, George sat down at the curb of the street and held his head. The pains and the smell of burned rubber, he said, were driving him crazy. Not long after this, during dinner one evening, the knife fell out of his hand, as though it had suddenly lost all control. At another meal George lost his equilibrium so much so that he was unable to bring his fork directly to his mouth, and the water spilled from his glass as he tried to drink.

Dr. Simmel finally decided to isolate George for a while from all friends and relatives, to remove from him all possible sources of friction. "Yip" Harburg, then leaving Beverly Hills for New York, turned his house over to George. Thereafter, from July 4 on, George was attended by his male nurse, and by his man, Paul. Ira and Leonore visited him for brief periods several times a day. Nobody else was permitted access to him. The seclusion seemed to do some good. George complained less about his headaches and even found the inclination to play the piano for brief sessions. But when George played the piano for Dr. Simmel on July 8, he was beginning to lose his coordination.

A few days after George had come to Harburg's house —on Friday, July 9—Ira and George Pallay dropped in for a moment to see how George was progressing. They found George asleep. They waited for him to awaken, but when he didn't they decided to leave and return later in the day.

At five o'clock that day, George finally awakened. He was so weak that he had to call his nurse to help him to the bathroom. Suddenly he slumped, collapsed, and fell into a coma as if he suffered a fit. His physical symptoms at that moment revealed to the nurse the unmistakable fact that had so long been explored and dismissed: George was the victim of a brain tumor.

Ira and Leonore were immediately informed of this startling development. They arrived at Harburg's just as George was being carried out on a stretcher to an ambulance. George tried to say something to Ira. From the incoherent mumble, Ira could make out only a single word: "Astaire."

George was rushed to the Cedars of Lebanon Hospital for surgery. The Los Angeles surgeon, Dr. Carl A. Rand, suggested calling in one of the country's foremost brain specialists, Dr. Walter E. Dandy. Hurried telephone calls to Dr. Dandy's office, home, and hospital failed to locate him. He was cruising somewhere on Chesapeake Bay with the Governor of Massachusetts on a private yacht that could not be reached.

George Pallay telephoned the White House and enlisted its aid in locating Dr. Dandy. On Saturday, two government destroyers were dispatched down the Chesapeake to locate the yacht. When it was found, Dr. Dandy was brought by special motorcycle escort to Cumberland, Maryland. There, in a three-way telephone conversation, Dr. Segall from Los Angeles authorized Dr. Dandy to come out to the Coast for the operation, while at the same time arrangements were made with Emil Mosbacher in New York for a private plane to stand by in readiness at the Newark airport for Dr. Dandy. Dr. Dandy was then rushed by another private plane to Newark.

While all this was going on, George's man, Paul, was waiting at the Burbank airfield at 9:00 P.M. Saturday to pick up the noted California surgeon, Dr. Howard Nafziger, who had been brought in for consultation. Dr. Nafziger had been found at Lake Tajoe where he was then vacationing. He arrived at the hospital at 9:30 P.M. where he was awaited by Ira and Leonore. After examining Gershwin, Dr. Nafziger found that the patient's pulse had fallen so low that an immediate operation was imperative; it was impossible to wait for Dr. Dandy. At 10:30 P.M. George was wheeled into the operating room for the preliminary surgery of opening a window in his head to locate the exact position of the tumor. This operation ended at midnight, when George was taken into the X-ray room where, after two and a half hours, the precise position of the cystic tumor was found to be the right temporal lobe of the brain. Gershwin was now prepared for the major operation. Meanwhile, at 11:45 P.M.—when Dr. Dandy arrived at the Newark airport—he was informed by Pallay of all the developments which now made it unnecessary for him to continue his flight west.

George was returned to the operating room at 3:00 A.M. Since Dr. Nafziger did not have his assistants or instruments, the operation was performed by Dr. Carl Rand, with Doctors Nafziger, Segall, and Eugene Ziskind attending. The operation lasted four hours. During all that time Arthur Lyons was in the operating room; Pallay waited outside. All the others were downstairs: Ira and Leonore, Henry Botkin, Moss Hart, Oscar Levant, Eugene Solow, Elizabeth Meyer, Arthur Kober, Alexander Steinert, and Lou and Emily Paley who had arrived in California only two days earlier.

As soon as the operation was over, Pallay learned from one of the attending physicians that George suffered from a cystic degeneration of a tumor on that part of the brain that could not be touched. There was not much hope for recovery. Even if George survived—which at the moment seemed doubtful—he would probably be disabled, or blind, or both for the rest of his days.

Pallay repeated the sad prognosis to Leonore as they drove back to 1019 North Roxbury Drive. Ira was driven back by Paul. At home, Leonore could not find the courage to tell Ira the truth. She insisted that all was well, that he should take some badly needed rest. Just then Max Dreyfus telephoned from New York. "What are they doing to my boy?" Dreyfus asked. Half-dazed, Ira told him: "George will be all right, Max. The operation was a success. There is nothing to worry about."

Ira, then, did not know that George was dying. A few hours later the hospital called to say that George had died at 10:35 A.M. without having regained consciousness.

Ira relayed the tragic news to his mother and his brother Arthur, who had been waiting at their telephone at 25 Central Park West. Frances Godowsky had to be reached by cable in Vienna, where she was then vacationing; until she received the message she had not even known that George was sick.

The first outsider to learn what had happened was George Jessel. He called the hospital Sunday morning to find out how Gershwin was doing and was informed that he had just died. Then the announcement came over the radio: "The man who said he had more tunes in his head than he could put down on paper in a hundred years is dead today in Hollywood. George Gershwin passed away today at the age of thirty-eight." It was in this way that many of George's lifelong friends—as well as the world of his admirers—were told of the tragedy. Harold Arlen and "Yip" Harburg heard the news on their car radio as they were driving in New York City; Harry Ruby, at breakfast aboard a ship from

Alaska; Jules Glaenzer, during his dinner in Deauville, France.

Kay Swift, who had been in continual touch with California when George was in the hospital, and later Saturday night when he was operated upon, said suddenly to her daughter at Sunday noon, "George is dead." Frantically she put through another call to Beverly Hills, and her worst fears were confirmed. Sammy Lee, the dance director who had been associated with so many Gershwin musicals, had a lunch date of two weeks' standing with Gershwin at the Brown Derby on the 11th; he was waiting for George to turn up when George Jessel stopped off at his table to tell him Gershwin was dead.

Expressions of grief and tributes to his greatness came from the many others who had been associated with him over the years—over the radio, in newspapers, by word of mouth, by letter. Serge Koussevitzky wrote, "Like a rare flower which blossoms forth once in a while, Gershwin represents a singularly original and rare phenomenon." George S. Kaufman told Isaac Goldberg that Gershwin's death was "the greatest tragedy I have ever known." Arnold Schoenberg said, "I know he is an artist, and a composer; he expressed musical ideas, and they were new." Eva Gauthier was convinced that "George Gershwin will live as long as music lives. He will never be forgotten and his place will never be filled." Paul Whiteman described Gershwin's art as "an enduring monument"; and Ferde Grofé said, "I may never again meet the like of Gershwin." Vernon Duke later wrote in his autobiography: "Death can be kind and it can be just; but it had no business taking our George, who was in full flower of his fine youth and who was unquestionably doing his best work." John O'Hara remarked poignantly: "George Gershwin

died on July 11, but I don't have to believe it if I don't want
to." Irving Berlin spoke in verse:

> As a writer of serious music
> He could dream for a while in the stars,
> And step down from the heights of Grand Opera
> To a chorus of thirty-two bars.

Gershwin died without learning that he had just received the highest honor that Italy could bestow on a foreign
composer: an honorary membership in the St. Cecilia Academy in Rome. He was the only American ever to be thus
honored. The announcement came while he was unconscious
in the hospital.

There was no will. Besides his belongings, furnishings,
and precious collection of paintings, he left almost $350,000
in securities, cash, and insurance (after debts). It all went
by New York law to his mother.

On July 13, the Mutual Broadcasting System broad-
cast a memorial concert to Gershwin, which included these
participants: Irving Berlin, Richard Rodgers, Lorenz Hart,
Cole Porter, Leopold Stokowski, Frances Langford, Merle
Armitage, Hoagy Carmichael, Arnold Schoenberg, and Fred
Waring. Conrad Nagel was the master of ceremonies. David
Broekman conducted the orchestra in Gershwin's music, and
Rabbi Edgar F. Magnin of Los Angeles delivered a brief
eulogy.

This was but one of the many tributes to Gershwin
heard over radio by way of giant networks and small local
stations, and on many different programs, as George Gershwin's body was brought by train from Los Angeles, where

it left on Monday morning, July 12, to New York where it arrived on Thursday morning, the 15th. After a few hours at the Riverside Memorial Chapel, Gershwin's body was taken to Temple Emanu-El on Fifth Avenue for funeral services at 2:00 P.M. that day.

Despite a downpour, almost four thousand of Gershwin's friends, colleagues, and admirers crowded the Temple, while another thousand lined both sides of Fifth Avenue outside. The crowd in the street was so dense that traffic was interrupted. Police lines had to be formed to keep the people in check. Many of those who had tickets for the services were unable to force their way through the crowd; one of these was Al Jolson, and not until a few of his friends forced a path for him was he able to get through.

The services opened with Bach's "Air" from the orchestral Suite No. 3, played on the organ by Gottfried H. Federlein. After Dr. Nathan A. Perilman, the rabbi, read two psalms, Ossip Giskin, cellist, played Schumann's "Träumerei." Then Rabbi Stephen S. Wise delivered a eulogy to "the singer of the songs of America's soul. . . . There are countries in Central Europe which would have flung out this Jew. America welcomed him and he repaid it with the gusto of a child and the filial tenderness of a son." More music— the slow movement from Beethoven's C-sharp minor String Quartet played by the Perolé Quartet and Handel's "Largo" on the organ—then a prayer by Dr. Perilman ended the services.

To the strains of the slow section of the *Rhapsody in Blue* played on the organ, the flower-covered coffin was carried out of the temple. The honorary pallbearers included Mayor La Guardia, Walter Damrosch, George M. Cohan, Edwin Franko Goldman, Gene Buck, Al Jolson, Vernon Duke, former Mayor James J. Walker, and Sam H. Harris. Behind the coffin came the immediate members of Gershwin's family.

The procession proceeded into the street where more than a thousand of Gershwin's admirers waited patiently in the rain to give him a last send-off. The funeral then made the journey to Hastings-on-Hudson where, to additional prayers, the body of George Gershwin was buried in Mount Hope Cemetery.

While these services were going on in New York, another service was taking place at the B'nai B'rith Temple in Hollywood, where Dr. Edgar F. Magnin officiated. The great of Hollywood came to pay their last respects, just as the equally great of Broadway were performing the same sad rite in New York. At the Hollywood service, Oscar Hammerstein read a poignant eulogy for his friend. It reads in part:

> Our friend wrote music
> And in that mold he created
> Gaiety and sweetness and beauty
> And twenty-four hours after he had gone
> His music filled the air
> And in triumphant accents
> Proclaimed to this world of men
> That gaiety and sweetness and beauty
> Do not die. . . .
> . . . .
> Some will want a statue erected for him
> He deserves this
> Some will want to endow a school of music
> In his name
> He deserves this

But his friends could add one more tribute:
In his honor
They could try to appreciate
And be grateful for
The good things in this world
In his honor
They could try to be kinder to one another. . . .
And this would be the finest monument of all.

There were also concerts on both coasts. The now-traditional all-Gershwin concert at the Lewisohn Stadium became a memorial on the evening of August 8. Alexander Smallens and Ferde Grofé conducted. The soloists included Ethel Merman, Todd Duncan, Anne Brown, and Harry Kaufman. During the intermission, Mrs. Charles S. Guggenheimer made a brief speech dedicating the concert to Gershwin's memory. The largest audience in the history of the Stadium concerts (20,223) rose in silent tribute; among them were George's mother and sister.

One month later, on September 8, a George Gershwin Memorial Concert was given in the Hollywood Bowl. A galaxy of musicians and stars had been gathered for the program, largely through the unsparing and indefatigable efforts of George Pallay. The conductors were Otto Klemperer, Nathaniel Shilkret, Victor Young, Nathaniel Finston, Charles Previn, Alexander Steinert, and José Iturbi. The soloists were Al Jolson (singing "Swanee"), Gladys Swarthout, Fred Astaire, Oscar Levant, Lily Pons, Ruby Elzy, Todd Duncan, Anne Brown, José Iturbi, and the Hall Johnson Choir. Those who paid homage to Gershwin through words rather than music were Edward G. Robinson (reading the Oscar Hammerstein tribute) and George Jessel. The concert reached the largest audience ever to hear a Gershwin program or, for that matter, any other musical program. For besides the capacity audience at the Hollywood Bowl there was a world-wide audience listening through the facilities of the Columbia Broadcasting System, which transmitted the concert on seven short-wave stations, the first time that any concert was broadcast on such an extensive network.

Just before George's death, he and Ira had discussed at some length the idea of building a permanent home in Beverly Hills. They delayed doing this because while Ira was all for staying in California, George was eager to get back to New York. They finally decided that Ira would build his home in Beverly Hills and that its grounds would include a small studio for George's use whenever he came to Hollywood to work or to visit.

These plans were frustrated by George's sudden death. Instead of building himself a new home, Ira purchased the house next door to the one he and George had rented on North Roxbury Drive—1021. It is the house he still occupies.

It was almost as if, even then, he did not want to get too far away from George.

postscript

SINCE 1937

The last piece of music Gershwin wrote was the song "Love Is Here to Stay" for *The Goldwyn Follies*. He was able to complete only five numbers for that production, and for some of these Vernon Duke, aided by Ira, had to provide the verses. Since two of these Gershwin songs are among his most beautiful—"Love Walked In" and "Love Is Here To Stay"—it is apparent that even in his last troublesome months there was no creative disintegration.

The Goldwyn Follies, a screen extravaganza with Andrea Leeds, Vera Zorina, Adolph Menjou, Kenny Baker, Ella Logan, and Bobby Clark, was released after Gershwin's death, in 1938. Since death kept George from writing the music for the ballet sequences, Ira suggested to Goldwyn that Gershwin's tone poem, *An American in Paris,* be adapted for the ballet; Ira even prepared a suitable scenario. Balanchine, who was in charge of the choreography, was delighted with the idea and went to work. But one day Goldwyn called Balanchine into his office to tell him that *An American in Paris* was too highbrow for a ballet. "What would the miners of Harrisburg, Pa., think of it?" Goldwyn asked. Balanchine answered firmly: "Mr. Goldwyn, I am not President Roosevelt, and I am not interested in what the miners of Harrisburg think." In any case, the *American in Paris* ballet went out of *The Goldwyn Follies.* Two short ballet sequences were substituted with new music by Vernon Duke.

The Goldwyn Follies was not the last important motion picture to contain Gershwin music. Two of his celebrated musicals were transferred to films in 1941 and 1943, respectively. The first was *Lady Be Good,* with Eleanor Powell, Ann Sothern, and Robert Young. Here three Gershwin songs from the original stage production were combined with numbers by other composers, including Jerome Kern's "The Last Time I Saw Paris" (lyrics by Oscar Hammerstein II), which won the Motion Picture Academy Award that year. In 1943 a screen remake of *Girl Crazy* starred Judy Garland and Mickey Rooney. In contrast to an earlier production in 1932, with Wheeler and Woolsey, this new version had virtually the complete Gershwin score.

Then Hollywood paid Gershwin the highest accolade it could bestow on a composer. It filmed his biography, *Rhapsody in Blue.* In telling the Gershwin story, the screen play by Sonya Levien, Howard Koch, and Elliott Paul—fol-

lowing the practice of most screen biographies—mixed some
truth with much fiction. The unifying theme in the story
was basically sound: the struggle in Gershwin to reconcile
his passion for jazz with his ideal of writing serious music;
his conflict of purpose in producing hits on the one hand and
good art on the other. Less convincing was the fabricated love
interest, which was made out of whole cloth. "Julie Adams"
was a soul mate whom Gershwin had met in his Tin Pan
Alley days and who became famous singing his songs. "Chris-
tine Gilbert" was a rich and cultured divorcée who finally
had to face the realization that Gershwin would never marry
her. No less fictitious were the picture of Gershwin's impover-
ished boyhood on the East Side; the portrait of his idealistic,
old-world music teacher, Prof. Frank, who wanted him to
remain true to his art; and the continual effort to ascribe
George's driving and indefatigable energy to an instinctive
awareness that he did not have long to live.

Robert Alda played George Gershwin; Herbert
Rudley, Ira; Morris Carnovsky, Papa Gershwin; Rosemary
de Camp, Mama; Charles Coburn, Max Dreyfus. Gershwin's
brother Arthur and his sister neither appeared nor were
mentioned. Paul Whiteman, Oscar Levant, Al Jolson, George
White, Rouben Mamoulian, Hazel Scott, and Anne Brown
portrayed themselves, while Maurice Ravel, Serge Rachmaninoff, Walter Damrosch, Igor Stravinsky, and Jascha Heifetz were played by others.

The crowning glory of the picture was, of course,
Gershwin's music—the most ambitious attempt to encompass
within a single production his greatest works. *Rhapsody in
Blue* was a monumental cavalcade of twenty-nine Gershwin
numbers, including all of the major serious works (some, of
course, in digest form); eighteen numbers were given fea-

tured treatment. There were two of Gershwin's earliest songs, "Swanee" and "Yankee Doodle Blues," and one of his last, "Love Walked In," together with most of the others with which his name is always linked.

When *Rhapsody in Blue* was released in July 1945, the country "plunged," as *Newsweek* reported, "into a season of Gershwin such as no composer has had before." Theater and night clubs throughout the country played Gershwin. All four radio networks dedicated special programs to him.

New Gershwin music emerged in *The Shocking Miss Pilgrim*, starring Dick Haymes and Betty Grable, in 1947. From completed or uncompleted manuscripts Gershwin had left behind, Ira, with the assistance of Kay Swift as musical editor, prepared a score that included nine songs never before published or performed—only one was a "find," "For You, For Me, For Evermore."

In 1951 MGM released the last major film with Gershwin music, and in some respects the best: *An American in Paris*. This is a love story about an American painter in Paris (Gene Kelly) and a Parisian girl he meets in a café (Leslie Caron, making her American screen debut). The American, however, is pursued by a wealthy socialite (Nina Foch) who promotes his career; and the Parisian girl is sought by a successful producer (Georges Guetary). True love is able to overcome all misunderstandings and obstructions. The climax of the picture—"the uncontested high point," as Bosley Crowther described it in the New York *Times*—was a twenty-minute modernistic ballet conceived by Gene Kelly, with swirling colors and lights and impressionistic settings, danced by Kelly and Leslie Caron to the music of *An American in Paris*. This tone poem was not the only Gershwin music in the jewel-studded score. There were also extracts from the

Concerto in F, and seven songs, two of them relatively un-familiar: "Tra-la-la," from *For Goodness Sake* (1922), and "By Strauss," originally interpolated in the Beatrice Lillie—Bert Lahr revue, *The Show Is On* (1936). The score also had a carry-over from *The Goldwyn Follies*, "Love Is Here To Stay," which now became a hit for the first time.

An American in Paris became the surprise selection of the Motion Picture Academy as the best picture of 1951 (either *A Streetcar Named Desire* or *A Place in the Sun* were expected to win the Oscar). This was the third time, since the inception of the awards in 1927-1928, that a musical was thus honored.

Other motion pictures had Gershwin music. In 1949 Fred Astaire and Ginger Rogers revived their hit from *Shall We Dance*, "They Can't Take That Away from Me," in *The Barkleys of Broadway* (which had Ira Gershwin's lyrics to Harry Warren's music). Three years later, the Gershwin song "Somebody Loves Me" provided the title for and was used in a Paramount musical starring Betty Hutton. Three later musicals also reached far back into the past for Gershwin favorites: *A Star Is Born* (Ira Gershwin here wrote the lyrics for Harold Arlen's songs) used "Swanee" as a major pro-duction number; *Three for the Money* featured "Someone To Watch Over Me" and "I've Got a Crush On You"; and "Someone To Watch Over Me" was also heard in *Young in Heart*. A Bob Hope musical, produced in 1956, was called *That Certain Feeling* and used that song as its theme.

Since 1937 some of Gershwin's music has appeared in new contexts and formats.

On October 18, 1940, the Ballet Russe de Monte Carlo presented at the 51st Street Theater in New York the world première of a new ballet, *The New Yorkers*. Its music was adapted and orchestrated by David Raksin from many of Gershwin's best-known songs and excerpts from other works, beginning with "Strike Up the Band" as an overture, and embracing "Let's Call the Whole Thing Off," the dog-walking sequence in *Damsel in Distress*, "I Got Rhythm," "Fascinating Rhythm," "Love Is Sweeping the Country," and two piano preludes. It was planned by Rea Irvin and Léonide Massine to be a "dioramic view of New York's café society in three scenes." The programmatic note goes on to explain:

> It presents a nocturnal adventure of the animated drawings made famous by Peter Arno, Helen E. Hokinson, William Steig, Otto Soglow and other artists' creations whose habitude are the pages of the *New Yorker*. To Central Park's Plaza come Arno's Colonel, Dowager and Timid Man; Hokinson's clubwomen; boys and girls; each intent on hotspotting. Venal headwaiters, baby-faced debutantes, keyhole columnists, Steig's "small fry," gullible gangsters, Thurber's introverts, Soglow's Little King, all these with gentle madness people the parade of New York after dark. The thread of the story is incidental to the portrayal of characters whose lives begin when the city goes to bed.

The choreography was by Massine, his second attempt to use Americana. Settings and costumes were by Carl Kent. In reviewing the performance, Irving Kolodin wrote in the *Sun* that Gershwin's music "remained the principal glory," and described that music as "some of the most vital . . . ever created on this island or for that matter in the rest of America."

Another posthumous ballet treatment of Gershwin's music, given in Gothenburg, Sweden, in 1954, was an elaborate choreographic interpretation of the Concerto in F.

The *Rhapsody in Blue* emerged in a new, and not too effective, symphonic dress on November 30, 1941, at a concert of the New York City Symphony, with Jean Morel conducting. This time the Rhapsody was adapted for violin and orchestra by Gregory Stone, and it was introduced by the violin virtuoso, Mishel Piastro.

Music from *Porgy and Bess* was also given fresh treatment. Beryl Rubinstein transcribed five of its principal songs for piano, and Jascha Heifetz for violin and piano. The most significant transcription, however, is A *Symphonic Picture* by Robert Russell Bennett. This work was commissioned by the celebrated conductor, Fritz Reiner, who felt that an excellent symphonic work might be built out of materials of the opera. Reiner even pointed out the excerpts he wanted included. In creating an integrated tone poem out of this music, Bennett was faithful to Gershwin's harmonic and orchestral intentions. The *Symphonic Picture* is made up of the following sequences, in the order of their appearance: Scene of Catfish Row with the peddler's calls; Opening Act II; "Summertime" and Opening of Act I; "I Got Plenty o' Nuttin'"; Storm Music; "Bess, You Is My Woman Now"; "It Ain't Necessarily So"; and the finale, "Oh Lawd I'm on My Way." Reiner conducted the world première with the Pittsburgh Symphony Orchestra in Pittsburgh on February 5, 1942.

Individual Gershwin songs and medleys have been orchestrated since Gershwin's death at various times by various musicians including Nathan van Cleve, Fred von Epps, Claude Thornhill, David Broekman, Irving Brodsky, George

B. Leeman, and Nathaniel Finston. One of the most significant of these new orchestrations was Morton Gould's symphonic adaptation of "I Got Rhythm," introduced by Gould himself leading an orchestra over the Columbia Broadcasting System, on March 22, 1944, and performed by the New York Philharmonic-Symphony under Artur Rodzinski the following October 9. The three piano preludes have also been transcribed for orchestra several times, notably by Roy Bargy, Gregory Stone, L. Raymond, and David Broekman; Jascha Heifetz arranged them for violin and piano; and the second prelude has been adapted for violin, cello and piano and for trumpet and piano by Gregory Stone, and for saxophone and piano by Sigurd Rascher.

Of the many performances of Gershwin's serious music in this country since 1937, two events should be singled out for special attention. The all-Gershwin concert at the Lewisohn Stadium on July 11, 1938—one of many concerts commemorating the second anniversary of his death—included the last of the Gershwin premières: *Dawn of a New Day*. This was an adaptation by Ira Gershwin and Kay Swift of two unpublished Gershwin songs—the verse of one, and the chorus of another—as the official march for the New York World's Fair, for which the payment of $3,000 was made by Grover Whalen.

On November 1, 1942, Arturo Toscanini conducted a work by Gershwin for the first time. For this occasion he selected the *Rhapsody in Blue,* and it was performed over the N.B.C. network by the N.B.C. Symphony Orchestra, with Benny Goodman as clarinet soloist and Earl Wild as pianist. Before undertaking this performance, Toscanini studied several different recordings, but the final result of his most painstaking study and preparation was, regrettably, neither good Toscanini nor good Gershwin. Virgil Thomson wrote in the *Herald Tribune* the following morning: "It got rough treatment. . . . It all came off like a ton of bricks. It was the *Rhapsody in Blue,* all right, as what rendition isn't? But it was as far from George's own way of playing the piece as one could imagine. . . . I was a little sorry . . . to hear this gay, sweet, rhapsodical number treated in a routine glamorizing that rubbed all the bloom off it and left its surface as shining and as glittery as a nickle plated Apollo Belvedere."

Most of the country's leading popular-orchestra conductors (some two dozen) wired congratulations to Toscanini for finally playing Gershwin, and Gershwin's mother was in the studio to thank the Maestro personally.

Toscanini was now completely won over to Gershwin. On November 14, 1943, he performed *An American in Paris,* and on April 2, 1944, the Concerto in F with Oscar Levant as soloist. On several different occasions Toscanini confided to Samuel Chotzinoff that in his opinion Gershwin's music "is the only *real* American music."

Since 1937 the name of George Gershwin has become such a symbol of creative achievement in America that it has been used by many different institutions, organizations, competitions, and so forth.

On April 22, 1943, the S.S. *George Gershwin* was christened at San Pedro, California, by Leonore Gershwin. Among others who were present were Ira Gershwin, Paul Whiteman, Marc Connolly, and Jesse Lasky.

In 1946 the Victory Lodge of B'nai B'rith established the Gershwin Memorial Contest "to promote tolerance through music." A prize of $1,000—plus publication royalties and an initial performance by the New York Philharmonic-Symphony—was to be given each year for the best short work submitted in a competition judged by Serge Koussevitzky (honorary member), Marc Blitzstein, Aaron Copland, William Schuman, Rabbi Judah Cahan, and Leonard Bernstein. The first winner was Peter Mennin for *Symphonic Allegro,* and the presentation of the award was made by Gershwin's mother at a concert of the New York Philharmonic-Symphony, Leonard Bernstein conducting, at the Metropolitan Opera House on March 27, 1945. Among later winners were Harold Shapero, Earl George, Ulysses Kay, Ned Rorem, Brian Dority, Robert Kurka, Ray Travis, Ralph Sweeney, George Rochberg, Kenneth Gaburo, and Ramiro Cortes.

A second competition, the George Gershwin Memorial Award, was instituted in Hollywood in 1947. Nick Bolin of Los Angeles was awarded $1,000 for *California Sketches* which was introduced at an otherwise all-Gershwin concert conducted by Paul Whiteman at the Hollywood Bowl on July 12, 1947. The curious fact about Bolin's winning this award is that the *Rhapsody in Blue* was the motivating force in his becoming a composer.

In 1946 the George Gershwin Memorial Collection of Music and Musical Literature was founded by Carl van Vechten at the Fisk University Library in Nashville, Tennessee. "The name of Gershwin was intended not only to honor a personal friend," explained Arna Bontemps, the University librarian, in the inaugural catalogue, "but also to recall the fact that this American belonged to a minority group, that as a composer he worked successfully in both the popular and the classical fields, and that much of his best music was inspired by Negro rhythms."

The George Gershwin Theater Workshop Arena, sponsored by a committee headed by Oscar Hammerstein II, was dedicated at Boston University on December 6, 1950. Emil Ellis of New York, on behalf of the Gershwin family, presented to the university two of Gershwin's paintings to be hung in the arena: a self-portrait and a water-color of Folly Beach, South Carolina. Two years later, on July 12, 1952, a George Gershwin Practice Hut was opened at Chautauqua Institute, at Chautauqua, New York. And on November 14, 1954, a George Gershwin Theater was dedicated at Brooklyn College, New York; on this occasion a new portrait of Gershwin by Henry Botkin was unveiled.

On July 11, 1937, Ira lost not only his brother but also his collaborator. They had been inseparable for years; their social and professional lives had been enmeshed. Nobody could fill George's place in Ira's life. For two years after George's death he was inconsolable. Work was out of the question—for the time being at any rate.

In 1940 he returned to his typewriter, and wrote the lyrics to Kurt Weill's music for the Moss Hart Broadway success *A Lady in the Dark*, starring Gertrude Lawrence. Songs like "The Saga of Jenny," "Tchaikovsky," and "Oh, Fabulous One in Your Ivory Tower" demonstrated that the master of the lyric had lost none of his precision and skill. Two years later, Ira became associated with the greatest song success (from the point of view of sales) of his entire career in "Long Ago and Far Away," one of several numbers in the motion picture *Cover Girl*, starring Rita Hayworth, for which Jerome Kern wrote the music. In the same year, 1943, he wrote the lyrics to music by Aaron Copland for *North Star*. Later efforts added to the skein of his successes: particularly, his songs with Kurt Weill for *Where Do We Go from Here* (which contains in "The Niña, the Pinta, and the Santa Maria" one of the most brilliant protracted verse sequences the screen has known); with Harry Warren for *The Barkleys of Broadway*, with Fred Astaire and Ginger Rogers; and with Harold Arlen for *A Star Is Born*, with Judy Garland, and *A Country Girl* with Bing Crosby. One of the songs from *A Star Is Born*, "The Man That Got Away," was one of the five nominated for the Academy Award in 1955.

Thus, since 1937, Ira Gershwin has succeeded in reassuming that imperial position among the song lyricists of this generation that he had previously occupied as George's collaborator.

appendixes

THE PLOT OF
Porgy and Bess

The setting is Catfish Row, a Negro tenement on Charleston's waterfront in South Carolina. A brief orchestral prelude, dissonant and brilliantly colored, suggests the pulse of activity, the restless movement of Catfish Row. In one corner of the court a crap game is taking place. In another, there is dancing. In a third, Clara is singing a tender lullaby to her child ("Summertime"). Serena entreats her husband, Robbins, not to join the crap game, but he is deaf to her entreaty. The voices of the gamblers, as they excitedly exhort the die to be kind to them, becomes a contrapuntal background to Clara's lullaby. Jake, her husband, impatient that the child is not yet asleep, snatches it from her arms and sings to it a ditty of his own which laments the fickleness of woman ("A Woman Is a Sometime Thing"). Into the seething activity of Catfish Row comes the honey man selling his ware with a street cry. After the orchestra makes a brief reference to the opening prelude, Porgy, the cripple, arrives in his goat cart. The men welcome him, but also jeer at him for being "soft" on Crown's girl, Bess. In a poignant and highly moving recitative, "When Gawd make cripple, He mean him to be lonely," Porgy describes the bleakness of his life; but he also insists he is soft on no woman. The appearance of Bess, on the arm of Crown, makes Porgy refer briefly to Jake's ditty that "a woman is a sometime thing." Crown is drunk. Soon he is further stimulated by the "happy dust" Sportin' Life gives him. When Crown joins the crap game he is in an ugly mood. Robbins wins one of the shoots and is about to scoop up his winnings when Crown seizes him by the wrist and prevents him. They fight. The people of Catfish Row cry out for them to stop, but the brawl grows more and more furious. Finally Crown seizes a cotton hook and kills his opponent. As Crown makes his escape, Serena throws herself on her dead husband's body. Shaking with fright, Bess is soothed by the "happy dust" Sportin' Life offers her; at the same time, Sportin' Life suggests to her that they go off to New York together. When she is alone, Bess seeks protection and a temporary home, but the people of Catfish Row are hostile to her and their doors are closed. Only the cripple, Porgy, is sympathetic. "Bess, Bess, Porgy will take you," he calls to her.

The scene now shifts to Serena's room where the mourners lament Robbins' death in a stirring threnody, "He's a-gone, gone, gone." Porgy makes a dramatic appeal to the mourners to fill the saucer with burial money. They comply—to the strains of another moving spiritual, "Overflow, Overflow," which then becomes the background music for a second dramatic appeal by

Porgy. The proceedings are disturbed by the arrival of a detective. He arrests Peter, one of the mourners, as a witness to the murder, and warns Robbins' widow to have the body buried the following day or it will be turned over to the medical students. With the detective gone, the mourners return to their lament, "Gone, gone, gone," and Serena gives voice to her terrible grief ("My Man's Gone Now"). When the undertaker arrives, he generously consents to bury Robbins for whatever money has been collected and to trust Serena for the rest. Descending chords in the orchestra, like the implacable tread of Fate, lead to Bess' exultant spiritual, "Oh, the train is at the station. . . . An' it's headin' for the Promised Lan'."

At the rise of the second-act curtain, Jake and other fishermen are repairing their nets. They sing a vigorous work song, swaying to its rhythms as if they were actually rowing a boat— "It take a long pull to get there." Porgy is sitting at the window watching them. His new-found happiness with Bess finds expression in the joyous refrain, "Oh I got plenty o' nuttin'." Others in Catfish Row remark on Porgy's happiness and how his love for Bess has changed him into a kind and beaming man. As if in confirmation, Porgy continues more joyfully than before with his song. Then the lawyer Frazier appears. For a dollar and a half he sells Bess a divorce from Crown—the usual fee for divorce is one dollar, but since the situation is complicated by the fact that Bess and Crown have never married, a higher fee is required. When Mr. Archdale, a white lawyer, arrives, he scolds Frazier for selling fake divorces, and he informs Porgy he has arranged for Peter's release from jail. As Mr. Archdale leaves, Porgy notices a buzzard flying overhead. In the "Buzzard Song" Porgy suggests it is an omen of impending disaster; the vivid orchestral background to his song emphasizes the feeling of doom that seizes Porgy and the rest of the crowd, which soon disperses with fear. Sportin' Life tries to get Bess to take more of his "happy dust" and once again urges her to come to New York. Porgy attacks Sportin' Life and drives him away. Porgy and Bess then speak of their love for each other in a rhapsodic duet, "Bess, You Is My Woman Now"; a highly expressive passage in the cello points up the tenderness of their feelings. Porgy then insists that Bess go off with the rest of Catfish Row to the lodge picnic taking place that day. Bess is hesitant, for she does not want to leave Porgy alone, but she finally yields to his persuasion. Catfish Row is now deserted, except for Porgy. "I got plenty o' nuttin'," he repeats triumphantly as the curtain is lowered. "I got my gal, got My Lawd, got my song."

The lodge picnic is held on Kittiwah Island. Primitive rhythms in the orchestra describe the abandoned gaiety. There is frenetic dancing and uninhibited singing. Several Negroes make music on mouth organs, combs, a washboard, and bones. Sportin' Life steps forward to give the crowd his cynical philosophy ("It Ain't Necessarily So"), much to the amusement of his audience. The picnic is about over, and Serena calls the people back to the boat. Before Bess can join them, Crown—who has been hiding on this very island—emerges furtively from a thicket and calls to her. She tries to tell him that she now belongs to Porgy, that Crown should seek out a younger girl. "Oh what you want wid Bess," she wails, against a strongly syncopated rhythm in the orchestra. But Crown still wants his girl. Breaking down her resistance, he drags her off into the woods.

A few bars of atmospheric music depict early dawn in Catfish Row. The fishermen are getting ready to go off to sea. As they depart, they repeat their work song, "It take a long pull to get there." After they leave, the court begins to resume its normal daily pulse. The strawberry woman and the crab man stroll in and out, shouting their street cries as they try to sell their wares. Peter, released from prison, arrives, bewildered by all that has happened to him. Bess, who has returned after two days on Kittiwah Island, is feverish and ill, and is being gently nursed back to health by Porgy. Serena prays for Bess' recovery with a dynamic "shout" that is punctuated with cries and exclamations from the rest of the women. The prayer is efficacious. Pale and weary, Bess comes out of her room to sit with Porgy outside their door. She confesses to Porgy that she has been with Crown and that she promised Crown to return to him. Porgy is ready to forget and forgive. When she tells him she is really in love with him alone, Porgy promises to protect her. A duet, "I Loves You Porgy," reaffirms the love each has for the other. The last strains of their song die out when the hurricane bells sound an ominous warning.

In the scene that follows, Serena's terrorized friends are in her room praying for their men out at sea. Porgy urges Clara to join in the singing, but Clara is oblivious to what is happening; she is singing softly to her baby a strain from "Summertime." In a sudden outburst of thunder and lightning, the door swings open, and Crown enters. He has come for Bess (the orchestra gently recalls a phrase from "Bess, You Is My Woman Now"). She insists she belongs to Porgy alone. Crown mocks the cripple, then becomes blasphemous. The shocked women continue their prayers more fervently than before, while Crown introduces a sacrilegious note into the praying by singing a vulgar blues melody ("A Red-Headed Woman Makes a Choochoo Jump Its Track"). The storm now erupts in full fury. From her seat at the window Bess sees that Jake's boat has overturned. Clara turns her baby over to Bess and rushes out to save her drowning husband. Bess cries out for a man to follow Clara and help her.

"Porgy, what you sittin' dere for," jeers Crown. Then Crown rushes to Clara's aid, but as he leaves he warns Bess he will come back for her.

The third act opens in Catfish Row. It is night; the court is filled with the poignant voices of women singing a plangent spiritual for their dead. Sportin' Life appears. He hints that Crown is still alive and that he will come for Bess, that a woman who has two men has no man at all. At the window of Porgy's room, Bess is lulling Clara's baby to sleep with a few bars of "Summertime." Suddenly Catfish Row becomes empty. In the dark, Crown appears and stealthily makes his way to Porgy's room. Quietly he calls to Bess. From the window emerges Porgy's hand with a long knife. As Crown approaches, Porgy plunges the knife in his rival's back; then Porgy strangles him. With Crown dead, Porgy exclaims jubilantly to Bess: "You got a man now. You got Porgy."

The next morning a detective, a coroner, and the police invade Catfish Row to question its inhabitants in order to un-cover Crown's murderer. The coroner insists that Porgy be taken to the police station to identify the dead man. Horrified that he must look at Crown's face, Porgy refuses to go and has to be dragged off. Once Porgy is gone, Sportin' Life tries to convince Bess that Porgy will be in jail a long, long time. He gives her some "happy dust" which she refuses. Then more ardently than ever—and with more extravagant promises of the bountiful life awaiting her—he tries to get her to go with him to New York ("There's a Boat That's Leavin' Soon for New York"). When Bess spurns him, he leaves a package of his "happy dust" outside her door in case she changes her mind. Bess' struggle with her will finally proves hopeless; she suddenly emerges from her room to snatch the package.

A week goes by. Porgy returns from jail in a jubilant mood.

He has finally been freed, and he is loaded with gifts for Bess and his friends. As he tells of his experiences, the orchestra recalls "Bess, You Is My Woman Now" as a rhapsodic song for strings—for Porgy is more deeply in love with Bess than ever. He calls to Bess but gets no answer. The embarrassment and discomfort of his friends arouse his suspicions and fears. He wails, "Oh Bess, oh where's my Bess." In a moving trio, Porgy continues to beseech his friends for information about Bess, while Serena and Maria try to convince him that he is well rid of her. It is only then that Porgy learns that Bess has gone to New York with Sportin' Life. Defiantly he calls for his goat cart. He intends to follow Bess to New York; he cannot live without her. When his friends realize they cannot dissuade him, they bid him farewell. The orchestra brings back a fragment from the opening prelude of the first act. With a dolorous spiritual on his lips, "Oh Lawd, I'm on my way to a Heavenly Land," Porgy sets forth on his long journey by cart. His friends join him in his song.

CONCERT WORKS BY GERSHWIN

1922

    135th Street, one-act opera, with libretto by B. G. De Sylva. Originally entitled *Blue Monday.* Première: *Scandals of 1922,* the Globe Theater, August 29, 1922 (one performance).

1924

    Rhapsody in Blue, for piano and orchestra. Première: Paul Whiteman and Orchestra, with the composer as soloist, Aeolian Hall, New York, February 12, 1924.

1925

    Concerto in F, for piano and orchestra. Première: New York Symphony Society, Walter Damrosch conducting, with the composer as soloist, Carnegie Hall, New York, December 3, 1925.

1926

Three Preludes, for piano solo. Première: The composer as soloist, Hotel Roosevelt, New York, November 4, 1926.

1928

An American in Paris, tone poem for orchestra. Première: New York Philharmonic-Symphony Society, Walter Damrosch conducting, Carnegie Hall, New York, December 13, 1928.

"In the Mandarin's Orchid Garden," concert song, with lyrics by Ira Gershwin. Première: Eleanor Marum, Blackstone Theater, Chicago, November 10, 1929.

1931

Second Rhapsody, for piano and orchestra. Première: Boston Symphony Orchestra, Serge Koussevitzky conducting, with the composer as soloist, Symphony Hall, Boston, January 29, 1932.

1932

Piano Transcriptions of 18 Songs. Published by Simon and Schuster, New York, 1932. SONGS: Swanee; Nobody But You; I'll Build a Stairway to Paradise; Do It Again; Fascinating Rhythm; Oh, Lady Be Good; Somebody Loves Me; Sweet and Low Down; That Certain Feeling; The Man I Love; Clap Yo' Hands; Do, Do, Do; My One and Only; 'S Wonderful Strike Up the Band; Liza; I Got Rhythm.

Cuban Overture, for symphony orchestra and Cuban percussion instruments. Originally entitled *Rhumba.* Première: Lewisohn Stadium Orchestra, Albert Coates conducting, Lewisohn Stadium, New York, August 16, 1932.

1934

    Variations on I Got Rhythm, for piano and orchestra. Première: Leo Reisman Orchestra, Charles Previn conducting, with the composer as soloist, Boston, January 14, 1934.

1935

    Porgy and Bess, grand opera in three acts, with libretto by DuBose Heyward, based on the play *Porgy,* by Dorothy and DuBose Heyward, and lyrics by DuBose Heyward and Ira Gershwin. Premiere: Colonial Theater, Boston, September 30, 1935.

STAGE PRODUCTIONS WITH
GERSHWIN'S MUSIC

1918

Half-Past Eight. Lyrics by Arthur Jackson. Opened and closed out-of-town. SONGS: There's Magic in the Air; Hong-Kong; The Ten Commandments of Love.

1919

Capitol Revue, a revue staged at the Capitol Theater, New York, and produced by Ned Wayburn for the opening of the theater. SONGS: Swanee (Caesar); Come to the Moon (Paley and Wayburn).

La, La Lucille. Book by Fred Jackson. Lyrics by Arthur Jackson, with additional lyrics by B. G. De Sylva. Produced by Alex A. Aarons at the Henry Miller Theater on May 26, 1919 (104 performances). With Jack Hazard and Janet Velie. SONGS: Nobody But You; When You Live in a Furnished Flat; The Best of Everything; Money, Money, Money; From Now on; Tee-Oodlc-Um-Bum-Bo; I Love To Be Loved by You; It's Great To Be in Love; There's More to the Kiss Than X-X-X (Caesar); Somehow It Seldom Comes True; The Ten Commandments of Love; The Love of a Wife.

The Morris Gest Midnight Whirl. Book and lyrics by B. G. De Sylva and John Henry Mears. Produced by Morris Gest at the Century Theater on December 27, 1919 (110 performances). With Bessie McCoy, Helen Shipman, and the Rath Brothers. SONGS: I'll Show You a Wonderful World; The League of Nations Depend on Beautiful Clothes; Baby Dolls; Let Cutie Cut Your Cuticle; Doughnut Song; Limehouse Nights; Poppyland.

1920

Broadway Brevities of 1920. Book by Blair Traynor and Archie Gottlier. Lyrics by Arthur Jackson. Produced by George LeMaire at the Winter Garden on September 29, 1920 (105 performances). With George LeMaire, Eddie Cantor, and Bert Williams. SONGS: Lu Lu; Snow Flakes; Spanish Love (Caesar).

The Scandals of 1920. Book by Andy Rice and George White. Lyrics by Arthur Jackson. Produced by George White at the Globe Theater on June 7, 1920 (318 performances). With Ann Pennington, Lou Holtz, Ethel Delmar, George White, Lester Allen, Doctor Rockwell. SONGS: My Lady; Idle Dreams; Everybody Swat the Profiteer; On My Mind the Whole Night Long; Scandal Walk; Come on and Kiss Me; I Love the Old Songs.

A Dangerous Maid. Book by Charles W. Bell. Lyrics by Arthur Francis (Ira Gershwin). Opened and closed out-of-town. SONGS: Boy Wanted; Dancing Shoes; Just To Know You Are Mine; The Simple Life; Some Rain Must Fall.

1921

The Scandals of 1921. Book by Bugs Baer and George White. Lyrics by Arthur Jackson. Produced by George White at the Liberty Theater on July 11, 1921 (97 performances). With George White, Ann Pennington, Lester Allen, Charles King, Lou Holtz. SONGS: I Love You; South Sea Isles; Where East Meets West; Drifting Along With the Tide; Just a Baby; Mother Eve (MacDonald and Hanley).

1922

George White's Scandals of 1922. Book by George White, W. C. Fields, and Andy Rice. Lyrics of E. Ray Goetz and B. G. De Sylva. Produced by George White at the Globe Theater on August 28, 1922 (88 performances). With W. C. Fields, Lester Allen, Winnie Lightner, Jack MacGowan, Ed Wynn, Paul Whiteman and Orchestra. SONGS: She Hangs out in Our Alley; Little Cinderelatives; I Found a Four-Leaf Clover; I Can Tell Where They're from When They Dance; I'll Build a Stairway to Paradise (De Silva and Arthur Francis); Just a Tiny Cup of Tea; Where Is the Man of My Dreams; My Heart Will Sail Across the Sea; The Moth for My Flame; The Grab Bag; Argentina. The one-act opera, *Blue Monday (135th Street)* was given a single performance, on opening night.

Our Nell, "a musical mellow drayma." Book and lyrics by A. E. Thomas and Brian Hooker. Music by Gershwin and William Daly. Produced by The Hayseed Productions, Inc., at the Nora Bayes Theater on December 4, 1922 (40 performances). GERSH-WIN's SONGS: Innocent Ingenue Baby; Walking Home with Angeline; Bye and Bye; My Old New England Home.

1923

George White's Scandals of 1923. Book by George White and William K. Wells. Lyrics by E. Ray Goetz, B. G. De Sylva, and Ballard MacDonald. Produced by George White at the Globe Theater on June 18, 1923 (168 performances). With Johnny Dooley, Lester Allen, Tom Patricola, Winnie Lightner. SONGS: Little Scandal Dolls; You and I in Old Versailles; Katinka; Lo-La-Lo; There Is Nothing Too Good for You; Let's Be Lonesome Together; Life of a Rose; Look in the Looking Glass; Where Is She?; Laugh Your Cares Away; Throw Her in High; On the Beach at How've You Been.

The Rainbow Revue (London). Book by Albert de Courville, Noel Scott, and Edgar Wallace. Lyrics by Clifford Grey. SONGS: Innocent Lonesome Blue Baby; Sweetheart I'm So Glad I Met You; Moonlight in Versailles; Goodnight My Dear; Sunday in London Town; Yankee Doodle Blues (Caesar and De Sylva); In the Rain; Oh Nina; Eastern Moon; Any Little Tune; Lady with Me; Give Me My Mammy; All Over Town.

1924

George White's Scandals of 1924. Book by George White and William K. Wells. Lyrics by B. G. De Sylva. Produced by George White at the Globe Theater on June 18, 1924 (192 performances). With Lester Allen, Tom Patricola, Winnie Lightner,

Will Mahoney. SONGS: I Need a Garden; Night Time in Araby; Year After Year; Somebody Loves Me (Ballard MacDonald); Tune in to Station J-O-Y; Rose of Madrid; Kongo Kate; I'm Going Back.

Lady Be Good. Book by Guy Bolton and Fred Thompson. Lyrics by Ira Gershwin. Produced by Aarons and Freedley at the Liberty Theater on December 1, 1924 (184 performances). With Fred and Adele Astaire, Walter Catlett, Cliff Edwards, and Ohman and Arden. SONGS: Hang on to Me; A Wonderful Party; The End of a String; We're Here Because; So Am I; Fascinating Rhythm; Oh, Lady Be Good; Linger in the Lobby; The Half of It Dearie Blues; Little Jazz Bird; Carnival; Swiss Miss.

Primrose (London). Book by Guy Bolton and George Grossmith. Lyrics by Ira Gershwin and Desmond Carter. SONGS: Till I Meet Someone Like You; Isn't It Wonderful; This Is the Life for a Man; When Toby Is out of Town; Some Far Away Someone; The Mophams; Four Little Sirens; Berkeley Square and Kew; Boy Wanted; Wait a Bit Susie; Naughty Baby; I Make Hay When the Moon Shines; Beau Brummel.

Sweet Little Devil. Book by Frank Mandel and Laurence Schwab. Lyrics by B. G. De Sylva. Produced by Laurence Schwab at the Astor Theater on January 21, 1924 (120 performances). With Constance Binney and Irving Beebe. SONGS: Strike, Strike, Strike; Lucky; Virginia, Don't Go Too Far; Someone Believes In You; Jijibo; Quite a Party; Under a One-Man Top; Hey, Hey, Let 'Er Go; Hooray for the U.S.A.; Sweet Little Devil; The Matrimonial Handicap; Pepita.

1925

Song of the Flame. Book and lyrics by Otto Harbach and Oscar Hammerstein II. Music by Herbert Stothart and Gershwin.

Produced by Arthur Hammerstein at the 44th Street Theater on December 30, 1925 (194 performances). With Tessa Kosta and Guy Robertson. GERSHWIN'S SONGS: Far Away; Song of the Flame; Woman's Work Is Never Done; Great Big Bear; Cossack Love Song; Midnight Bells; Tartar; You May Wander Away; You Are You.

Tell Me More. Book by Fred Thompson and William K. Wells. Lyrics by B. G. De Sylva and Ira Gershwin. Produced by Alex A. Aarons at the Gaiety Theater on April 13, 1925 (32 performances). With Alexander Gray and Phyllis Cleveland. SONGS: Mr. and Mrs. Sipkin; Three Times a Day; When Debbies Go By; Why Do I Love You?; Kickin' the Clouds Away; Love Is in the Air; My Fair Lady; Tell Me More; In Sardinia; Baby; Ukelele Lorelei.

Tip Toes. Book by Guy Bolton and Fred Thompson. Lyrics by Ira Gershwin. Produced by Aarons and Freedley at the Liberty Theater on December 28, 1925 (194 performances). With Queenie Smith, Allen Kearns, Robert Halliday, Andrew Tombes, and Jeanette MacDonald in a minor role. SONGS: Waiting for the Train; Nice Baby, Come to Papa; Looking for a Boy; Lady Luck; When Do We Dance; These Charming People; That Certain Feeling; Sweet and Low Down; Our Little Captain; Tip Toes; It's a Great Little World; Nightie Night.

1926

Oh Kay. Book by Guy Bolton and P. G. Wodehouse. Lyrics by Ira Gershwin. Produced by Aarons and Freedley at the Imperial Theater on November 8, 1926 (256 performances). With Gertrude Lawrence, Oscar Shaw, Victor Moore, and Harland Dixon. SONGS: The Woman's Touch; Don't Ask; Dear Little Girl; Maybe; Clap Yo' Hands; Do, Do, Do; Bride and Groom; Someone To Watch Over Me; Fidgety Feet; Heaven on Earth; Oh Kay.

1927

Funny Face. Book by Paul Gerard and Fred Thompson. Lyrics by Ira Gershwin. Produced by Aarons and Freedley at the Alvin Theater on November 22, 1927 (244 performances). With Fred and Adele Astaire, Victor Moore, and Allen Kearns. SONGS: Birthday Party; Once; 'S Wonderful; Funny Face; High Hat; Let's Kiss and Make Up; In the Swim; He Loves and She Loves; Tell the Doc; My One and Only; Sing a Little Song; The Babbitt and the Bromide; Dance Alone with You; The World Is Mine.

1928

Rosalie. Book by Guy Bolton and William Anthony McGuire. Lyrics by Ira Gershwin and P. G. Wodehouse. Additional songs by Sigmund Romberg. Produced by Florenz Ziegfeld at the Ziegfeld Theater on January 10, 1928 (335 performances). With Marilyn Miller, Bobbe Arnst, Frank Morgan, Jack Donahue. GERSHWIN'S SONGS: Show Me the Town; Say So; Let Me Be a Friend to You; Yankee Doodle Rhythms; Oh Gee, Oh Joy; New York Serenade; How Long Has This Been Going on?

Treasure Girl. Book by Vincent Lawrence and Fred Thompson. Lyrics by Ira Gershwin. Produced by Aarons and Freedley at the Alvin Theater on November 8, 1928 (68 performances). With Gertrude Lawrence, Clifton Webb, Walter Catlett, Paul Frawley. SONGS: Skull and Bones; Oh So Nice; According to Mr. Grimes; A Place in the Country; K-ra-zy for You; I Don't Think I'll Fall in Love Today; Got a Rainbow; I've Got a Feelin' I'm Fallin'; What Causes That; What Are We Here for; Where's the Boy? Here's the Girl.

1929

Show Girl. Book by William Anthony McGuire based on J. P. McEvoy's novel of the same name. Additional songs by Jimmie Durante. Lyrics by Ira Gershwin and Gus Kahn. Produced by Florenz Ziegfeld at the Ziegfeld Theater on July 2, 1929 (111 performances). With Ruby Keeler, Clayton, Jackson and Durante, Joseph McCauley, Harriet Hoctor, and Duke Ellington. GERSHWIN'S SONGS: Happy Birthday; My Sunday Fella; How Could I Forget; Lolita; Do What You Do; Spain; One Man; So Are You; I Must be Home by Twelve O'Clock; Black and White; Harlem Serenade; Home Blues; Following the Minstrel Band; Liza. *An American in Paris* was used for a ballet sequence.

Strike Up the Band. Book by Morrie Ryskind and George S. Kaufman. Lyrics by Ira Gershwin. Produced by Edgar Selwyn at the Times Square Theater on January 14, 1930 (191 performances). With Clark and McCullough. SONGS: I Mean to Say; A Typical Self-Made American; Soon; A Man of High Degree; Three Cheers for the Union; This Could Go on for Years; If I Became President; What's the Use of Hanging Around with You; He Knows Milk; Strike Up the Band; In the Rattle of Battle; Military Dancing Drill; Mademoiselle in New Rochelle; I've Got a Crush on You; How About a Boy Like Me; Ring a Ding a Ding-Dong Bell; I Want To Be a War Bride; Yankee Doodle Rhythm; Seventeen and Twenty-One; Nobody.

1930

Girl Crazy. Book by Guy Bolton and John McGowan. Lyrics by Ira Gershwin. Produced by Aarons and Freedley at the Alvin Theater on October 14, 1930 (272 performances). With Ethel Merman, Ginger Rogers, Allen Kearns, and Willie Howard. SONGS: Bidin' My Time; The Lonesome Cowboy; Could You Use

Me?; Broncho Busters; Barbary Coast; Embraceable You; Sam and Delilah; I Got Rhythm; Land of the Gay Caballero; But Not for Me; Treat Me Rough; Boy What Love Has Done to Me; Cactus Time in Arizona.

1931

Of Thee I Sing. Book by Morrie Ryskind and George S. Kaufman. Lyrics by Ira Gershwin. Produced by Sam H. Harris at the Music Box Theater on December 26, 1931 (441 performances). With William Gaxton, Victor Moore, Lois Moran, June O'Dea, George Murphy. The first musical to win a Pulitzer Prize for drama. SONGS: Wintergreen for President; Who Is the Lucky Girl To Be; The Dimple on My Knee; Because, Because; Never Was There a Girl So Fair; Some Girls Can Bake a Pie; Love Is Sweeping the Country; Of Thee I Sing; Here's a Kiss for Cinderella; I Was the Most Beautiful Blossom; Hello, Good Morning; Who Cares; Garçon, S'il Vous Plaît; The Illegitimate Daughter; The Roll Call; Jilted; Posterity Is Just Around the Corner; Trumpeter Blow Your Horn.

REVIVAL: May 5, 1952. Produced by Chandler Cowles and Ben Segal at the Ziegfeld Theater. With Jack Carson, Paul Hartmann, Betty Oakes, and Lenore Lonergan.

1933

Let 'Em Eat Cake. Book by Morrie Ryskind and George S. Kaufman. Lyrics by Ira Gershwin. Produced by Sam H. Harris at the Imperial Theater on October 21, 1933 (90 performances). With William Gaxton, Victor Moore, Lois Moran, and Philip Loeb. SONGS: Wintergreen for President; Tweedledee for President; Union Square; Shirts by Millions; Comes the Revolution; Mine; Cloistered from the Noisy City; On and On and On; Let

'Em Eat Cake; Blue, Blue, Blue; Who's the Greatest; No Comprenez, No Capish; Up and At 'Em; That's What He Did; I Know a Foul Ball; Throttle Throttlebottom; A Hell of a Fix; Let 'Em Eat Caviar; Hanging Throttlebottom in the Morning.

Pardon My English. Book by Herbert Fields. Lyrics by Ira Gershwin. Produced by Aarons and Freedley at the Majestic Theater on January 20, 1933 (46 performances). With Lyda Roberti, Jack Pearl, George Givot. SONGS: Three-Quarter Time; The Lorelei; Pardon My English; Dancing in the Streets; So What; Isn't It a Pity; My Cousin from Milwaukee; Hail the Happy Couple; The Dresden Northwest Mounted; Luckiest Man in the World; I Want to Be There; Tonight; Where You Go, I Go; He's Not Himself.

STAGE PRODUCTIONS WITH

INTERPOLATED GERSHWIN SONGS

1916

The Passing Show of 1916. Book and lyrics by Harold Atteridge. Music by Sigmund Romberg and Otto Motzaw. Produced by the Shuberts at the Winter Garden on June 22, 1916 (140 performances). With Ed Wynn, Fred Walton, Stella Horban, Herman Timberg, and the Ford Sisters. SONG: The Making of a Girl.

1918

Hitchy Koo of 1918. Book and lyrics by Glen MacDonough. Music by Raymond Hubbell. Produced by Raymond Hitchcock at the Globe Theater on June 6, 1918 (68 performances). With Leon Errol, Irene Bordoni, and Raymond Hitchcock. SONG: You —oo Just You (Caesar).

Sinbad. Book and lyrics by Harold Atteridge. Music by Sigmund Romberg and Al Jolson. Produced by the Shuberts at the Winter Garden on February 14, 1918 (164 performances). With Al Jolson. SONGS: Swanee (Caesar); Dixie Rose (Caesar and De Sylva).

1919

Good Morning Judge. Book by Fred Thompson based on Pinero's *The Magistrate.* Music by Lionel Monckton and Howard Talbott. Produced by the Shuberts at the Shubert Theater on February 6, 1919 (140 performances). With Molly and Charles King. SONGS: I Was So Young (Caesar and Bryan); There's More to the Kiss Than X-X-X (Caesar).

Lady in Red. Book and lyrics by Anne Caldwell. Music by Robert Winterberg. Produced by John J. Slocum at the Lyric Theater on May 12, 1919 (48 performances). With Adele Rowland. SONG: Something about Love (Paley).

1920

Dere Mabel. SONG: We're Pals (Caesar).

Ed Wynn Carnival. Book and songs by Ed Wynn. Produced by J. C. Whitney at the New Amsterdam Theater on April 5, 1920 (64 performances). With Ed Wynn. SONG: Oh How I Love to Be Loved By You (Paley).

Look Who's Here. Book by Frank Mandel. Lyrics by Edward Paulson, with additional lyrics by Cecil Lean. Music by Silvio Hein. Produced by the Spiegels, Inc., at the 44th Street

Theater on March 2, 1920 (87 performances). With Cleo May-field and George Mack. SONG: Some Wonderful Sort of Someone (Green).

Sweetheart Shop. Book and lyrics by Anne Caldwell. Music by Hugo Felix. Produced by Edgar J. MacGregor and William Moore Patch at the Knickerbocker Theater on August 31, 1920 (55 performances). With Helen Ford. SONG: Waiting for the Sun to Come Out (Caesar).

1921

The Perfect Fool. Book, lyrics, and music by Ed Wynn. Produced by A. L. Erlanger at the George M. Cohan Theater on November 7, 1921 (256 performances). With Ed Wynn. SONG: My Log Cabin Home (Caesar and De Sylva).

1922

For Goodness Sake. Book by Fred Jackson. Lyrics by Arthur Jackson. Music by William Daly and Paul Lannin. Produced by Alex A. Aarons at the Lyric Theater on February 20, 1922 (103 performances). With Fred and Adele Astaire. SONGS: Someone; Tra-la-la.

The French Doll. Book and lyrics by A. E. Thomas, adapted from a French play by Armont and Gerbidion. Produced by E. Ray Goetz at the Lyceum Theater on February 20, 1922 (120 performances). With Irene Bordoni. SONG: Do It Again (De Sylva).

Spice of 1922. Book and lyrics by Jack Lait. Produced by Arman Kaliz at the Winter Garden on July 6, 1922 (73 performances). With George Price, Valeska Suratt, Arman Kaliz. SONG: Yankee Doodle Blues (Caesar and De Sylva).

1923

   The Dancing Girl. Book and lyrics by Harold Atteridge and Irving Caesar. Music by Sigmund Romberg. Produced by the Shuberts at the Winter Garden on January 24, 1923 (126 performances). With Marie Dressler, Trini, and Tom Burke. SONGS: The American Boy of Mine; Cuddle Me as We Dance; Why Am I Sad?; Pango Pango.

   Little Miss Bluebeard. Book and lyrics by Avery Hopwood. Music by various composers. Produced by Charles Frohman and E. Ray Goetz at the Lyceum Theater on August 28, 1923 (175 performances). With Irene Bordoni. SONG: I Won't Say I Will (De Sylva and Jackson).

   Nifties of 1923. Book and lyrics by Sam Bernard and William Collier. Produced by Charles Dillingham at the Fulton Theater on September 25, 1923 (47 performances). With Bernard Collier, Van and Schenck, Ray Dooley, Frank Crumit, and Helen Broderick. SONGS: Nashville Nightingale (Caesar); At Half-Past Seven (De Sylva).

1926

   Americana. Book and lyrics by J. P. McEvoy. Music by various composers. Produced by Richard Herndon at the Belmont Theater on July 26, 1926 (224 performances). With Lew Brice, Roy Atwell, Charles Butterworth, and Helen Morgan. SONG: That Lost Barber-Shop Chord (Ira Gershwin).

1936

   The Show Is On. Book by David Freedman and Moss Hart. Music by various composers. SONG: By Strauss (Ira Gershwin).

GERSHWIN SCORES FOR
MOTION PICTURES

1931

   Delicious. A Fox Production starring Janet Gaynor and Charles Farrell. Directed by David Butler. SONGS: Delishious; Blah, Blah, Blah; Somebody from Somewhere; Katinkitschka. An orchestral interlude was the basis of the *Second Rhapsody.*

1937

   Damsel in Distress. An RKO Production starring Fred Astaire and Joan Fontaine. Directed by George Stevens. SONGS: Foggy Day; Things Are Looking Up; I Can't Be Bothered Now; Nice Work If You Can Get It.

Shall We Dance. An RKO Production starring Fred Astaire and Ginger Rogers. Directed by Mark Sandrich. SONGS: Slap That Bass; Let's Call the Whole Thing Off; They Can't Take That Away from Me; Shall We Dance; They All Laughed; I've Got Beginner's Luck.

1938

The Goldwyn Follies. A United Artists Production with Vera Zorina, Adolphe Menjou, Andrea Leeds, and others. Directed by George Marshall. SONGS: Love Walked In; Our Love Is Here to Stay; I Love To Rhyme; Just Another Rhumba; I Was Doing All Right.

1945

Rhapsody in Blue. A Warner Brothers Production. The screen biography of George Gershwin, starring Robert Alda as the composer, and with Joan Leslie, Alexis Smith, Charles Coburn, Oscar Levant, and many others. Directed by Irving Rapper. SONGS: Swanee; Yankee Doodle Blues; 'S Wonderful; Somebody Loves Me; The Man I Love; Embraceable You; Summertime; It Ain't Necessarily So; Oh, Lady Be Good; I Got Rhythm; Love Walked In; Clap Yo' Hands; Do It Again; I'll Build a Stairway to Paradise; Liza; Someone To Watch Over Me; Bidin' My Time; Delishious; I Got Plenty o' Nuttin'. ALSO: *Rhapsody in Blue; An American in Paris;* Concerto in F.

1947

The Shocking Miss Pilgrim. A 20th Century Fox Production, starring Betty Grable and Dick Haymes. Directed by George Seaton. SONGS: Aren't You Kinda Glad We Did; For You, For Me, For Evermore; But Not in Boston; Stand Up and Fight; Changing

My Tune; One, Two, Three; Sweet Backward; Waltz Me No Waltzes; Waltzing Is Better Than Sitting Down; Back Bay Polka.

1951

An American in Paris. An MGM Production starring Gene Kelly and Leslie Caron, with Oscar Levant and Nina Foch. Directed by Vincent Minnelli. It won the Academy Award as the best picture of the year. SONGS: I Got Rhythm; Embraceable You; 'S Wonderful; By Strauss; Tra-la-la; Our Love Is Here To Stay; I'll Build a Stairway to Paradise. ALSO: Concerto in F; *An American in Paris.*

MOTION PICTURES ADAPTED
FROM GERSHWIN MUSICALS
(*with Gershwin Music*)

1932

    Girl Crazy. An RKO Production starring Wheeler and Woolsey. Directed by William A. Seiter. SONGS: Could You Use Me?; Embraceable You; Sam and Delilah; I Got Rhythm; But Not for Me.

1940

    Strike Up the Band. An MGM Production starring Mickey Rooney, Judy Garland, and Paul Whiteman and His Orchestra. GERSHWIN'S SONGS: Strike Up the Band.

1941

Lady Be Good. An MGM Production starring Eleanor Powell, Robert Young, and Ann Sothern. Directed by Norman Z. McLeod. GERSHWIN'S SONGS: Hang on to Me; Fascinating Rhythm; Oh, Lady Be Good. Jerome Kern's The Last Time I Saw Paris (Oscar Hammerstein II), introduced in this picture, won the Academy Award.

1943

Girl Crazy. An MGM Production, starring Mickey Rooney and Judy Garland. Directed by Norman Taurog. SONGS: Treat Me Rough; Sam and Delilah; Bidin' My Time; Embraceable You; Fascinating Rhythm; I Got Rhythm; But Not for Me; Barbary Coast; Cactus Time in Arizona.

vii

THE GREATEST SONGS OF

GEORGE GERSHWIN

(and the stars who introduced them)

A Woman Is a Sometime Thing. Introduced by Edward Matthews
in *Porgy and Bess.*

The Babbitt and the Bromide. Introduced by Adele Astaire in
Funny Face.

Bess, You Is My Woman Now. Introduced by Todd Duncan and
Anne Brown in *Porgy and Bess.*

Bidin' My Time. Introduced by The Foursome in *Girl Crazy.*

Boy, What Love Has Done to Me. Introduced by Ethel Merman
in *Girl Crazy.*

But Not For Me. Introduced by Ginger Rogers and Willie
Howard in *Girl Crazy.*

Clap Yo' Hands. Introduced by Betty Cooper and Harland Dixon in *Oh Kay*.

Do, Do, Do. Introduced by Gertrude Lawrence in *Oh Kay*.

Do It Again. Introduced by Irene Bordoni in *The French Doll*.

Embraceable You. Introduced by Ginger Rogers and Allen Kearns in *Girl Crazy*.

Fascinating Rhythm. Introduced by Fred and Adele Astaire in *Lady Be Good*.

I Got Plenty o' Nuttin'. Introduced by Todd Duncan in *Porgy and Bess*.

I Got Rhythm. Introduced by Ethel Merman in *Girl Crazy*.

I'll Build a Stairway to Paradise. A production number in the *Scandals of 1922*.

It Ain't Necessarily So. Introduced by John W. Bubbles in *Porgy and Bess*.

I've Got a Crush on You. Introduced by Gordon Smith and Doris Carson in *Strike Up the Band*.

Lady Be Good: *see* Oh, Lady Be Good.

Let's Call the Whole Thing Off. Introduced by Fred Astaire and Ginger Rogers in *Shall We Dance*.

Liza. Introduced by Ruby Keeler and Nick Lucas in *Show Girl*.

Looking for a Boy. Introduced by Queenie Smith in *Tip Toes*.

(The) Lost Barber-Shop Chord: *see* That Lost Barber-Shop Chord.

Love Is Here To Stay. Introduced by Kenny Baker in *The Goldwyn Follies*.

Love Is Sweeping the Country. Introduced by George Murphy and June O'Dea in *Of Thee I Sing*.

Love Walked In. Introduced by Kenny Baker in *The Goldwyn Follies*.

(The) Man I Love. Originally intended for *Lady Be Good,* and then for the first version of *Strike Up the Band,* but deleted from both productions. Introduced by Adele Astaire at the Philadelphia tryout of *Lady Be Good* in 1924. Sung by Eva Gauthier at a recital in Derby, Connecticut, 1925.

Mine. Introduced by William Gaxton in *Let 'Em Eat Cake.*

Nobody But You. Introduced by Helen Clark, Lorin Baker, and chorus in *La, La Lucille.*

Of Thee I Sing. Introduced by William Gaxton and Lois Moran in *Of Thee I Sing.*

Oh, Lady Be Good. Introduced by Walter Catlett in *Lady Be Good.*

Our Love Is Here To Stay: *see* Love Is Here To Stay.

Sam and Delilah. Introduced by Ethel Merman in *Girl Crazy.*

So Am I. Introduced by Fred and Adele Astaire in *Lady Be Good.*

So Are You. Introduced by Eddie Foy, Jr., and Kathryn Hereford in *Show Girl.*

Somebody Loves Me. Introduced by Winnie Lightner in *George White's Scandals of 1924.*

Someone To Watch Over Me. Introduced by Gertrude Lawrence in *Oh Kay.*

Soon. Introduced by Margaret Schilling in *Strike Up the Band.*

Stairway to Paradise: *see* I'll Build a Stairway to Paradise.

Strike Up the Band. Introduced by Jim Goff and chorus in *Strike Up the Band.*

Summertime. Introduced by Abbie Mitchell in *Porgy and Bess.*

Swanee. Introduced as a production number at the Capitol Theater Revue, but made famous by Al Jolson in *Sinbad.*

Sweet and Low Down. Introduced by Andrew Tombes, Gertrude McDonald, and Amy Revere in *Tip Toes.*

'S Wonderful. Introduced by Adele Astaire and Allen Kearns in *Funny Face.*

That Certain Feeling. Introduced by Queenie Smith and Allen Kearns in *Tip Toes*.

That Lost Barber-Shop Chord. Introduced by Louis Lazarin and the Pan American Quartet in *Americana*.

There's a Boat That's Leavin' Soon for New York. Introduced by John W. Bubbles in *Porgy and Bess*.

They Can't Take That Away From Me. Introduced by Fred Astaire in *Shall We Dance*.

(A) Typical Self-Made American. Introduced by Dudley Clements, Jerry Goff, and chorus in *Strike Up the Band*.

Who Cares. Introduced by William Gaxton and Lois Moran in *Of Thee I Sing*.

Wintergreen for President. Introduced by the ensemble in *Of Thee I Sing*.

RECOMMENDED RECORDINGS
OF GERSHWIN'S MUSIC

I. CONCERT WORKS

An American in Paris
New York Philharmonic-Symphony under Artur Rodzinski (Columbia ML-4026); André Kostelanetz and His Orchestra (Columbia ML-4458); NBC Symphony under Toscanini (Victor LM-9020); RCA Victor Symphony under Leonard Bernstein (Victor LM-1031).
See also: Omnibus Albums—The Serious Gershwin.

Concerto in F
Pittsburgh Symphony under William Steinberg, with Leonard Pennario as soloist (Capitol P-8219); New York Philhar-

monic-Symphony under André Kostelanetz, with Oscar Levant as soloist (Columbia ML-4879); Cincinnati Symphony under Tor Johnson with Alec Templeton as soloist (Remington 199-184) Montovani and Orchestra, with Julius Katchen as soloist (London LL-1262).

See also: Omnibus Albums—The Serious Gershwin.

Cuban Overture

André Kostelanetz and His Orchestra (Columbia ML-4481).

Porgy and Bess

COMPLETE OPERA: Lawrence Winters, Camilla Williams, Inez Matthews, Avon Long, J. Rosamund Johnson Chorus, with Lehman Engel conducting. (Columbia SL-162).

EXCERPTS: Todd Duncan, Anne Brown, Jessye Choir, etc., with Alexander Smallens conducting (Decca 7006–8042); Risë Stevens, Robert Merrill, Shaw Chorale, etc. (Victor LM-1124); Cab Calloway, Helen Thigpen, and others (Victor LPM-3158).

A *Symphonic Picture,* by Robert Russell Bennett: Pittsburgh Symphony under Fritz Reiner (Columbia ML-2019); Indianapolis Symphony under Fabien Sevitzky (Bluebird LBC-1059); New York Philharmonic-Symphony under André Kostelanetz (Columbia ML-4804); Minneapolis Symphony under Antal Dorati (Mercury 50016).

See also: Omnibus Albums—The Serious Gershwin.

Preludes for Piano

Oscar Levant, soloist (Columbia ML-2073).

Transcribed for violin and piano: Jascha Heifetz, soloist (Decca DL-7003).

See also: Omnibus Albums—The Serious Gershwin.

Rhapsody in Blue
> Philadelphia Orchestra, under Eugene Ormandy, with Oscar Levant as soloist (Columbia ML-4026); André Kostelanetz and His Orchestra, with Alec Templeton as soloist (Columbia ML-4455); Paul Whiteman and His Orchestra, with Leonard Pennario as soloist (Capitol H-302); Montovani and Orchestra, with Julius Katchen as soloist (London LL-1262).
> *See also:* Omnibus Albums—The Serious Gershwin.

Second Rhapsody
> Morton Gould and His Orchestra, with Oscar Levant as soloist (Columbia ML-2073).

Variations on I Got Rhythm
> Morton Gould and His Orchestra, with Oscar Levant as soloist (Columbia ML-2073).

II. MUSICAL COMEDY SCORES

Girl Crazy
> COMPLETE SCORE. Mary Martin, Louise Carlyle, Eddie Chappell, with orchestra and chorus directed by Lehman Engel. (Columbia ML-4475).

Of Thee I Sing
> PRINCIPAL EXCERPTS. Jack Carson, Hartman, and the original 1952 Broadway cast. (Capitol S-350).

III. MOTION-PICTURE SCORES

An American in Paris
> Gene Kelly, Leslie Caron, and Oscar Levant (MGM E-93).

Girl Crazy
> Judy Garland, Mickey Rooney, and others (Decca 5412).

IV. SONG COLLECTIONS

Bing Crosby Sings Songs by George Gershwin

Bing Crosby and Orchestra (Decca DL-5081). CONTENTS: Embraceable You; They Can't Take That Away from Me; Love Walked in; Summertime; It Ain't Necessarily So; I Got Plenty o' Nuttin'; Somebody Loves Me; Maybe.

Dorothy Kirsten Sings Songs of George Gershwin

Dorothy Kirsten with Percy Faith and his orchestra and chorus. (Columbia ML-2129). CONTENTS: Embraceable You; Soon; Do, Do, Do; Mine; Love Is Here To Stay; Someone To Watch Over Me; Love Walked In; I've Got a Crush on You.

Ella Sings Gershwin

Ella Fitzgerald (Decca DL-5300). CONTENTS: Someone to Watch Over Me; My One and Only; But Not for Me; Looking for a Boy; I've Got a Crush On You; How Long Has This Been Going On?; Maybe; Soon.

Embraceable You: A Tribute to George Gershwin

Wally Stotts Orchestra (Epic LG-1009). CONTENTS: Embraceable You; Strike Up the Band; Someone To Watch Over Me; Somebody Loves Me; Liza; Summertime; Love Is Here To Stay; The Man I Love.

Gems from Gershwin

Jane Froman, Felix Knight, Sunny Skylar, and orchestra under Nathaniel Shilkret (Victor LPT-3055). CONTENTS: Excerpts from *Of Thee I Sing, Girl Crazy, Lady Be Good, Tip Toes, Porgy and Bess,* and other songs.

Gershwin Jazz Concert

Eddie Condon and his orchestra, with Lee Wiley, Jack Teagarden, Bobby Hackett, and others (Decca DL-5137). CON-

TENTS: Somebody Loves Me; 'S Wonderful; My One and Only; Oh, Lady Be Good; Someone To Watch Over Me; The Man I Love; Swanee; I'll Build a Stairway to Paradise.

Gershwin Plays Gershwin

George Gershwin at the piano, with Fred Astaire (Heritage 0073). CONTENTS: Clap Yo' Hands; Do, Do, Do; Fascinating Rhythm; Sweet and Low Down; Hang on to Me; That Certain Feeling; I'd Rather Charleston; Someone To Watch Over Me; The Half of It Dearie Blues.

Gershwin Rarities, Vol. 1

Kaye Ballard, David Craig, Betty Gillet, accompanied by David Baker and John Morris (Walden 302). CONTENTS: They All Laughed; Things Are Looking Up; Isn't It a Pity; Funny Face; Aren't You Kind of Glad We Did; Soon; Shall We Dance; Stiff Upper Lip; Seventeen and Twenty-One; Kickin' the Clouds.

Gershwin Rarities, Vol. 2

Louise Carlyle, Warren Galjour, accompanied by the John Morris Trio (Walden 303). CONTENTS: Where's the Boy; That Certain Feeling; Let's Kiss and Make Up; Oh, So Nice; I Want To Be a War Bride; Nice Work If You Can Get It; Foggy Day; How Long Has This Been Going On; Nightie Night; Sweet and Low Down.

Heifetz Plays the Music of Gershwin

Transcribed for violin and piano by Jascha Heifetz. Jascha Heifetz, with Emanuel Bay at the piano (Decca DL-7003). CONTENTS: Summertime; A Woman Is a Sometime Thing; My Man's Gone Now; It Ain't Necessarily So; Tempo di Blues; Bess, You Is My Woman Now; 3 Preludes.

Music of George Gershwin

André Kostelanetz and His Orchestra (Columbia ML-2026). CONTENTS: Embraceable You; Fascinating Rhythm; The Man I Love; 'S Wonderful; Maybe; Someone To Watch Over Me; Oh, Lady Be Good; Soon.

Music of George Gershwin

George Gershwin, Fred Astaire, Hildegarde, Larry Adler, and others (Columbia AAL-39). CONTENTS: The Man I Love; Do, Do, Do; My One and Only; 'S Wonderful; Half of It Dearie Blues; Fascinating Rhythm; Sweet and Low Down; Summertime; Bess, You Is My Woman Now; It Ain't Necessarily So; I Got Plenty o' Nuttin'; There's a Boat That's Leavin' Soon for New York.

Oscar Peterson and Buddy de Franco Play Gershwin

Oscar Peterson, Buddy de Franco, and orchestra conducted by Russ Garcia. Supervised by Norman Granz (Norgren MGM-1016). CONTENTS: I Got Rhythm; I Was Doing All Right; The Man I Love; It Ain't Necessarily So; Bess, You Is My Woman Now; Someone to Watch Over Me; 'S Wonderful; Strike Up the Band; They Can't Take That Away From Me.

The Popular Gershwin

Eddie Fisher, Eartha Kitt, June Valli, Lou Monte, Jaye P. Morgan, Dinah Shore, Sauter-Finegan Orchestra, Hugo Winterhalter and His Orchestra, Henri René and His Orchestra, Glenn Miller and His Orchestra, and others (Victor LPM-6000). CONTENTS: 29 songs.

Songs of George Gershwin (transcribed for piano)

Eddy Duchin (Columbia CL-6103). CONTENTS: The Man I Love; Someone to Watch Over Me; Love Walked In; Embraceable You; 'S Wonderful; Somebody Loves Me; Summertime; They Can't Take That Away From Me.

Transcriptions of 18 Songs

Piano transcriptions by George Gershwin. Leonid Hambro, soloist (Walden 200). CONTENTS: See page 331.

V. OMNIBUS ALBUMS

The Life and Music of George Gershwin

Produced by David Ewen. This is a chronological presentation of Gershwin's works, which includes all his serious music, and over 60 songs (Columbia FL-230).

The Serious Gershwin

Morton Gould and His Orchestra, and Morton Gould as piano soloist (Victor LM-6033). CONTENTS: *Rhapsody in Blue;* 3 Piano Preludes; *Concerto in F; An American in Paris; Porgy and Bess*—Piano Solo from Act I, Scene I; Suite from *Porgy and Bess* (arranged by Morton Gould).

BIBLIOGRAPHY

books on George Gershwin

(AMERICAN)
Armitage, Merle (editor). *George Gershwin*. New York: Longmans, Green & Co., 1938. A memorial volume to which thirty-eight of Gershwin's friends and colleagues contributed reminiscences and tributes.

Ewen, David. *The Story of George Gershwin*. New York: Henry Holt & Co., 1943. A biography for young people.

Goldberg, Isaac. *George Gershwin*. New York: Simon and Schuster, 1931. Written while Gershwin was still alive, and with his best work to come. It was an extension of three articles originally published in *Ladies Home Journal*, based exclusively on material derived from conversations with George and Ira Gershwin.

(FOREIGN)

Chalupt, René. *George Gershwin; le musicien de la Rhapsody in Blue*. Paris: Amiot, Dumant, 1948.

Ewen, David. *George Gershwin; Leben und Werk*. Zurich, Leipzig, Wien: Amalthea Verlag, 1955. A translation of the young people's biography listed above.

Pool, Rosey E. *Een Nieuw lied voor America; het leven van George Gershwin*. Amsterdam: Tilburg-Nederlands Boekhus, 1951.

Pugliaro, M. *Rapsodia in blue; l'arte e l'amore nella vita di George Gershwin*. Turin: S.A.S., 1951.

Schipke, Brigitte. *George Gershwin und die Welt seiner Musik*. Freiburg: Drei Ringe Musikverlag, 1955. A monograph.

Schoorl, Bob. *George Gershwin: van Broadway tot Carnegie Hall*. Amsterdam: A. J. G. Strengholt, 1952.

some books in which George Gershwin is discussed

Bagar, Robert, and Biancolli, Louis. *The Concert Companion*. New York: McGraw Hill & Co., 1947. Program notes of the major serious works.

Bolton, Guy, and Wodehouse, P. G. *Bring On the Girls*. New York: Simon and Schuster, 1953. Behind-the-scenes glimpses of the writing and production of several early Gershwin musicals.

Cerf, Bennett. *Try and Stop Me*. New York: Simon and Schuster, 1944. A chapter on Gershwin filled with anecdotes.

Cross, Milton, and Ewen, David. *The Milton Cross Encyclopedia of Great Composers*. Two volumes. New York:

Doubleday and Co., 1953. The section on Gershwin includes his biography, a general comment on his music, and analytical notes of his most important serious works.

Duke, Vernon. *Passport to Paris.* Boston: Little, Brown & Co., 1955. Intimate glimpses of George and Ira Gershwin by one who was a friend of both.

Ewen, David (editor). *The Book of Modern Composers.* New York: Alfred A. Knopf, Inc. Second Edition, Revised and Enlarged, 1950. The book contains a brief biography, a Personal Note by Isaac Goldberg, an extract from an article by Gershwin expounding his esthetic theories, and an essay on Gershwin by John Tasker Howard.

Ewen, David. *The Complete Book of 20th Century Music.* New York: Prentice-Hall, Inc., 1952. A brief biography, a critical evaluation, and program notes for his major serious works.

Ewen, David. *Men of Popular Music.* New York: Prentice-Hall, Inc. Revised Edition, 1952. A profile on Gershwin.

Howard, John Tasker. *Our Contemporary Composers.* New York: Thos. Y. Crowell, 1941. A brief biography and criticism of principal works.

Jessel, George. *This Way, Miss.* New York: Henry Holt & Co., 1955. Includes a brief tribute to Gershwin.

Levant, Oscar. *A Smattering of Ignorance.* New York: Doubleday & Co., 1940. The last chapter is an informal portrait of Gershwin by one of his closest friends and most famous interpreters.

Nichols, Beverly. *Are They the Same at Home.* New York: George H. Doran, 1927. Includes an early personal portrait of Gershwin.

O'Connell, Charles. *Victor Book of Overtures, Tone Poems.* New York: Simon and Schuster, 1950. Contains an analysis of *An American in Paris.*

Osgood, Henry O. *So This Is Jazz*. Boston: Little, Brown & Co., 1926. Many sections are devoted to an evaluation of Gershwin's place in jazz.

Rosenfeld, Paul. *Discoveries of a Music Critic*. New York: Harcourt, Brace & Co., 1936. One of the chapters is a critical evaluation of Gershwin's music.

Schillinger, Frances. *Joseph Schillinger: A Memoir by His Wife*. New York: Greenberg, 1949. Includes an account of Gershwin's study with Joseph Schillinger.

Seldes, Gilbert. *The Seven Lively Arts*. New York: Harper & Bros., 1924. Includes one of the earliest tributes to Gershwin's significance.

Slonimsky, Nicolas. *Lexicon of Musical Invective*. New York: Coleman-Ross Co., 1953. Includes interesting derogatory criticisms of several serious Gershwin works.

Smith, Cecil. *Musical Comedy in America*. New York: Theater Arts Books, 1950. A source for Gershwin's major musical comedies.

Spaeth, Sigmund. *A History of Popular Music in America*. New York: Random House, Inc., 1948. A source for Gershwin's songs and musical comedies.

Thomson, Virgil. *The Musical Scene*. New York: Alfred A. Knopf, 1945. Excellent critiques of the 1941 revival of *Porgy and Bess* and the Toscanini performance of the *Rhapsody in Blue*.

Veinus, Abraham. *Victor Book of Concertos*. New York: Simon and Schuster, 1948. Analyses of the *Rhapsody in Blue* and Concerto in F.

Whiteman, Paul, and McBride, Margaret. *Jazz*. New York: J. H. Sears & Co., 1926. Contains a first-hand account of the première of the *Rhapsody in Blue*.

selected magazine articles

Behrman, S. N. "Troubadour." *New Yorker*, May 1929. A "Profile."

Bernstein, Leonard. "A Nice Gershwin Tune." *Atlantic Monthly*, April 1955. The author enters into an imaginary colloquy with the professional manager of a music-publishing firm, and offers his personal views about Gershwin's serious works.

Braggioti, M. "Gershwin Is Here To Stay." *Etude*, February 1953.

Duke, Vernon. "Gershwin, Schillinger, and Dukelsky." *Musical Quarterly*, January 1947.

Ewen, David. "Gershwin Would Be Surprised." *Harper's Magazine*, May 1955. A study of the growth of Gershwin's fame since his death.

Ewen, David. "The Stature of George Gershwin." *American Mercury*, January 1950.

Goldberg, Isaac. "Gebrüder Gershwin." *Vanity Fair*, June 1932.

Goldberg, Isaac. "George Gershwin and Jazz." *Theatre Guild Magazine*, March 1930.

Jacobi, Frederick. "The Future of Gershwin." *Modern Music*, November-December 1937.

Kilenyi, Edward. "George Gershwin as I Knew Him." *Etude*, January 1951. Reminiscences by Gershwin's teacher.

Marek, George. "Rhapsody in Blue after Twenty-Five Years." *Good Housekeeping*, February 1949.

O'Hara, John. "American in Memoriam." *Newsweek*, July 15, 1940.

Pollak, R. "Gershwin." *American Magazine of Art*, September 1937.

Taubman, Howard. "Why Gershwin Tunes Live on." New York *Times Magazine*, September 28, 1952.

Thomson, Virgil. "George Gershwin." *Modern Music*, November-December 1935.

Woollcott, Alexander. "George the Ingenuous." *Cosmopolitan*, November 1933.

index